Managing water for peace
in the Middle East

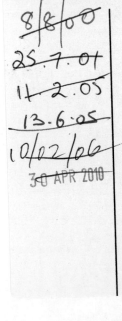

Note to the reader from the UNU

The programme area of the United Nations University (UNU) on Sustaining Global Life-support Systems responds to the priorities identified in the "Agenda 21" emanating from the United Nations Conference on Environment and Development (UNCED), held in Rio de Janeiro, Brazil, in 1992. Within this programme area, the programme on Integrated Studies of Ecosystems aggregates issues of environmentally sustainable development from the entry point of the capacity of ecosystems and their ability to support, resist, or recuperate from the long-term impact of major transformations. Projects within this programme approach issues from three perspectives: One focus is on integrated studies of fragile ecosystems and other vulnerable regions in given geographical zones—mountains and lowlands, and fragile ecosystems in critical zones. A second set of projects covers improved methods of measuring and monitoring sustainability and environmental management. A third comprises sectoral studies of critical resources such as forests, oceans, biodiversity resources, and waters.

As a part of its activities concerned with water as a critical resource, the UNU is continuing to organize a series of projects that work to harness the inextricable link between water and geopolitics in arid and volatile regions. The aim is to identify the issues in disputes concerning water resources, select alternative scenarios that could lead to the solution of the complex problems related to water issues, and recommend processes through which the countries concerned are likely to agree on mutually satisfactory solutions to the problems.

The Middle East Water Forum held in Cairo, Egypt, in 1993, organized by the UNU, produced an authoritative book on the subject, entitled *International Waters of the Middle East: From Euphrates–Tigris to Nile*. The forum proved highly successful and contributed, informally but importantly, to the progress of the Middle East peace talks. The present book has emerged as a part of the UNU's continuing efforts in this field and is one of a series of books related to water issues and conflict resolution.

Managing water for peace in the Middle East: Alternative strategies

Masahiro Murakami

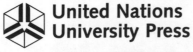

**United Nations
University Press**

TOKYO · NEW YORK · PARIS

United Nations University Press
The United Nations University, 53-70, Jingumae 5-chome,
Shibuya-ku, Tokyo 150, Japan
Tel: (03) 3499-2811   Fax: (03) 3406-7345
Telex: J25442   Cable: UNATUNIV TOKYO

Typeset by Asco Trade Typesetting Limited, Hong Kong
Printed by Permanent Typesetting and Printing Co., Ltd., Hong
Kong
Cover design by Jonathan Gullery/Abel Graphics, Thornwood,
New York, USA

UNUP-858
ISBN 92-808-0858-3
05000 P

Contents

Contents

Abbreviations

International organizations and agencies

DTCD	Department of Technical Cooperation for Development (UN)
FAO	Food and Agriculture Organization of the United Nations
UNDP	United Nations Development Programme
UNEP	United Nations Environment Programme
UNESCO	United Nations Educational, Scientific and Cultural Organization
UNRWA	United Nations Relief and Works Agency for Palestine Refugees in the Near East
WHO	World Health Organization
WMO	World Meteorological Organization

Academic and professional associations

AGU	American Geophysical Union
AWWA	American Water Works Association
IDA	International Desalination Association
IHP/IHD	International Hydrological Programme/Decade
IWRA	International Water Resources Association
NWSIA	National Water Supply Improvement Association (USA)

Projects

EGMC	East Ghor Main Canal
INWC	Israel National Water Carrier

MDS   Mediterranean–Dead Sea (canal/conduit)
PG   Palestine Grid

Desalination technology

CA   cellulose acetate
ED   electrodialysis
EDR   electrodialysis reversal
ME   multi-effect evaporation
MSF   multi-stage flash evaporation
RO   reverse osmosis
VC   vapour compression

Units of measurement

gal.   (US) gallon(s)
GWh   gigawatt hour(s)
ha   hectare(s)
km^2 square kilometre(s)
km^3 cubic kilometre(s)
kV   kilovolt(s)
kVA   kilovolt ampere(s)
kW   kilowatt(s)
kWh   kilowatt hour(s)
m^3 cubic metre(s)
m^3/sec cubic metre(s) per second
MCM   million cubic metres
mgd   million gallons per day
mg/l   milligram(s) per litre
mig   million imperial gallons
MW   megawatt(s)
MWh   megawatt hour(s)
μm   micrometre(s) (micron[s])
ppm   part(s) per million
psi   pound(s) per square inch

Miscellaneous

BOD   biochemical oxygen demand
CFU   colony-forming unit(s)
CIS   Commonwealth of Independent States (former Soviet Union, since
           1991)
EDTA   ethylene diamine tetra-acetic acid
El.   ground elevation
JD   Jordanian dinar(s)
KD   Kuwaiti dinar(s)
M&I   municipal and industrial

Abbreviations

O&M	operation and maintenance
PLO	Palestine Liberation Organization
TDS	total dissolved solids
UAE	United Arab Emirates

1

Introduction

1.1 Background

Limitations on water, one of the scarcest resources in an arid region, are likely to have a significant impact on the economic development of all countries of the Middle East. Middle East water-resource issues are also likely to have a significant impact on the future political framework of the region in the aftermath of the Gulf war of 1990–91 and the peace agreements between Israel and the Palestine Liberation Organization of September 1993 and Israel and Jordan of October 1994. The scarcity of water and the high cost of its development have long been recognized in arid regions, especially in the Arabian Gulf countries, where neither surface water nor renewable fresh groundwater are available. The demand for water to serve expanding third-world populations continues to increase, however, while fresh-water supplies are finite, and it is becoming more and more difficult to develop them on a renewable basis. Almost all fresh and renewable waters such as rivers, streams, lakes, and groundwater, which are termed "conventional water" or "traditional water," have already been exploited or will be fully developed in the countries of the Middle East and North Africa by the end of this century.

Few regions of the planet offer a more varied physiography or a

1

richer mix of ethnicities, religions, languages, societies, cultures, and politics than the Middle East. At the same time, no segment of the globe presents its diverse aspects in such an amalgam of conflicts and complexities. Out of this compound, one issue emerges as the most conspicuous, trans-boundary, and problematic—water. Its scarcity and rapid diminution are most keenly felt in places where there also happen to exist some of the fiercest national animosities. River waters in the Middle East in particular are a conflict-laden determinant of both the domestic and external policies of the region's principal actors. However, as one of the leaders of the Palestine Liberation Organization stated in the early 1990s, "Water is more important than oil or politics"; so politics may not remain a constraint to water development much longer.

As water shortages occur and full utilization is reached, policies tend to be framed more and more in zero-sum terms, adding to the probability of discord, and it would seem to be unavoidable that the severity of Middle Eastern water problems will continue to increase significantly. In the already overheated atmosphere of political hostility, the lack of sufficient water to satisfy burgeoning human, developmental, and security needs among all the nations of the Middle East has heightened ambient tensions. By the end of the 1990s Israel, Jordan, and the West Bank and Gaza, or Palestine, will have lost virtually all of their renewable sources of fresh water if current patterns of consumption are not quickly and radically altered. In these circumstances, the Jordan River system, which includes the Al-Wuheda dam scheme on a major tributary of the Yarmouk River, unquestionably holds the greatest potential for conflict.

Despite the many political complications in the Middle East, there is a recent history of tacit, although limited, cooperation over multinational river development even among the bitterest opponents on the Nile, Euphrates, and Jordan Rivers:

» Egypt and the Sudan created a model of cooperation in their 1959 Nile Waters Agreement, which not only governs the sharing of the Nile's waters but contains an instrument for settling controversies by negotiation. This could serve as a model for other river systems in the application of technology to alleviate water problems.

» Turkey has often threatened to cut the flow of the Euphrates. But Iraq and Syria managed to arrive at an arrangement over the operation of the Tabqa dam in 1975. Turkey agreed with Syria on the operation of the Ataturk dam in 1987, by releasing 500 m³/sec

2

$(15.8 \times 10^9 \text{ m}^3$ per year) of water to the Syrian border. However, the water was used as a political weapon to force Syria to curtail its support for Kurdish activists in south-east Anatolia.

» Israel and Jordan—before Israel's invasion of Lebanon and her troublesome stand on clearing out obstructions to the intake of Jordan's East Ghor canal—had more or less informally agreed to share the Jordan River system within the framework of the 1955 Johnston Plan (Naff and Matson 1984).

Multinational river development has been a keen concern of water-resource planners throughout the world, especially in developing countries in arid regions. One example has been Turkey's ambitious proposal for the "Peace Pipeline" project in 1987, to transfer water from the Seyhan and Ceyhan river systems in south-eastern Turkey to the Euphrates basin and to other countries downstream. This project would require the construction of a series of dams, water tunnels, and the world's longest international water pipeline system, with a total length of about 6,550 km and a capacity of 6 million cubic metres a day (Gould 1988). It has been shown to be technically though not yet economically feasible. The project would involve the crossing of several political boundaries, however, and is likely to be postponed until some of the most pressing political issues of the Arab world, including international water-rights problems between Turkey, Syria, and Iraq, have been solved. Transboundary river development may not take place this century, but planning and the easing of water disputes will certainly form an important part in political discussions to determine the future pattern of boundaries to be redrawn in any future peace settlements.

In arid regions, the potential resources of fresh and/or good-quality water are limited because of the scantness of rainfall and the very high potential evaporation, exceeding the potential rainfall by ten times or more. Further, as is becoming increasingly apparent, salinity pollution resulting from irrigated agriculture, which is not a recent phenomenon but an age-old problem, has an important indirect effect on water quality.

Scientists of the former Soviet Union have reported that the Caspian and Aral Seas are in retreat because excessive irrigation withdrawals are reducing inflow from their catchments. The Aral Sea has already shrunk dramatically in size; the water level has dropped by three metres since 1960, reducing its size by some 18,000 km^2. In the meantime the reduced inflow from the two major rivers, the Sir Darya and the Amu Darya, with enhanced salinity from irrigation returns, has already increased its salinity up to 1,000 ppm of total dissolved solids (Meybeck et al. 1990).

Basin irrigation has been practised on the flood plain of the Tigris and Euphrates Rivers since 4000 B.C. Lack of drainage has repeatedly caused a build-up of salts in soil and water that has inhibited food production and indeed that contributed to the decline of Sumerian culture. More recently the modern development of irrigation in arid regions has suffered from a variety of salinity-pollution problems. Problem areas have included the Indus River basin in South-West Asia, the Tigris-Euphrates basin in the Middle East, the Nile in North Africa, the Murray River in Australia, and the Colorado River in the United States (Meybeck et al. 1990).

Since the 1950s the Colorado River has been seriously contaminated by irrigation return flows and highly saline pumped drainage water from the Wellton-Mohawk irrigation project in south-western Arizona. By 1961 the salinity of the river had reached a level that was unacceptable to the government of Mexico. In 1973 the International Boundary and Water Commission required the US government to improve, enhance, and protect the quality of water available in the Colorado River for use in the United States and Mexico. The agreed-upon salinity level could only be attained by either bypassing saline drainage or desalting the brackish water before it returned to the river. Since water is a precious resource in the semi-arid areas of southern Arizona, a decision was made to reclaim a major portion of the Wellton-Mohawk drainage by a desalination plant—the world's largest reverse-osmosis desalting facility, with an installed capacity of 72.4 million gallons, or 274,000 m^3, per day (Applegate 1986).

In some of the more arid parts of the Middle East, in particular the Gulf states, where good quality water is either not available at all or is extremely limited, desalination of seawater has been commonly used to solve the problems of water supply for municipal and industrial (M&I) uses. Owing to the rapid increase in demand for water in the Arabian Gulf countries—Saudi Arabia, Kuwait, the United Arab Emirates, Qatar, Bahrain, and Oman—where the potential for development of conventional water resources such as fresh surface water and renewable groundwater is extremely limited, other alternatives such as waste-water reclamation and desalination processes have been developed since the 1960s. Saudi Arabia, Kuwait, Qatar, and Bahrain are using non-renewable groundwater resources in large quantities, causing depletion of these valuable resources. Although conventional water resources such as renewable groundwater and surface run-off are available in Oman, the United Arab Emirates, and Saudi Arabia, these resources have yet to be developed sustainably in an integrated water-resources planning context.

A huge amount of non-renewable or fossil fresh groundwater is stored in the Palaeozoic to Mesozoic-Neogene (Nubian) sandstones which underlie wide areas in the Arabian peninsula in Saudi Arabia and Jordan and in the eastern Sahara desert in Egypt and Libya. The dominance and importance of the non-renewable groundwater reserves in national water planning may be seen in the 1985–90 development plans of Saudi Arabia and Libya.

Saudi Arabia is one of the world's leaders in the production of wheat for self-sufficiency in food, but is heavily dependent on the use of non-renewable groundwater. Agricultural water demand in Saudi Arabia in 1985 amounted to 8×10^9 m^3 per year, while the demand for water for urban, rural, and industrial (M&I) use was 1.6×10^9 m^3 per year (MAWSA 1985). It was estimated that the total annual demand will increase to 16.5×10^9 m^3 by the year 2000, of which 14×10^9 m^3 will be for agriculture and 2.5×10^9 m^3 for M&I use. The huge water demand for agriculture is based on the kingdom's policy of self-sufficiency in food and on the use of non-renewable groundwater for growing grain, which generally requires 2,000–3,000 tons of water per ton of grain (Akkad 1990; SWCC 1990).

Groundwater development and/or mining in the Nubian sandstones of the inland desert depressions of Libya for the "Great Man-Made River" project will be a key element in Libya's development strategy for the twenty-first century. The Libyan government began construction in 1984–1986 (first and second phases), with the aim of abstracting groundwater in the inland desert at a rate of 2×10^9 m^3 per year (66 m^3/sec) in total. The water is to be conveyed over 600 km north to farms on the Mediterranean coast by the world's largest water pipeline system, with a total length of 4,000 km (Beaumont et al. 1988). The life of the Nubian sandstone aquifer can only be estimated to be between 20 and 200 years, owing to the lack of data for estimating groundwater recharge through wadi beds and/or depressions during occasional and temporary flash floods. The total pipeline system is therefore designed on the assumption of an aquifer life of 50 years.

The Egyptian government began non-renewable groundwater development in the Nubian sandstone aquifer in the inland Sahara desert in the mid-1950s with the New Valley project, which aims to expand the cultivated area in the Kharga and Dakhla oases. The construction

5

of deep production wells in the Dakhla oasis was completed by 1966, which increased the combined installed capacity of shallow and deep systems up to 190 million m^3 per year, but the yield had decreased to a level of 159 million m^3 per year by the end of 1969. The Egyptian authorities are planning to augment the extraction till it reaches 2,400 million m^3 per year by the year 2000 (Shahin 1987). The extraction of the target volume will lead to further decline of the piezometric head and cessation of the artesian flow. The project is also faced with the human problem that many of the managerial staff do not like living in such isolated areas.

Desalination of brackish water and seawater is a key element of non-conventional water-resources development. The ocean holds 1.34 × 10^9 km^3 of seawater, which accounts for 96.5% of the earth's total water reserves of 1.39 × 10^9 km^3. In some of the drier parts of the Middle East, in particular the Arabian Gulf states, where conventional good-quality water is not available or is extremely limited, desalination of seawater has been commonly used to solve problems of water supply arising from increasing demand for municipal and industrial uses. The cost of desalting brackish groundwater is competitive, while for seawater it is invariably high, being largely influenced by petroleum prices. Two-thirds of the world's desalting plants are located in the oil-rich states of the Middle East, which can afford the price of massive quantities of desalting equipment.

A hydro-power scheme for a Mediterranean–Dead Sea canal, with multiple socio-economic and political ramifications, was proposed by Israel in 1980. The plan was to convey water from the Mediterranean to the Dead Sea via canals and tunnels, utilizing the difference in elevation of almost 400 m to generate 600 MW of electricity. In addition, it was proposed to use the water to cool nuclear power stations rated at 1,800 MW, and to investigate the feasibility of generating 1,500 MW from the Dead Sea as a solar pond (Naff and Matson 1984). However, there has been no provision for sharing resources with other countries and no effort at joint development. The project was soon put aside, owing to strong opposition from Arab states and others, and following the confusion and drop in world oil market prices in 1984. Recently, however, discussion of the Mediterranean–Dead Sea canal or a Red Sea–Dead Sea canal has been revived by worldwide attention to the need for clean energy and safeguarding the global environment and the peace negotiations among Israel, Palestine, and Jordan.

Israel has experienced much difficulty in making additional water supplies available since the late 1960s, when it was using as much as

95% of the total renewable water sources available in its territory (Beaumont et al. 1988). Almost half of Israel's total water supply is dependent on water that has been diverted or pre-empted from Arab sources outside its pre-1967 boundaries (Naff and Matson 1984). The main effort has to be shifted to making more efficient use of available supplies rather than increasing the capacity of hydraulic structures.

In neighbouring Jordan, almost all the renewable waters will be fully exploited by the mid or late 1990s, when the ongoing Al-Wuheda dam project on the Yarmouk River is completed. This is the largest tributary not yet fully developed in the Jordan River system. After construction of the diversion tunnel in late 1989, the project was stopped by strong opposition from the Israeli government, which is the administrator of occupied Palestine, or the West Bank.

Priority in water-resource development in each state is still given to developing its own resources, not only conventional fresh-water resources such as renewable groundwater and surface water but also non-conventional water resources such as fossil groundwater, brackish groundwater, seawater, saline drainage water, and treated sewage effluents. The potential contribution of marginal waters to meet the anticipated water demand in Israel and Jordan will be a unique initiative. Another option will be the diversion of water from the existing system from one use to another—from agriculture to M&I, as has been done in large population centres in Arizona in the United States, and in some cases from general M&I to domestic drinking water—to make the best use of scarce resources.

Non-conventional water resources need to be developed properly in an integrated planning context such as a national water master plan. By the first decades of the twenty-first century almost all states in arid regions will be facing severe water shortages in urban centres as populations continue to grow. Water-resources planning for the twenty-first century in arid regions may therefore include the following techno-political alternatives:

>> water conservation and diversion of existing water systems from one use to another;
>> development of non-conventional water resources—including desalination of brackish water and seawater and the use of treated sewage—and water-energy co-generation, such as
  — the lower Jordan River brackish-water reclamation scheme with RO desalination (the Peace Drainage Canal),
  — the Mediterranean–Dead Sea Conduit scheme,
  — the Aqaba seawater pumped-storage scheme for co-generation;

7

≫ multinational fresh-water transfer or importation by pipeline, tankers, barges, or floating water bags, including
— the Ceyhan/Seyhan–Middle East Peace Pipeline, including a smaller pipeline or canal to the Jordan watersheds (Kolars and Wolf 1993),
— diversion of the Nile to Gaza and Israel,
— Manavgat–Mediterranean, using tugs and bags as carriers (Savage 1990),
— other bilateral options, including diversion of the Euphrates from Iraq to north Jordan, diversion of the Shatt al-Arab from Iraq to Kuwait, and diversion from Iran to Qatar,
≫ other marginal non-conventional measures, including weather modification, dual distribution systems, and rain harvesting.

There are now several changes in the political situation since the Iraqi invasion of Kuwait in 1990 and Israel's peace agreements with the PLO and Jordan that may form part of a comprehensive resolution of the Israel-Arab problem. This may make integrated development not only technically and economically feasible but politically desirable and urgent.

1.2 Objectives, concepts, and scope

This study attempts to evaluate some new non-conventional approaches to water resources which need to be taken into account in building the new peace in the Middle East. These new approaches, including techno-political alternatives, offer the opportunity to introduce new applications of well-tried technology to solve long-standing water problems which are at the centre of many of the potential sources of conflicts.

It introduces the following five concepts:

(1) *integration of development alternatives in the context of a water master plan*, including applications of non-conventional water resources for arid regions;

(2) *co-generation of clean energy and water*, including solar-hydro, groundwater-hydro, and hydro-powered reverse-osmosis desalination;

(3) *the strategic use of non-conventional water resources for sustainable development*, including brackish water, seawater, and reclaimed waste water;

(4) *techno-political alternatives and joint development with the sharing of resources for the multinational development* of the Jordan River and Dead Sea basin;

(5) *water-resources planning for peace* in the context of Israel-Palestine-Arab issues.

Arid zones occupy about one-third of the land area of the earth, and include both some advanced countries and many developing countries in North and South America, North and South-West Africa, the Middle East, Central Asia, West Asia, and Australia. This study is not a worldwide review of arid-zone hydrology and water-resources development but a case study on water-resources planning in the developing countries of the Middle East. In this study, the term "Middle East" includes the whole geographical region including Kuwait, Jordan, Palestine, and Israel, where the peace of the world has been at risk for the last forty years or more.

1.3 Organization of the book

Chapter 2 reviews arid-zone hydrology and problems, and the constraints to water-resources development and management in the arid zone, including non-conventional water-resources development alternatives.

Section 2.1 reviews the definition of "arid zone" and the causation of arid zones in a global context of the water cycle and balance. Sections 2.2–2.5 describe the nature of the hydrology and riparian issues of major multinational rivers in the Middle East such as the Tigris-Euphrates, Indus, Nile, and Jordan Rivers. Section 2.6 examines the world's first major effort to control river salinity problems by installing the world's largest reverse-osmosis desalinating plant at Yuma on the lower reaches of the Colorado River. Section 2.7 describes large-scale non-renewable or fossil groundwater development projects that are being carried out in Saudi Arabia, Egypt (the New Valley project), and Libya (the Great Man-Made River project). Sections 2.8 and 2.9 describe desalination practices in the Arabian peninsula, including brackish-groundwater desalination by reverse osmosis in Bahrain and seawater distillation in the Arabian Gulf countries. Section 2.10 describes pioneer groundwater-hydro projects in Chile and Libya. Section 2.11 describes the world's first solar-hydro and seawater pumped-storage schemes in Egypt. Section 2.12 summarizes the review studies in the chapter and suggests some of the implications of developing marginal waters as non-conventional water resources in the arid region.

Chapters 3 to 5 are studies of the application of water-resources planning for peace that attempt to conceive sustainable water-resources development plans, including non-conventional alternatives,

9

for Kuwait, Jordan, Palestine, and Israel, where the peace of the world is at risk.

The desalination of brackish groundwater and seawater is the main topic of these studies, taking into account energy saving made possible by recent innovations in reverse-osmosis (RO) membrane technology. A new co-generation approach is proposed to demonstrate a way that potential energy can be used in developing a water-resources system, including use of groundwater and seawater, which has not been utilized before in the context of conventional water-resources development. This approach aims to coordinate (1) groundwater hydro-power, (2) solar-evaporation and hydro-power, and (3) hydro-powered RO desalination in an integrated regional development context.

The study, which was carried out in 1990–1991, aims to identify a water-resources planning approach to provide the foundations for a peace negotiation and/or settlement by the use of shared resources and their joint development by Israel, Palestine, and Jordan, while taking into account the various recent changes in the political situation in the Middle East since the 1990–91 Gulf war.

Chapter 3 considers the application of hydro-powered RO desalination to the development of marginal water resources in Kuwait and a case study on brackish groundwater development with hybrid RO. The unit water costs have been estimated to compare the cost effectiveness of various desalination methods, including the conventional thermal multi-stage flash process and the membrane process with hydro-powered RO.

Sections 3.1–3.3 describe the physiography, hydrology, and water resources of Kuwait. Sections 3.4 and 3.5 describe experimental RO desalination projects which have been undertaken in Kuwait since 1985 on both seawater and brackish groundwater. Section 3.6 sets out a proposal for applying hydro-powered RO desalination to brackish-groundwater development in the south-western part of Kuwait. Section 3.7 presents a water master plan study for the development of marginal water resources in Kuwait.

Chapter 4 considers the application of non-conventional water-resources development to a national water master plan for Jordan. Jordan has only a limited potential for renewable water-resources development, and this will be exhausted by the mid to late 1990s. There are, however, various development alternatives for both conventional waters, such as surface water and groundwater, and non-conventional waters, including brackish water, seawater, and urban waste water.

Sections 4.1–4.3 describe the background and water-resources

10

development and management of Jordan. Section 4.4 provides an inventory of potential non-conventional water resources in Jordan. Section 4.5 describes a key proposal for co-generation by brackish-groundwater RO desalination and groundwater-hydro to sustain the non-renewable and renewable water-resources system in southern Jordan. Section 4.6 presents a master plan study on non-conventional water use in the context of a national water master plan for Jordan.

Chapter 5 discusses integrated water-resources development and management of the Jordan River system, with the aim of mitigating the historical complexities, commonalities, and conflicts between Israel and the Arab states. Techno-political alternatives in a context of co-generation are shown to provide an opportunity for sharing resources and joint development between Israel, Palestine, and Jordan.

Sections 5.1–5.2 describe the background and water resources of Israel. Section 5.3 is a review of Jordan River development and Israel's water-resources development and management. Section 5.4 provides a case study on the joint Israel/Jordan Mediterranean–Dead Sea conduit scheme, which is a key proposal for co-generation, coupling RO seawater desalination with a solar-evaporation hydro scheme. Section 5.5 is a master plan study on multinational water-resources development and management, including options for water importation between Israel and other Middle East states. Section 5.6 is a proposal for a hybrid seawater pumped-storage scheme with hydro-powered RO desalination as a strategic non-conventional water-energy co-generation alternative for inter-state regional economic development for peace for the riparian states of the Gulf of Aqaba.

Chapter 6 contains concluding remarks and recommendations for further study.

Appendix A describes the state of the art in reverse-osmosis desalination, which has important implications for water-resources planning in the twenty-first century.

Appendix B describes the physiography of Jordan and Israel.

Appendix C gives a historical review of the multinational development of the Jordan River system, including notes on negotiations over water-allocation problems between Israel and other riparian states from 1948 to 1967.

Appendix D gives some recommendations for the future planning of joint development and management of the Jordan River system.

Figs. 1.1 and 1.2 are key maps which will be useful for reference throughout the book.

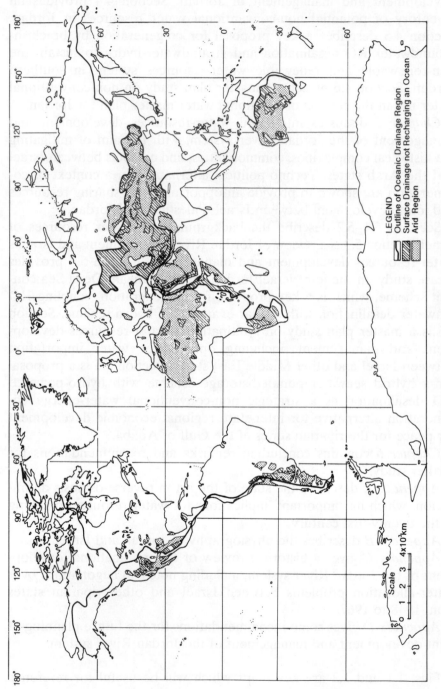

Fig. 1.1 World ocean catchment and arid zone

LEGEND
Outline of Oceanic Drainage Region
Surface Drainage not Recharging an Ocean
Arid Region

Scale
0 1 2 3 4×10⁵km

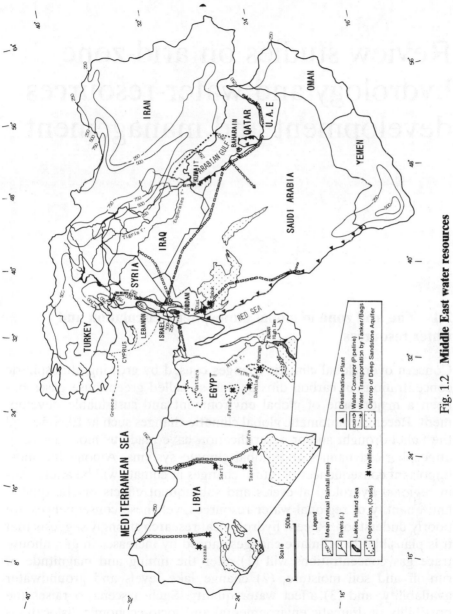

Fig. 1.2 **Middle East water resources**

13

2

Review studies on arid-zone hydrology and water-resources development and management

2.1   The arid zone in global atmospheric circulation and water resources

Concern over global climatic changes caused by growing atmospheric concentrations of carbon dioxide and so-called greenhouse gases has been a major issue of global environment and sustainable development. Recent symptomatic global climatic changes such as El Niño and the Sahel drought and/or desertification have made us more aware of atmospheric dynamics and global climate systems. Among the most important consequences of future changes in climate will be alterations in regional hydrological cycles and subsequent effects on the quality and quantity of regional water resources, yet these consequences are poorly understood. Recent hydrological research strongly suggests that it is plausible that climatic changes caused by increases in greenhouse trace gas concentrations will (1) alter the timing and magnitude of run-off and soil moisture, (2) change lake levels and groundwater availability, and (3) affect water quality. Such a scenario raises the possibility of dramatic environmental and socio-economic dislocations and has widespread implications for future water-resources planning and management.

By looking at the variations of climate and hydrological conditions in geological time, we can simulate the analogies of future greenhouse conditions which may cause significant changes in water availability. Nicholson and Flohn (1980), using a variety of palaeoclimatic records, suggested that there have been significant climatic changes in the Sahel region that can be related to possible driving forces in global atmospheric circulation, which may explain the huge amount of fossil groundwater resources stored in the extensive Nubian sandstones of the Sahara desert during the Late Pleistocene age.

Water differs markedly from most other natural resources by its remarkable property of continuous renewal in the water cycle, the main link in which is water exchange between oceans and the land. The world ocean is a gigantic evaporator, which, in this natural cycle, is the main source of fresh water. The fresh water falls as atmospheric precipitation and is the source of all water flows and water accumulation on land. The greater part of the water on the earth, approximately 97.5%, is salt water and water that is mineralized.

The volume of fresh water amounts to 35,029,000 km^3, or 2.52% of the total uncombined water on the earth. Rivers and streams account for 0.006%, fresh-water lakes for 0.26%, and water contained in the atmosphere for 0.001% of the total quantity of fresh water. The rest of the fresh-water component occurs as soil moisture, permanent snow cover, marshes, and active groundwater (Korzun et al. 1976). Since the end of the nineteenth century the attention of many scientists has been directed to the problem of the connection between atmospheric precipitation, run-off, and evaporation in river basins. Water-resources development in the twentieth century has been directed to exploiting rivers and streams, lake water, and groundwater, which have had to be exclusively fresh. Saline waters such as seawater and brackish water, of which the storage potential is estimated to be as much as 97.5% of all the water on the earth (Korzun et al. 1976), may suggest their increasingly important role in the water-resources planning of arid to semi-arid countries in the twenty-first century.

2.1.1 Causation of the arid zone

On a world scale there is a sharp fall in rainfall near 30° latitude in both hemispheres (see the horse latitudes in fig. 2.1), and in places, notably on the west coast of Chile and Peru, rainfall is almost or entirely unknown (fig. 2.2). Since this aridity affects oceans as well as continents, it is apparent that there must be some process whereby rainfall is suppressed, for there is no shortage of water for evaporation.

15

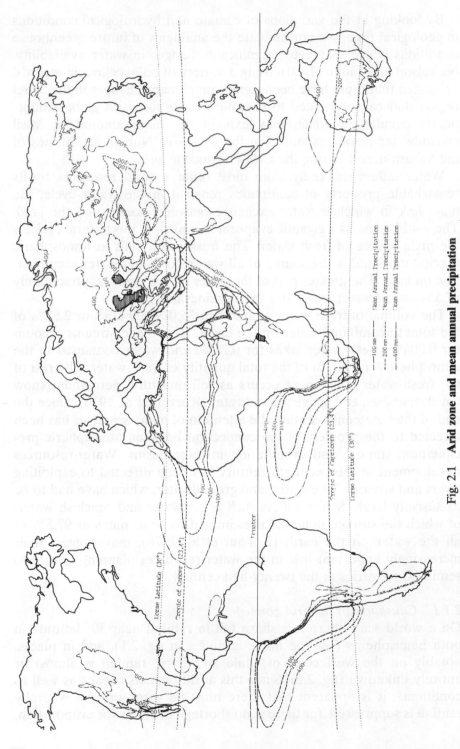

Fig. 2.1 Arid zone and mean annual precipitation

Horse Latitude (30°)

Tropic of Cancer (23.4°)

Equator

Tropic of Capricorn (23.4°)

Horse Latitude (30°)

— Mean Annual Precipitation

—— Mean Annual Precipitation

——— Mean Annual Precipitation

—— 100 mm

—— 200 mm

——— 400 mm

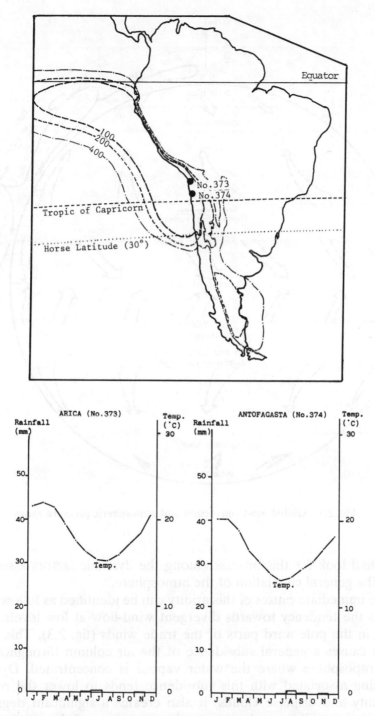

Fig. 2.2 **Arid-region climate graphs (Arica and Antofagasta, Chile)**

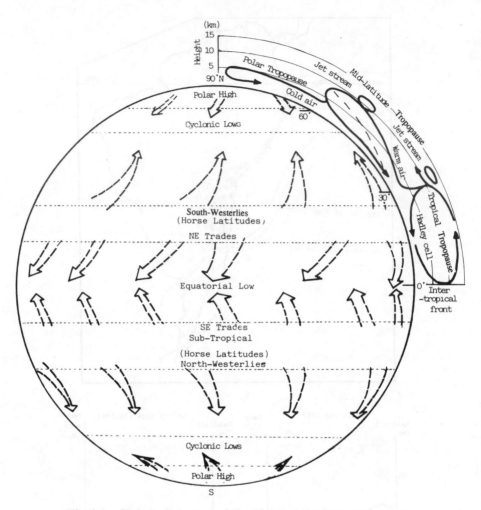

Fig. 2.3 **Global wind convection and atmospheric pressure zones**

We shall look for this process among the dynamic factors associated with the general circulation of the atmosphere.

The immediate causes of this aridity can be identified as follows: The first is the tendency towards divergent wind-flow at low levels, especially in the pole-ward parts of the trade winds (fig. 2.3). This divergence causes a general subsidence of the air column throughout the low troposphere where the water vapour is concentrated. Dynamic warming associated with this subsidence tends to lower the relative humidity and disperse clouds; it also creates a significant degree of hydrostatic stability, so that convection currents and shower-type precipitation are inhibited. At sea the trade winds have a shallow, moist

18

layer of moving air capped by a stable or inversion layer above which the air is very dry. Over land, as in the Sahara, northern Mexico, Australia, and much of the Middle East (in summer), the dryness may extend to ground level. Hence surface divergence, general subsidence, low humidities, and an absence of deep convection form a causally connected sequence over much (but not all) of the subtropical world. The second cause of aridity, not truly independent of the first, is the existence of high-pressure zones near the latitudes of 30° north and south (figs. 2.4 and 2.5). Over the ocean, this high pressure is recorded at sea level, but inland it may be necessary to ascend to levels of 2–3

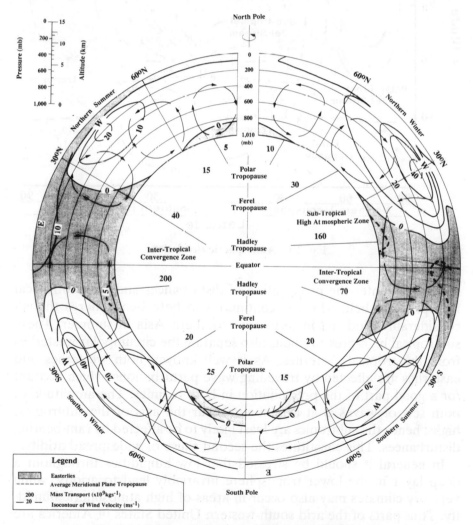

Fig. 2.4 **Schematic global circulation and tropopauses**

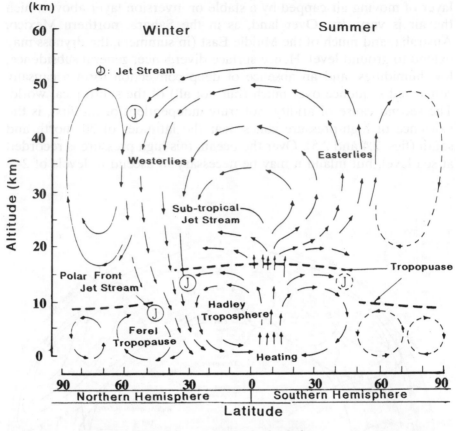

Fig. 2.5 **Atmospheric circulation**

km to encounter the propagation of disturbances and the subtropical high-pressure belt, which is continuous in both hemispheres though considerably modified in form over southern Asia in summer. These subtropical high-pressure belts also separate the circumpolar westerlies from the tropical easterlies. As is well known, both westerlies and easterlies are affected by travelling wave perturbations, which account for a good part of the precipitation in both regimes. The amplitude of both sets of waves is at a minimum near the axis of the subtropical highs; hence the subtropics are least likely to be affected by rain-bearing disturbances. This constitutes the second cause of widespread aridity.

In general it should be stressed that low humidities throughout a deep layer in the lower troposphere invariably lead to aridity, while very dry climates may also occur in areas of high atmospheric humidity. Thus parts of the arid south-western United States of America are dry not because of low humidities but because of the ineffectiveness of rain-making disturbances (Benton and Estoque 1954).

A further point is that remoteness from the sea is not a guarantee of drought; high moisture contents occur deep in the interior of Amazonia, more than 2,000 km from the ocean along any possible direct streamline, and rainfall is heavy. Yet extremely low rainfalls occur in many areas along oceanic coasts, as in Chile, Peru, Morocco, and south-west Africa (see figs. 2.1 and 2.2). The point is, of course, that local sources of evaporation play a very small role in precipitation, which tends in most instances to fall from moist air streams whose humidity has been derived from very remote surfaces.

The aridity of the subtropics thus emerges as an aspect of world climate dependent on deep-seated features of the earth's general atmospheric circulation. It does not arise from local or man-made circumstances but from natural causes involving exceedingly large energy transformations and momentum transports. It has not been conceived that the regime can be significantly altered by human intervention. Discussion today in the early 1990s, however, is based on the world-wide concern with global climatic changes, which may be due to the substantial increases of carbon dioxide caused by industrialization since the Second World War.

It is equally unlikely that any past climatic epoch can have experienced a complete absence of subtropical aridity. As we have seen, the maintenance of the mid-latitude westerlies absolutely requires the existence of compensating easterlies in the tropics. Similarly the transfer of momentum and heat northward in the tropics requires the existence of a Hadley cell (figs. 2.3–2.5), with subsidence (and hence low humidity and drought) at some subtropical latitude. Hence it seems likely that the arid zone can have been no more than constricted in extent and driven a few degrees towards the equator at the height of recent glacial development; it can hardly have been eliminated altogether (Hare 1964).

2.1.2 Definition and classification of the arid zone
Deserts have been mapped in regions as diverse as low and high latitude zones, inland continents, and coastal zones. Cold deserts, which are situated in high mountain ranges or high-latitude zones, are not included in this study, which deals with warm deserts situated between the tropics and the temperate zones.

One of the simplest classifications of dry climates takes 10 inches (250 mm) as the dividing line between arid and semi-arid and 20 inches (500 mm) between semi-arid and humid (refer to fig. 2.1). Although these criteria are scorned by many scientific geographers and climatologists, they are actually not bad for the standard climatic classifications.

Most classifications today use combinations of temperature and precipitation, in order to make some allowance for the increasing evaporation with higher temperatures. De Martonne (1926, 1942) and Koppen (1923) both used figures of mean annual precipitation (P) and temperature (T). The basic de Martonne formula gives an index of aridity (I) which is a true sliding scale without artificial break points: $I = P/(T + 10)$. Koppen's formula has rigid break points, but these are varied according to the season of maximum rainfall. The margin between arid and semi-arid would be R (rainfall) $= T + 11$. Koppen's formulas were an attempt to assign climatic values to the limits of the main vegetation types of the world.

Another approach analyses the temperature and precipitation ratios of individual months. The monthly indices, including mean monthly precipitation (P_m) and temperature (T_m), are then summarized into an annual figure. Thus, de Martonne's index becomes the total of twelve monthly indices, each of which is calculated as $12P_m/(T_m + 10)$.

Thornthwaite's basic system is more complex, but uses only mean monthly temperature and precipitation to arrive at a figure for estimated potential evapotranspiration (PEt) (Thornthwaite 1948). The arid regions are classified on the basis of an aridity index (AI) which assumes (1) $AI = 0$ when $P = PEt$, (2) $AI = -100$ when $P = 0$, (3) $AI = +100$ when P is much greater than PEt, with the following zone classifications corresponding to the AI ranges indicated:

— semi-temperate, 0 to -10,
— semi-arid, -20 to -40,
— arid, less than -40.

This method has been widely used by climatologists owing to its simple methodology. For the irrigation engineer, however, the method of estimating the parameters for potential evapotranspiration was found to be not accurate enough to be used for design purposes. Thornthwaite has introduced soil factors to the point that his latest indices can no longer be considered purely climatic (Thornthwaite and Mather 1957).

An early version of the concept of evaporation balance was devised by Albrecht Penck (1910), who used the geomorphic factor of hydrographic balance for a broad climatic classification. De Martonne (1942) drew a world map upon such a basis.

Emberger (1955) uses mean annual precipitation (P), mean daily maximum temperature of the warmest month (M), and mean daily minimum temperature of the coldest month (m), all combined into a single moisture quotient (Q) using the following formula:

$$Q = \frac{2P}{(M+m)(M-m)} \times 1,000$$

Unlike the formulae of Koppen, Thornthwaite, or de Martonne, Emberger's moisture quotient cannot be used by itself to make a valid climatic map. His maps appear to be based on his profound knowledge of vegetation, not on the mapping of climatic data. After mapping the vegetation zones, he determines the associated moisture quotients and other climatic values within the zones. Thus, the northern limit of his arid zone in north-west Africa varies from a moisture quotient of 16 to one of 40. In characterizing the climate of his stations, he uses the actual mean daily minimum temperature of the coldest month, as well as the moisture quotient. His maps for north-west Africa, which he calls bioclimatic zone maps, are of fundamental value for all geographers and climatologists. Because of the accuracy and detail of his mapping, the maps form a valuable test of the vegetation validity of any climatic system. A simple check shows, for example, that de Martonne's index of 10 would serve fairly well as the northern limit of Emberger's Mediterranean arid bioclimatic zone.

Meigs, a former chairman of the Arid Zone Commission of the International Geographical Union, made a global arid zone map in 1951 (fig. 2.6), whose zonal classifications have been widely used in arid-zone research since World War II. Meigs's classification is based on regional temperatures (mean monthly maxima and minima) and the duration of dry periods. His arid index map distinguishes three subregions: extremely arid, arid, and semi-arid. The extremely arid region, which receives zero annual rainfall for twelve months of continuous observation, occupies about 4% of the land area of the earth. The arid region, which has a minimum of one month of rainy season, covers about 15% of the land area of the earth. The semi-arid region has a rainy season with 100–200 mm of rainfall and occupies about 14.6% of the land area of the earth (Goudie and Wilkinson 1977).

2.1.3 Global atmospheric circulation and climatic changes in the arid zone

In the last twenty years low rainfall in the Sahel, possibly related to climatic changes, has reduced water availability in North Africa. Fol-

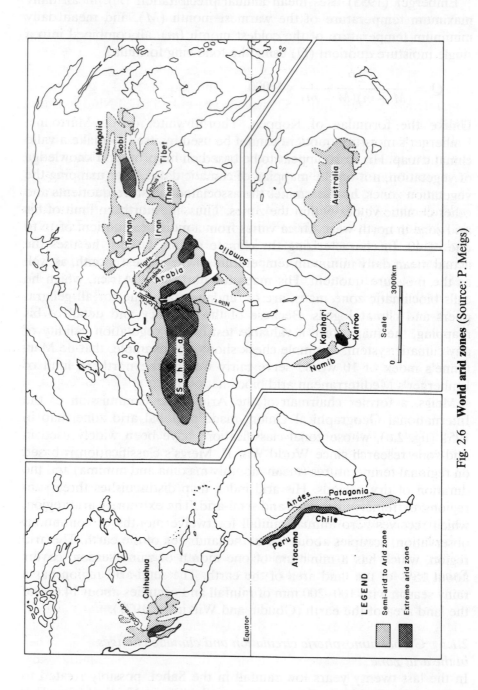

Fig. 2.6 **World arid zones** (Source: P. Meigs)

LEGEND

Semi-arid to Arid zone

Extreme arid zone

land and Palmer (1986) noted that there is a strong inverse relation-ship between worldwide sea surface temperature (SST) and Sahelian rainfall. The SST has been rising since the late 1960s, which period corresponds with decreasing rainfall in the Sahelian region. The present increase in SST is considered likely to be linked to global climatic change, which suggests the warming of the climate by the greenhouse effect. However, the rising SST may also be linked to El Niño southern oscillations.

El Niño events occurred in 1972–73, 1976–77, and 1982–83, result-ing in drought in the Sahel. Failure or weakening of the Guinea mon-soon seriously reduced the rainfall in the Ethiopian highlands. Most of the major rivers of North Africa originate in the Central African uplands, the Atlas Ranges, and the Ethiopian highlands (see section 2.2.4). More than 80% of the Nile's water originates in the Ethiopian highlands. The reservoir level in Lake Nasser has fallen by more than 18 meters in the last seven years owing to the African drought (WPDC 1988). As a result, usable effective storages are only one-fifth (20×10^9 m^3) of the 1979 level.

The increasing albedo is another climatic factor that affects water resources. Desertification has increased the albedo level in the catch-ment area of northern African rivers. The net effect of a high albedo level is that the sun's energy is reflected to the atmosphere to heat the air, causing increased evaporation and transpiration, resulting in a decrease in the potential water resources.

2.1.4 *Palaeoclimatology and water-resources planning*

About 10,000 years B.P. the global climate was moist and cooler, indi-cating atmospheric carbon dioxide concentrations between 260 and 290 mg/l. The earth was covered with 6.2 billion hectares of forest as compared to 4.1 billion hectares today at the end of the last (fourth) glacial age (Matthews 1983).

Nicholson and Flohn (1980) explored water availability in Africa using a variety of palaeoclimatic records. They suggest that parts of the Sahel region were drier 18,000 years before the present (B.P.), became moister and cooler with frequent rains in the period 10,000–4,500 years B.P., and then became drier again up to the present. Similarly, Good-friend et al. (1986) explored the palaeoclimatic evidence for climatic changes in the area of the Jordan River basin and the Dead Sea. They identified large fluctuations in the level of the Dead Sea, its terminal lake, in the Late Pleistocene period up to 4,300 years B.P.

Reconstructions of the record back several centuries can provide

valuable information on both past climatic conditions and the vulner-
ability of our water resources system to future changes. In a striking
example, Stockton and Jacoby (1976) used tree rings to extend the
run-off record in the Colorado River basin back more than 400 years,
using carbon-13 (^{13}C) isotope in tree rings as the environment tracer
(fig. 2.7). This kind of study has direct water management and policy

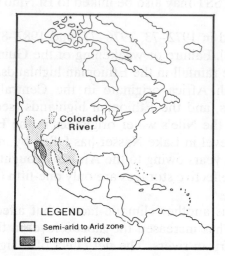

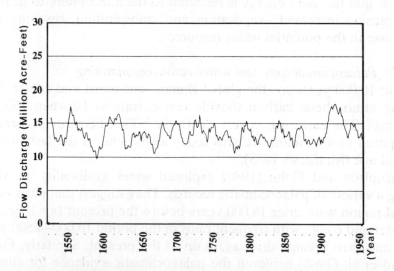

Fig. 2.7 **Palaeohydrology of the Colorado River basin.** 400-year
run-off record reconstructed from ^{13}C in tree rings, plotted as a
10-year moving average (1 acre-foot = 1,234 m³). Note the anom-
alously high run-off during the early twentieth century; this short
period was used to determine allocations for the 1922 Colorado River
Compact. (Source: Stockton and Jacoby 1976)

implications. For example, the original 1922 Colorado River water allocation was based on the hydrological record available at that time: namely about 30 years from the late 1890s to the early 1920s. In 1976, when the historical record was reconstructed back to the middle 1500s, the period from 1890 to the 1920s stood out as a time of abnormally high run-off. The 400-year record now shows that more water was allocated to users than is likely to be available on a long-term average basis. If the long-term record had been available in 1922, such over-allocation might not have occurred. These changes can also be related to possible driving forces in the global atmospheric circulation.

PALAEO-CARBON DIOXIDE AND THE GREENHOUSE EFFECT. The atmospheric carbon dioxide concentrations in air particles trapped in the 2,200 metre Vostock ice cores have been analysed to examine the historical changes of the climate since 160,000 years B.P (Matthews 1983). These Antarctic ice cores also provide temperature information for the same period based on the oxygen isotope (^{18}O) ratio. The derived temperature changes closely match changes in carbon dioxide concentrations (fig. 2.8).

Gammon et al. (1985) reviewed the history of atmospheric carbon dioxide from 100 million years ago to the present. During the Cretaceous age (100 million years B.P) the carbon dioxide level was perhaps as high as several thousand parts per million; then it dropped to 200–300 mg/l during the glacial-interglacial cycles of the past few million years through 10,000 years B.P. Since the nineteenth century, the carbon dioxide level has increased to about 350 mg/l, which could be owing to the accelerated burning of fossil fuels as an energy source (see fig. 2.9). North America, western Europe, and the former USSR and Soviet-bloc countries produce 67.4% of the world's carbon dioxide emissions to sustain their industrial activities (Rotty and Masters 1985).

COHMAP AND GCMs. The scientists of the Cooperative Holocene Mapping Project (COHMAP) have assembled a global array of well-documented palaeoclimatic data and general circulation models (GCMs). The GCM, which was developed to look at soil moisture in the mid-continental region of the United States of America, has shown that significant drying may occur if the concentration of carbon dioxide in the earth's atmosphere is doubled (Manabe and Wetherald 1986). GCM-generated hydrological data suffer from two major limitations: (1) the spatial resolution of GCMs is too coarse to provide hydrological information on a scale typically of interest to a hydrologist, and

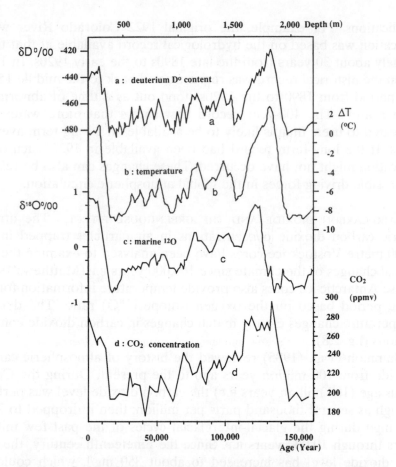

Fig. 2.8 **Carbon dioxide concentrations in Vostock ice cores.** The upper scale gives the depth of the core; the lower scale indicates the time (in years) of the various records. (Source: Loruis et al. 1988)

(2) hydrological parameterizations in GCMs are very simple and often do not provide the detailed information necessary for water-resources planning (WMO 1987). The hybrid COHMAP-GCM model simulates historical worldwide climatic changes in the atmosphere, geosphere, and biosphere that accompanied the transition from glacial to inter-glacial conditions during the past 18,000 years with geological and palaeo-ecological evidence (COHMAP members 1988), the results of which are to be used not for predicting the changes in water resources systems in future but for understanding changes in global climate on a geological time scale.

To assess the implications of the greenhouse effect for water

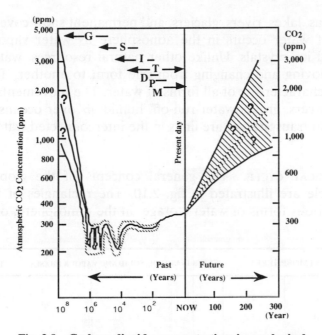

Fig. 2.9 **Carbon dioxide concentration in geological time scale.** (*G*) geological carbon cycle model; (*S*) ocean sediment cores; (*I*) trapped air bubbles in ice cores; (*T*) ^{13}C isotopic studies of tree rings; (*D*) direct chemical measurements of the past century; (*P*) spectroscopic plates from the Smithsonian Solar Constant Program; (*M*) Mauna Loa record and subsequent precise atmospheric CO_2 measurements by non-dispersive infrared spectroscopy (Source: Gammon et al. 1985)

resources in the arid to semi-arid regions, regional-scale details of future changes are needed for temperature, precipitation, evaporation, soil moisture, and other hydro-climatological variables. It is simply assumed that increasing concentrations of greenhouse gases will have an adverse effect on water resources in tropical and temperate arid zones.

2.1.5 Nature of the hydrological cycle and global water balance
Hydrology is concerned with the occurrence and movement of water on the earth. Water is one of the commonest substances in nature. It occurs in chemically combined forms, in free states, and in the biosphere. The free states include groundwater and soil moisture in the upper layer of the lithosphere and in the soil cover, and water in

29

oceans, seas, lakes, rivers, glaciers, and permanent snow cover. A small amount of water occurs in the atmosphere as water vapour, water drops, and ice crystals. Unlike other natural resources, water is continually moving and changing from one form to another. The movement is a characteristic of all forms of water. The movements of ocean currents, rivers, groundwater run-off, humid air over oceans and continents, and transpiration are links in the interconnected water cycle of nature.

HYDROLOGICAL CYCLE. The general concepts of the global hydrological cycle are illustrated in fig. 2.10. The rectangles of the figure denote various forms of water storage: in the atmosphere, on the sur-

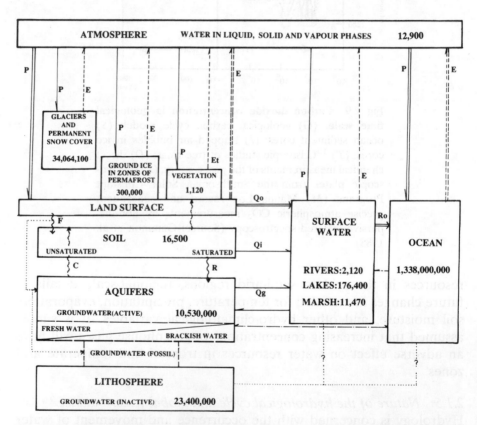

Fig. 2.10 **The global hydrological cycle.** Numbers represent the volume of water reserves in cubic kilometres. (*P*) rainfall/precipitation; (*E*) evaporation; (*Et*) evapotranspiration; (*F*) filtration/infiltration from surface to unsaturated soil; (*Qo*) overland flow; (*Qi*) lateral interflow; (*Qg*) groundwater outflow; (*R*) groundwater recharge; (*Ro*) run-off to ocean; (*C*) capillary rise from groundwater (Data source: Korzun 1976)

face of the ground, in the unsaturated soil moisture zone, in the groundwater reservoir below the water table, in the channel drainage network, and in the oceans. The arrows in the diagram denote the various hydrological processes responsible for the transfer of water from one form of storage to another.

Thus the precipitable water (W) in the atmosphere may be transformed by precipitation (P) to water stored on the surface of the ground. In the reverse direction, water may be transferred from the surface of the ground by evaporation (E) or from the unsaturated soil by transpiration through vegetation and subsequent evaporation from the leaf surface (Et).

Some of the water on the surface of the ground will infiltrate through the surface into the unsaturated soil (F), but some of it may find its way as overland flow (Qo) into the channel network. During precipitation, if the field moisture deficit of the soil which has arisen since the previous precipitation is substantially satisfied, then there will be either recharge (R) to the groundwater or else lateral interflow (Qi) through the saturated soil into the channel network.

Groundwater storage is depleted by groundwater outflow (Qg), which enters the channel network and supplies streamflow during dry periods. During prolonged droughts, soil moisture may be replenished by capillary rise (C) from groundwater to the unsaturated zone and subsequent loss to the atmosphere by evapotranspiration.

Overland flow (Qo), lateral interflow (Qi), and groundwater outflow (Qg) are all combined and modified in the channel network to form the run-off (Ro) from the area for which the balance is being calculated. These various hydrological processes form the subject matter of physical hydrology.

GLOBAL WATER BALANCE. The quantities of water in the ocean, atmosphere, ice masses, lakes, and rivers may be evaluated without too much difficulty. It is more difficult to determine the amounts contained in living organisms and in the lithosphere. The figure of greatest uncertainty is that for inactive groundwater. A general idea of the world water reserves is shown in table 2.1. The total reserves are preliminarily estimated to be about 1,386 million km³. The breakdown of the volume of each form of water is shown below (Korzun et al. 1978):

>> *Ocean and seas.* The volume of water in the ocean is estimated to be 1,338 million km³ by assuming that the ocean covers an area of 361.3 million km² with an average depth of about 3.7 km. This represents about 96.5% of the total water reserves of the earth.

31

Table 2.1 **World water reserves**

	Volume (km³)	Share of world reserves	
		Share of total water (%)	Share of fresh water (%)
Atmospheric water	12,900	0.001	0.01
Glaciers and permanent snow cover	24,064,000	1.74	68.7
Ground ice in zones of permafrost strata	300,000	0.022	0.86
Water in rivers	2,120	0.0002	0.006
Water in lakes (fresh, 91,000 km³)	176,400	0.013	0.26
Water in marshes	11,470	0.0008	0.03
Soil moisture	16,500	0.001	0.05
Active groundwater (in aquifers), including brackish and fossil	10,530,000	0.76	30.1
Inactive groundwater (in lithosphere)	23,400,000	1.7	—
World ocean	1,338,000,000	96.5	—

Source: Korzun et al. 1976.

>> *Glaciers and permanent snow cover.* The amounts of water in the ice of the polar regions and in the glaciers of mountainous regions are estimated to be about 24 million km³, which accounts for 68.7% of the earth's total resources of fresh water.

>> *Inactive groundwater.* Substantial amounts of water are stored in the lithosphere. The inactive groundwater in the earth's crust—that is, gravity water contained in the pores and cracks of saturated strata—is estimated to be 23.4 million km³ by assuming an effective porosity of 5%–15% and a maximum depth of 2,000 m.

>> *Active groundwater.* The depths of fresh-water accumulations vary, depending on local geological characteristics. By assuming an effective depth of aquifers between 200 and 600 m, the volume of active groundwater is preliminarily estimated to be 10.53 million km³, which is 30% of the total volume of fresh water.

>> *Soil moisture.* Soil moisture is more closely related to weather conditions than is groundwater. During the wet seasons, moisture is stored in the soil, while it is removed by evaporation and tran-

spiration in the dry seasons. The storage of moisture in the soil is estimated to be 16,000 km^3, by assuming a soil layer of 2 m thick with 10% of moisture on average.

» *Lakes and reservoirs*. There are numerous lakes in the world. Large lakes with an area of more than 100 km^2 may store 95% of the total reserves in all lakes in the world. The total water volume in the world's 145 large lakes amounts to 168,000 km^3, which is 95% of the world's total of 176,000 km^3. Of this, 91,000 km^3 is in fresh-water lakes, while approximately half the water (85,000 km^3) is salty. Most of the salty lake water is concentrated in large lakes without outlet, such as the Dead Sea, the Caspian Sea, and the Aral Sea.

Intensive construction of large dams, especially since the Second World War, has created large reservoirs on major rivers. The total capacity of the 10,000 reservoirs of the world amounts to about 5,000 km^3, with a net capacity of about 2,000 km^3, which now controls approximately 14% of the total annual river run-off of 445,000 km^3.

» *Marshes*. Marshes occur in many areas of the earth. These are mostly peat marshes in countries with temperate climates and their equivalents in tropical and equatorial areas. The total amount of marsh water in the world is preliminarily estimated to be 11,000 km^3.

» *River channels*. The total water storage in river channels of the world at any given moment is estimated at 2,000 km^3, which accounts for only 0.006% of all fresh water. However, it is of great importance to development as a renewable source for water supply.

» *Atmosphere*. Water is contained in the atmosphere in the form of water vapour, water drops, and ice crystals. The total moisture in the atmosphere amounts to about 12,000 km^3, which is equivalent to 25 mm of water if spread over the whole surface of the globe.

2.1.6   Remarks on global water reserves and water resources

The total amount of water in the hydrological cycle is constant and can neither be increased nor diminished. From the global-scale water-budget study outlined above, it looks as though there is more than enough fresh water to meet the demands of human survival, both now and in the foreseeable future. However, water is often available in the wrong place, at the wrong time, or in the wrong quality. This uneven distribution is highlighted in the arid regions. In many of the countries in the Middle East, the hydrological cycle is being disturbed by over-exploitation, depletion, or deterioration of the fresh waters in rivers and groundwater aquifers.

Salt waters, including seawater and brackish waters in rivers and aquifers, have been conceived as either useless or harmful and as being outside the scope of water-resources planning except where neither conventional river water nor groundwater of good quality exists. The volume of conventional fresh-water reserves on the earth, however, is minimal compared with other forms of water such as seawater, which accounts for 96.5% of the total water on the earth. Potential ground-water reserves are estimated to be as high as 30% of the total fresh-water reserves. However, brackish water is predominant in the major aquifers of the arid region owing to the minimal rainfall and hence minimal groundwater recharge.

Most of the known conventional water resources such as river water and groundwater of good quality or low salinity have already been developed or will soon be fully exploited in most countries of the Middle East. Non-conventional waters such as seawater and brackish waters, including both surface and groundwater, therefore, seem likely to play an increasingly important role in water-resources planning of the arid region for the twenty-first century, when the advances and innovations of desalting technologies, including reverse osmosis applications, are taken into account to save energy and cost.

2.2 The Tigris and Euphrates Rivers

Despite the great size of the Middle East, there are only three rivers that can be classified as large by world standards—the Nile, the Euphrates, and the Tigris. The watersheds of both the Euphrates and the Tigris are situated within the Middle East, predominantly in the countries of Turkey, Syria, and Iraq (fig. 2.11).

The Euphrates, which is the longest inter-state river in western Asia, has been developed since 4000 B.C. Several ancient civilizations in Mesopotamia were supported by basin irrigation from the Tigris and Euphrates Rivers. Owing to the extremely arid climate, however, the farm lands on the Mesopotamian alluvials have suffered from salt accumulation and waterlogging problems since 2400 B.C., during the Sumerian age. This ancient civilization disappeared with the abandonment of irrigation-canal systems. The washing out of accumulated salts, or leaching as it is called, can be carried out only with an efficient

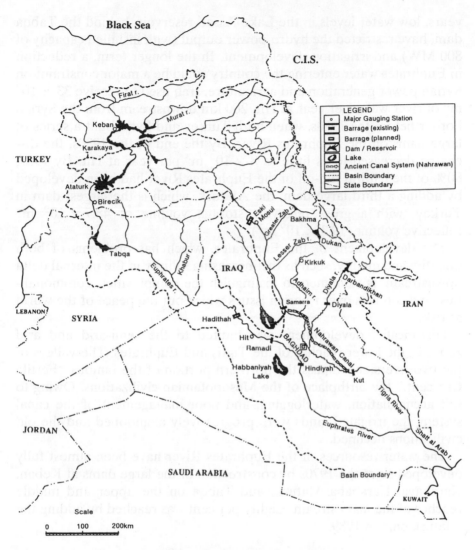

Fig. 2.11 **The Tigris-Euphrates basin**

drainage system, which requires careful water management to sustain the irrigation system.

Before Turkey began building large dams on the Euphrates, the river's average annual flow at the Turkish-Syrian border was about 30×10^9 m^3. To this, a further 1.8×10^9 m^3 is added in Syria from the Khabour River, a major tributary. On several occasions in recent

35

years, low water levels in the Lake Assad reservoir, behind the Tabqa dam, have restricted the hydro-power output (with installed capacity of 800 MW) and irrigation development. In the longer term, a reduction in Euphrates water entering the country could be a major constraint on Syrian power generation and agriculture. Iraq used to receive 33×10^9 m^3 of river water per year at Hit, 200 km downstream from the Syrian border before the 1970s, when both Turkey and Syria built a series of large dams on the Euphrates River. By the end of the 1980s, the discharge decreased to as little as 8×10^9 m^3 per year at Hit. By 1989, 80% of the natural run-off of the Euphrates River had been developed by adding a third large dam, the Ataturk, which is the largest dam in Turkey, with a gross reservoir storage volume of 48.7×10^9 m^3 (effective volume, 19.3×10^9 m^3).

The development of the Euphrates, which has problems of both quantity and quality, such as the increasing salinity in the internal delta downstream, is examined to distinguish the complexities, commonalities, and conflicts over riparian issues which put the peace of the world at risk.

Historically, development was limited to the semi-arid and arid zones of the lower reaches of the Tigris and Euphrates. The valleys of the two rivers encompass the northern portion of the famous "Fertile Crescent," the birthplace of the Mesopotamian civilizations. Owing to salt accumulation, waterlogging, and poor management of the canal system, the irrigated lands were progressively abandoned and the old civilizations declined.

The water resources of the Euphrates River have been almost fully developed since the 1970s by construction of the large dams at Keban, Karakaya, Karababa/Ataturk, and Tabqa on the upper and middle reaches of the main stream. Eighty per cent was reached by adding the Ataturk dam in 1989.

2.2.1 The river basin

The Tigris-Euphrates basin lies primarily in three countries—Turkey, Syria, and Iraq (see fig. 2.11). Both the Tigris and Euphrates rivers rise in the mountains of southern Turkey and flow south-eastwards, the Euphrates crossing Syria into Iraq and the Tigris flowing directly into Iraq from Turkey. The main stream of the Euphrates in Turkey is called the Firat, and it has four major tributaries—the Karasu, the Murat, the Munzur, and the Peri. After leaving Turkey, the Euphrates has only one large tributary, the Khabur, which joins the main stream in Syria. By contrast, the Tigris has four main tributaries, all of which unite with the main stream in Iraq. The largest of these, the Great Zab, has its source in Turkey, while the Lesser Zab and the Diyala originate in Iran. All of the catchment of the Adhaim, which is the smallest stream, is in Iraq. In southern Iraq the Tigris and the Euphrates unite to form the Shatt al-Arab, which in turn flows into the Arabian Gulf.

The lengths of the main streams are 2,330 km for the Euphrates, 1,718 km for the Tigris, and 190 km for the Shatt al-Arab. The catchment area of the basin is 423,800 km², of which 233,000 km² is that of the Euphrates, 171,800 km² of the Tigris, and 19,000 km² of the Shatt al-Arab (Shahin 1989).

The hydrographic and hydrological characteristics vary greatly over the basin. Rainfall in the Turkish headwaters area is abundant, but seasonal. However, from about 37°N, the river runs through arid country in Syria and Iraq.

2.2.2 Hydrology

The main sources of the Euphrates river flows in Turkey are found in the four tributaries, all of which originate at altitudes of about 3,000 m or more in the mountainous areas of eastern Turkey. Hydrological study was initiated in 1927–1929 by installing the first pluviometric stations in the basin of the Firat, the uppermost part of the Euphrates. Long-term records indicate an average annual precipitation of about 625 mm in the Keban basin, decreasing to approximately 415 mm in the lower Firat basin.

The upper part of the Euphrates basin has a catchment area of 63,874 km² at the confluence of the Firat and the Murat near the Keban, which produces 80% of the total annual flow at Karababa/ Ataturk (fig. 2.12). The average flow at Keban station over the 31 years of records (1936–1967) was 648 m³/sec, with the lowest flow of 136 m³/sec in September 1961 and the maximum flood of 6,600 m³/sec in May 1944. The long-term annual average discharge at the Karababa/Ataturk dam site is estimated to be 830 m³/sec. (Doluca and Pircher 1971).

The Firat has a relatively regular regime, characterized by two months of very high average flow in April and May and a period of eight dry months from July to February. The annual flow varies considerably from year to year, including extremely low flow records between July 1957 and January 1963, during which the average flow decreased to only 83% of the long-term average. The average winter flows, varying between 200 and 300 m³/sec, increase in February from early spring rains at lower elevations. The increase continues during

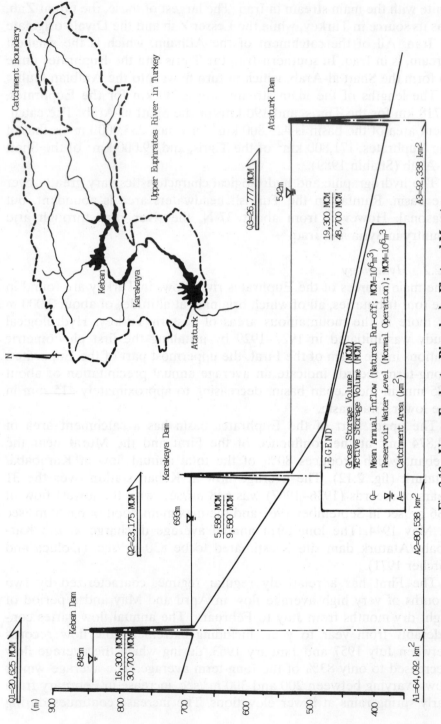

Fig. 2.12 Upper Euphrates River basin: Firat and Murat

March, when the snow begins to melt, and in April and May monthly average flows of 2,000 m³/sec and more are reached, with maximum floods occurring between mid-April and early May under the combined effect of melting snow and rains. The flow rapidly diminishes after June, reaching its minimum values in September and sometimes October.

The flows of the Tigris and Euphrates in Iraq are largely dependent on the discharges in Turkey. Much of the discharge of the Tigris results from the melting snow accumulated during the winter in Turkey. However, winter rains, which are common in late winter and early spring, falling on a ripe snowpack in the highlands, can greatly augment the flow of the main stream and its tributaries, giving rise to the violent floods for which the Tigris is notorious. The period of greatest discharge for the Tigris system as a whole is from March through May and accounts for 53% of the mean annual flow. The highest mean monthly discharge takes place during April. Minimum flow conditions are experienced from August through October and make up 7% of the annual discharge. The mean annual flow of the Tigris is 48.7×10^9 m³ in total at its confluence with the Euphrates, which includes 13.2×10^9 m³ from the Greater Zab, 7.2×10^9 m³ from the Lesser Zab, and 5.7×10^9 m³ from the Diyala (Shahin 1989; Beaumont et al. 1988).

The total flow of the Euphrates is not as great as that of the Tigris, although the river regimes are similar. It, too, rises in the highlands of Turkey and is fed by melting snows, to an even greater extent than the Tigris, but it lacks the major tributaries which the Tigris has. In Iraq, the period of maximum flow on the Euphrates is shorter and later than that of the Tigris and is usually confined to the months of April and May. Discharge during the two months accounts for 42% of the annual total. Minimum flows occur from August through October and contribute only 8.5% of the total discharge. The mean annual runoff of the Euphrates is 35.2×10^9 m³ at its confluence with the Tigris (Shahin 1989; Beaumont et al. 1988).

These mean values, however, conceal the fluctuations in discharge that can occur from year to year, for it must be remembered that both floods and drought are themselves of variable magnitude. Schematic regime hydrographs of the Tigris and Euphrates are shown in fig. 2.13.

2.2.3 *Euphrates River development and salinity problems*
The Euphrates River, which is the longest multinational river in Western Asia, has been developed since 4000 B.C. Several ancient civ-

39

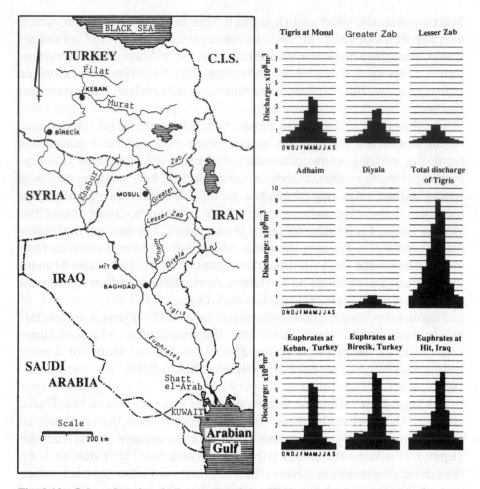

Fig. 2.13 Selected regime hydrographs of the Tigris and Euphrates Rivers (Source: Beaumont et al. 1988)

ilizations in Mesopotamia were supported by basin irrigation from the Tigris and Euphrates Rivers. Owing to the extremely arid climate, however, the farm lands on the Mesopotamian alluvials have suffered from salt accumulation and waterlogging problems since Sumerian times. These ancient civilizations disappeared with the abandonment of irrigation-canal systems.

One of the major reasons for the success of this complex irrigation network was the establishment of an efficient system of drainage, which prevented waterlogging of the soil and consequent salination of the land. Throughout the lowland as a whole, drainage was achieved by supplying irrigation water from the Euphrates in the west and the

Nahrawan canal in the east (fig. 2.11). This permitted the Tigris, which was situated between the two, to function as a drain, and to collect water from the adjacent agricultural lands. So efficient was this system that it supported widespread cultivation of the land in the region for many years without a serious decline in land quality. The maximum limits of agricultural expansion in the Diyala plains seem to have been attained during the Sassanian period (A.D. 226–637). With the collapse of Sassanian rule, a marked deterioration in agricultural conditions occurred, which continued almost unchecked for centuries. The reasons for the agricultural decline are complex, but a major one was probably the decreasing effectiveness of the central government, which meant that the necessary reconstruction and maintenance of the irrigation networks tended to lapse. Progressive siltation of the major canals occurred, reducing the efficiency of water transmission, and the irrigation control works fell into disrepair. By the time of the Mongol invasions of the twelfth and thirteenth centuries A.D., the abandonment of the once fertile land was almost complete.

The term "hydraulic civilization" has been used to describe societies similar to those in the alluvial lowlands of Iraq, which required large-scale management of water supplies by the bureaucracies of central governments for widespread agriculture to be feasible.

Although the agricultural recovery of the Tigris-Euphrates lowlands began during the late nineteenth century, with the rehabilitation of a number of the ancient canals, it was not until the early part of the twentieth century that the first modern river-control work, the Al-Hindiyah barrage (1909–1913) was constructed on the Euphrates. Its original function was to divert water into the Al-Hillah channel, which was running dry, but later, following reconstruction in the 1920s, it was also used to supply other canals. Between the two world wars, considerable attention was given to the Euphrates canal system, and many new channels were constructed and new control works established. Development on the Tigris tended to come later. The building of the Al-Kut barrage began in 1934 but was not completed until 1943, while on the Diyala, a tributary of the Tigris, a weir was constructed in 1927–1928 to replace a temporary earth dam that had to be rebuilt each year following the winter flood. The weir allowed six canals to be supplied with water throughout the year.

Following the Second World War, river-control schemes tended to concentrate on the problems of flood control. Two of the earliest projects, completed in the mid-1950s, were situated towards the upper part of the alluvial valley. The Samarra barrage was constructed on the Tigris River with the objective of diverting flood waters into the

41

Tharthar depression to provide a storage capacity of 30×10^9 m³. A similar scheme was also built on the Euphrates, where the Al-Ramadi barrage diverted flood waters into the Habbaniyah reservoir and the Abu Dibis depression. It had been hoped that stored water from these two projects might be used for irrigation during the summer months, but it was discovered that the very large evaporation losses, together with the dissolution of salts from the soils of the depressions, seriously diminished water quality and rendered it unsuitable for irrigation purposes. In conjunction with the barrages on the main streams themselves, two major dams were constructed on tributaries of the Tigris. The Dukan dam, with a reservoir storage capacity of 6.3×10^9 m³, was completed on the Lesser Zab River in 1959, while further south, on the Diyala River, the Darbandikhan dam, with 3.25×10^9 m³ of storage, was opened in 1961.

The Tigris and Euphrates Rivers are the main sources of water in Iraq. Because of flood irrigation, 1,598,000 ha of land have been affected by salinity, and the government is trying to reclaim this land (fig. 2.14). Before the 1970s, when both Turkey and Syria built a series of large dams on the Euphrates, Iraq received 33×10^9 m³ of river water per year at Hit, 200 km downstream from the Syrian border. By the end of the 1980s, the flow discharge at Hit had decreased to as little as 8×10^9 m³ per year (WPDC 1987).

Before Turkey began building large dams on the Euphrates, the river's average annual flow at the Turkish-Syrian border was about 30×10^9 m³. To this, a further 1.8×10^9 m³ is added in Syria from the Khabur River (Beaumont 1988). On several occasions in recent years, low water levels in the Lake Assad reservoir, behind the Tabqa dam (fig. 2.11), have restricted the hydro-power output (with an installed capacity of 800 MW) and irrigation development. In the 1970s Syria was planning to reclaim 640,000 ha or more in the Euphrates basin. However, progress has been slow, and only about 61,000 ha of new land either has been brought into cultivation or will be in the near future. The water requirement for this area is minimal and can at present easily be supplied from the 12×10^9 m³ Lake Assad reservoir or from the river's flow. In the longer term, however, a reduction of the Euphrates water entering the country could be a major constraint on Syrian power generation and agriculture.

In 1989, 80% of the natural run-off of the Euphrates River was developed by closing the Ataturk dam, the biggest dam in Turkey, with a gross reservoir storage volume of 48.7×10^9 m³ (effective volume, 19.3×10^9 m³) as shown in fig. 2.12.

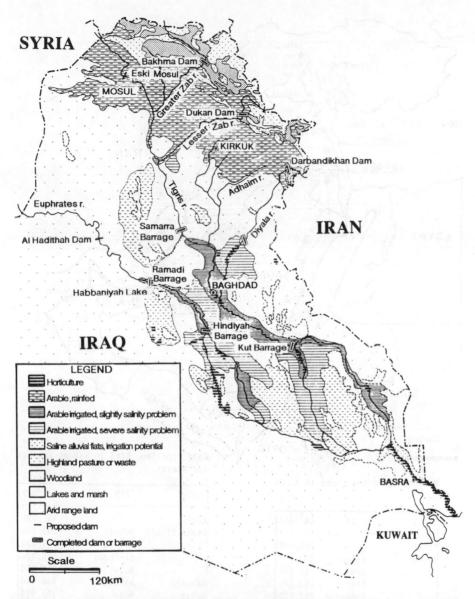

Fig. 2.14 **Salinity map of the Tigris-Euphrates delta** (Source: Beaumont et al. 1988)

2.2.4   *The Peace Pipeline project*

An inter-basin development plan was studied in the context of Tur-key's ambitious "Peace Pipeline" project in 1987, which would include the transfer of fresh water from the Seyhan, Ceyhan, and Euphrates basins by a series of dams and diversion tunnels to supply countries in

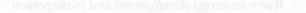

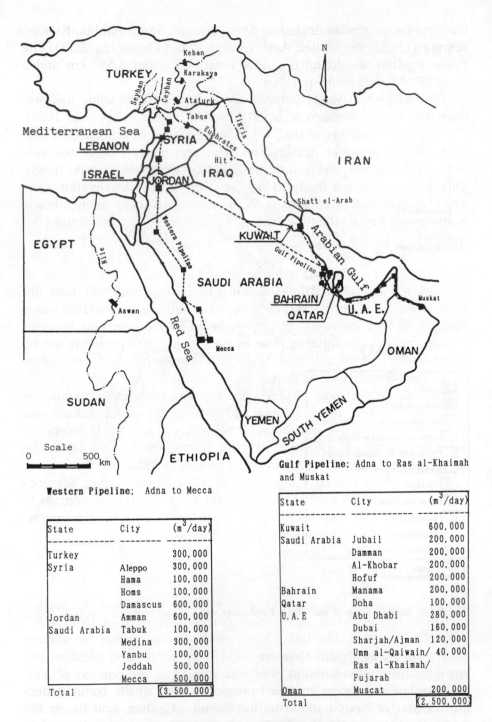

Western Pipeline; Adna to Mecca

State	City	(m³/day)
Turkey		300,000
Syria	Aleppo	300,000
	Hama	100,000
	Homs	100,000
	Damascus	600,000
Jordan	Amman	600,000
Saudi Arabia	Tabuk	100,000
	Medina	300,000
	Yanbu	100,000
	Jeddah	500,000
	Mecca	500,000
Total		(3,500,000)

Gulf Pipeline; Adna to Ras al-Khaimah and Muskat

State	City	(m³/day)
Kuwait		600,000
Saudi Arabia	Jubail	200,000
	Damman	200,000
	Al-Khobar	200,000
	Hofuf	200,000
Bahrain	Manama	200,000
Qatar	Doha	100,000
U.A.E	Abu Dhabi	280,000
	Dubai	160,000
	Sharjah/Ajman	120,000
	Umm al-Qaiwain/ Ras al-Khaimah/ Fujairah	40,000
Oman	Muscat	200,000
Total		(2,500,000)

Fig. 2.15 The Peace Pipeline scheme

the Arabian peninsula, including Syria, Jordan, Saudi Arabia, Kuwait, Bahrain, Qatar, the United Arab Emirates, and Oman (fig. 2.15). The Peace Pipeline would have a total length of about 6,550 km and a capacity of 6 million m^3 per day.

The unit cost of water pumped along the Peace Pipeline has preliminarily been estimated at US$0.84–US$1.07 per m^3 (Gould 1988). The economic viability of the project was assessed by comparison with conventional seawater desalination. The unit water cost of the seawater desalination was simply assumed at US$5/$m^3$ (Gould 1988). This, however, is not likely to represent the actual desalination cost, which should now take into account recent advances in membrane technologies for desalination such as reverse osmosis (see sections 2.8 and 2.9).

2.2.5 Political constraints and feasibility

Fresh water supplies are finite, and it is becoming more and more difficult to undertake projects that include the shifting of available water supplies to new areas of demand, especially if the project involves crossing political boundaries. The Peace Pipeline will probably not be a key application for individual states but an option in water-resources planning at a multinational level.

The total project cost of the Peace Pipeline has been estimated at US$21 × 10^9 (1990 price, *Economist* 1990), which would make it one of the most expensive transboundary projects in the world (compare the Euro tunnel, at US$15 × 10^9; the Itaipu dam, US$9 × 10^9; the Mediterranean–Dead Sea solar-hydro project, US$2 × 10^9).

Water politics will be a key issue in transboundary river development in the Middle East. There is as yet no political commitment to the Peace Pipeline, but this project and variations on it remain options for consideration in the ongoing peace process.

2.3 The Indus River

The Indus, one of the mightiest rivers of the world and the second longest in western Asia, has a mean annual discharge of 207.5 × 10^9 m^3 (ECAFE 1966). The Indus River system has ten times the volume of flow of the Colorado River in the United States and Mexico, and more than three times that of the Nile.

Alluvial plains in the middle to lower reaches of the Indus system have been developed to form the largest irrigation scheme in the world. Approximately 16,000 km of canals have been constructed to irrigate over 9 million ha (Buras 1967). This irrigation project covers the greater part of a vast plain covered with fine-textured alluvial soil overlying coarser sediments extending deep (ten to hundreds of metres) downward to the bedrock of an ancient valley.

The development of the irrigation project was mostly carried out after 1850, but elements of an ancient flood irrigation channel can still be found. Most of the canals were excavated through the surface soil to the more pervious underlying fine sand, so that a large proportion of the surface water diverted through these canals seeped underground. The sediment, which forms an extensive aquifer, was continuously recharged by the leaking irrigation canals, so that the groundwater table rose continuously. In many areas, this rise was estimated to be approximately 30 cm per year. As a result, in much of the Indus plain the groundwater level was near the soil surface. Proper aeration of the soil could not take place, and, with the prevailing arid climatic conditions, capillary action and evapotranspiration moved salts from the subsurface up to the root zone of crops and to the land surface. Thus once-fertile lands have so deteriorated that crops can no longer be grown. In the 1950s and 1960s, the salinity and waterlogging problems became so serious that intensive research was carried out by international agencies, headed by the Harvard University Water Resources Group, focusing on aquifer utilization and management, including the mining of groundwater.

During successive stages of development of the irrigation systems in the Indus valley, little attention was given to land drainage, and emphasis was put on maximizing the extent of irrigated land. Integrated management of the underlying aquifer system in line with the surface-subsurface drainage is now being used successfully to control salinity and reclaim irrigated land.

2.3.1 The river basin

The Indus rises in Tibet, in the snow-clad Kailas range of the Himalayas, about 5,500 m above mean sea level. The catchment area extends over four countries—China, India, Pakistan, and Afghanistan—with the portion in Pakistan accounting for more than 50% of the total. The Indus basin lies in the subtropical zone; the Tropic of Cancer passes through its southernmost part, while its northern edge reaches the latitude 37°N (see fig. 2.16).

The Indus cuts through mountain ranges forming a narrow gorge and deep channel from the headwaters until an important tributary,

Fig. 2.16 **The Indus River basin**

the Kabul River, joins it from the west near Attock. A few kilometres above the town of Mithankot, the Indus is joined by its most important tributary, the Panjnad River, which carries the waters of five main tributaries—the Jhelum, the Chenab, the Ravi, the Beas, and the Sutlej. The river slope from the headwaters to Attock is approximately 1/300; from Attock to Mithankot it is 1/4,000; and from Mithankot to the sea it averages 1/7,000. The total length of the Indus is about 2,900 km. The drainage area of the whole system is approximately 970,000 km².

The northern region of the basin, where the Indus and its main tributaries originate, is fully covered with rugged sky-high mountains and glaciers, comprising an area of about 452,000 km². Because of the steep and barren slopes of these mountains, the erosion is very heavy, ranging according to locality from about 400 to over 4,000 tons per km² annually, with an average of about 1,500 tons. Lower down, the basin comprises vast plains formed and separated from each other by the five main tributaries. Further down from Mithankot, the Indus valley is covered with alluvium built up by the deposition of silt carried down by the river. The delta begins from Kotri, about 185 km from the sea, where the land is almost level and the soil is generally infertile. Closer to the sea is marshy land and mangrove forests which are generally flooded during high tides.

2.3.2 Hydrology

As noted, the Indus basin lies in the subtropical zone. In the plains, the average temperature during winter is about 21°C in Karachi and about 15°C in Lahore. Summer, the hottest season, is from May to August, and average temperature ranges from about 29°C in May to about 34°C towards the end of June or early July, when the maximum temperature often rises above 27.7°C. Despite the mighty Indus, the Indus plain is semi-arid. There are significant extremes of rainfall in the basin. The area around Sukkur and Mithankot receives only about 100 mm of rain a year, while, at Murree, a hill station at 2,280 m elevation, the annual precipitation is about 1,270 mm. The precipitation, inclusive of snow, is many times heavier in the hilly region than in the plains. The mid-hill area, with elevations from about 1,200 m to 2,500 m, where the south-west monsoon generally strikes the mountain mass, has the heaviest rainfall, averaging about 1,250–1,500 mm a year. At higher and lower elevations, the rainfall decreases rapidly and the air is correspondingly drier and clearer. The rainfall further decreases rapidly from north to south in the plains, from about 550 mm of annual rainfall in the foothills to only about 100 mm at Mithankot and Sukkur. Below Sukkur, the rainfall increases a little owing to the maritime air, reaching about 200 mm along the sea coast. The mean annual rainfall over the Indus plains is less than 250 mm.

Due to the uneven distribution of precipitation over the basin, the Indus and its tributaries receive most of their flow from the mountains. The flows are subject to extreme variations; the maximum summer discharge is over 100 times the winter minimum. During July and August, all the rivers attain their peaks, discharging a considerable volume of water to the sea (see fig. 2.17).

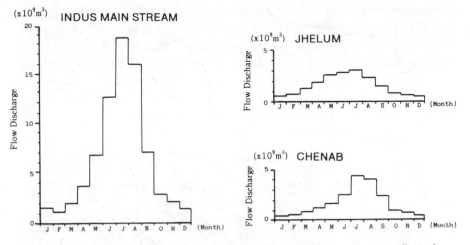

Fig. 2.17   **Average monthly flow of the Indus River and its two largest tributaries**

The mean annual run-off of the Indus is 207×10^9 m³, with a yearly maximum of 264×10^9 m³ and minimum of 171×10^9 m³. The Indus main stream carries about 110.3×10^9 m³ per year, while the major tributaries Jhelum, Chenab, Beas, Sutlej, Ravi carry 27.85×10^9 m³, 29×10^9 m³, 15.65×10^9 m³, 16.8×10^9 m³, and 7.9×10^9 m³ respectively. Thus the main stream alone carries a little more than half of the total discharge of the system. When combined with the Jhelum and Chenab, it carries a little more than fourth-fifths of the overall total, while the Ravi, Beas, and Sutlej together deliver a little less than one-fifth. The run-off coefficients are as high as 58%–82% (ECAFE 1966).

2.3.3   *Water-resources development*
As rainfall is scarce in the plains, where the cultivable areas lie, agriculture on the Indus plains has to depend almost exclusively on an irrigation system utilizing the river flows.

Many weir and canal systems were built on the Indus and its tributaries from the middle of the nineteenth century onwards, the first of which was the Upper Bari Doab canal, built between 1850 and 1859 to bring water from the Ravi River at Madhopur to the upper half of the *doab*, or inter-river land, in the vicinity of Lahore. By 1947, when India and Pakistan achieved independence as separate countries, the Indus water system had already been developed to provide irrigation to about 10.9 million ha, but it is remarkable that no storage reservoirs had yet been built in a system serving the world's largest irrigation area. Among the major hydraulic works built before 1947 were the

49

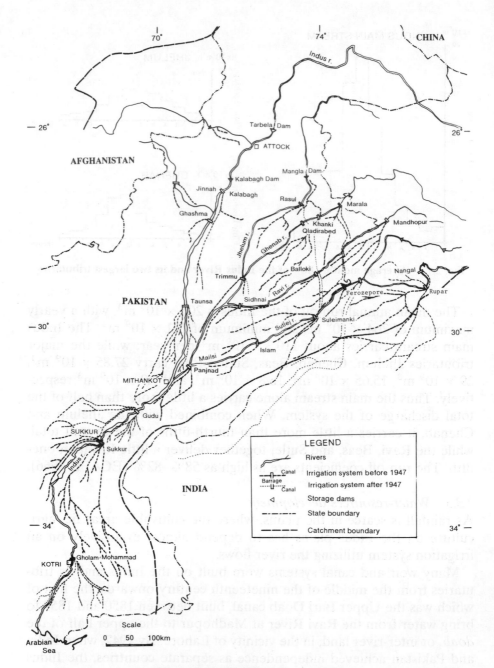

Fig. 2.18 **Indus River development**

following (see fig. 2.18):
— on the Indus: Paharpur canal, Sukkur barrage (North-West, D.
  Unhar, Begari, Ghoti canals);

50

— on the Jhelum: Upper Jhelum canal (Rasul barrage);
— on the Chenab: Upper Chenab canal (Marala barrage), Lower Chenab canal (Khanki barrage):
— on the Jhelum and Chenab: Trimmu barrage, Rangpur canal, Haveli-Sidhnai canal, Panjnad barrage and canal, Abasia canal;
— on the Ravi: Madhopur barrage (Upper and Central Bari Doab canals), Balloki barrage (Lower Bari Doab canal);
— on the Sutlej and Beas: Ferozepore barrage (Eastern and Bikaner canals), Suleimanki barrage (Pakpattan, Fordwah, and E. Sadifia canals), Islam barrage (Mailsi, Qaimpur, and Bahawal canals);
— on the Swat: Upper and Lower Swat canals;
— on the Kabul: Kabul River canal.

Because the new international boundary cut across the common canal system of Punjab, leaving one part in India and the other in Pakistan, controversy on the use of the canal waters arose soon after the Partition. It took twelve years of patient negotiation before the controversy was settled by the Indus Waters Treaty in 1960. Between 1947 and 1960 intensive river development was carried out, including the following:

— on the Indus: Thal canals, Taunsa barrage (Dera Ghazi Khan and Muzaffargarh canals), Gudu barrage (Desert, D. Unhar, Begari, and Ghoti canals), Kotri barrage (Fuleli and Pinyari canals);
— on the Jhelum: Lower Jhelum canal (Rasul barrage);
— on the Ravi: Upper Bari Doab canal extensions;
— on the Beas: Shah Nehar and Hoshiarpur canals;
— on the Sutlej and Beas: Rajasthan canal;
— on the Kabul: Warsak dam;
— on the Kurram: Kurram Garhi weir.

The following major works were undertaken through the Indus Basin Development Fund (IBDF) and its successor, the Tarbela Development Fund:

— on the Jhelum: Mangla dam;
— on the Jhelum, Chenab, Ravi, and Sutlej: Trimmu-Sidhnai-Mailsi-Bahawal link canal system, Rasul-Qadirabad-Balloki-Suleimanki link canal system;
— on the Indus and Jhelum: Chashma barrage, Chashma-Jhelum link canal;
— on the Indus and Chenab: Taunsa-Panjnad link canal;
— on the Indus: Tarbela dam.

It was originally intended that the IBDF would finance tube-well drainage works to compensate for leakage from the link canal systems, but at the choice of the Pakistan government the tube-well programme was financed by other means and the savings to the IBDF were put towards construction of the Tarbela dam.

2.3.4 Salinity and waterlogging problems

During successive stages of development of the irrigation systems, emphasis was put on maximizing the extent of irrigated land. In the Indus valley, as in all other flat valleys in the world, the natural surface and subsurface drainage is poor. Since there were not enough drainage channels, most of the rainwater and canal seepage percolated down to lower depths. As time passed, the groundwater table got higher and higher by steps, and finally, in the 1950s and 1960s it came close to the ground surface and has thus caused waterlogging in many large areas. Proper aeration of the soil could not take place and the capillary action and evapotranspiration moved salts from the subsurface up to the root zone of the crops and to the land surface. Thus, once-fertile lands so deteriorated that crops could no longer be grown.

In the former Punjab area in Pakistan, 5 million ha have already gone out of cultivation due to salinity caused by waterlogging, 690,000 ha are in an advanced stage of deterioration, and 2 million ha are affected to a lesser degree (fig. 2.16). Since 1954, extensive groundwater and salinity investigations have been undertaken. As a result of these investigations, recommendations were made to install a great number of deep wells to lower the groundwater level, and to use the pumped water for flushing the salts from the ground surface down to the drains provided as well as to the lower layer of soil. Moreover, the pumped water is used to supplement the existing canal supplies for irrigation.

In 1959 the Water and Power Development Authority, established in 1958 to take charge of all water and power development in Pakistan, launched its first reclamation project in Rechna Doab, in the districts of Gujarawala, Sheikhupura, and Lyallpur. The project comprised about 1,800 tube wells in a gross commanded area of 480,000 ha. The average volume of groundwater pumped was about 1.85×10^9 m^3 per year. In 1961 a second project was launched in Chai Doab, including 3,300 tube wells in a gross commanded area of 920,000 ha, with an average pumping volume of about 2.5×10^9 m^3 per year. The Authority has continued this salinity-control and reclamation work to remove the catastrophic threat to the well-being of the people of Pakistan.

The extent of salinity and a schematic diagram of salinity-control land reclamation in the lower Indus valley, using conjunctive aquifer

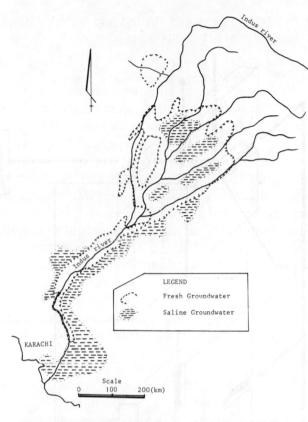

Fig. 2.19A **Saline groundwater in the Indus valley**
(Source: Buras 1967)

management with surface and subsurface drainage measures, are
shown in figs. 2.19A and 2.19B.

2.4 The Nile River

Despite the great area of the Middle East, there are only three rivers,
the Nile, the Euphrates, and the Tigris, that can be classified as large
rivers by world standards. Of these, the Nile, which is the world's
longest river, receives most of its discharge from precipitation falling
well outside the Middle East on the upland plateau of East Africa and
the highlands of Ethiopia (fig. 2.20).

The Nile is the whole life of Egypt. The country owes its existence to
the river, which provides water for agriculture, industry, and domestic
use. Cultivation is dependent on irrigation from the river.

53

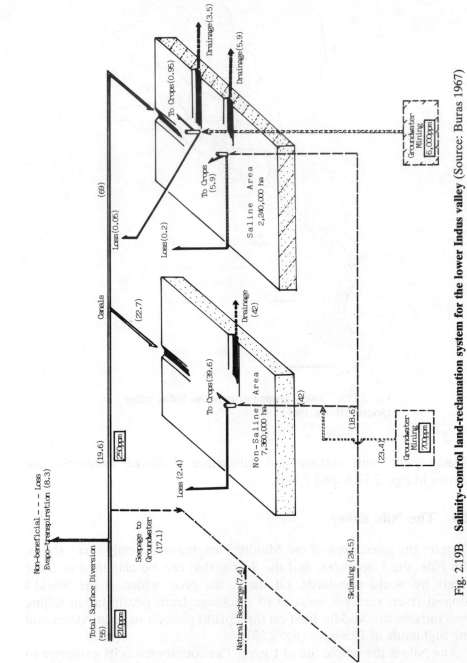

Fig. 2.19B   Salinity-control land-reclamation system for the lower Indus valley (Source: Buras 1967)

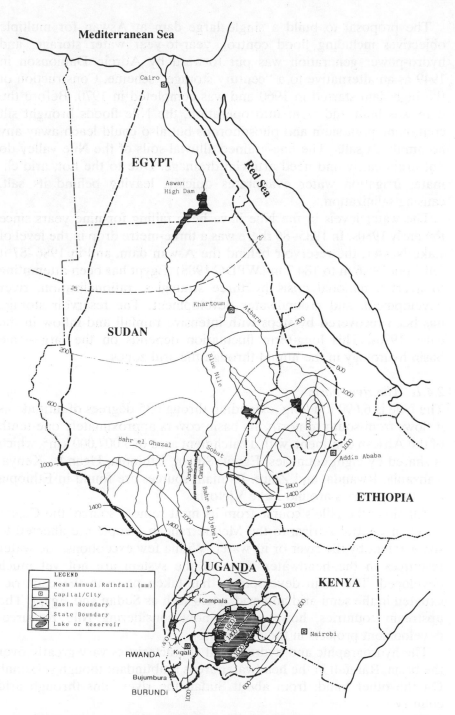

Fig. 2.20   **The Nile River basin**

The proposal to build a single large dam at Aswan for multiple objectives including flood control, year-to-year water storage, and hydro-power generation was put forward by Adrein Danionson in 1949 as an alternative to a "century storage" scheme. Construction of the high dam started in 1960 and was completed in 1970. Before the dam was built and went into operation, the Nile floods brought silt containing potassium and phosphorous but also could leach away any accumulated salts. The fine-grained alluvial soils of the Nile valley do not drain easily and need artificial drainage. Due to the hot, arid climate, irrigation water evaporates quickly, leaving behind its salt, causing salinization.

The water levels in the Nile have been falling for nine years since the early 1980s. In 1985–86 there was a three-metre drop in the level of Lake Nasser, the reservoir behind the Aswan dam, and in 1986–87 it fell from 195.6 m to 184.7 m (WPDC 1988). Egypt has been attempting to avert a national crisis by three strategies: rationalization, river development, and groundwater development. The reservoir storage has been recovered by steps with intensive rainfall and inflow in the early 1990s. This long-term fluctuation depends on the large-scale basin hydrology in the humid through the arid zones.

2.4.1   The river basin

The Nile is 6,690 km long, extending through 35 degrees of latitude as it flows from south to north. Its basin covers approximately one-tenth of the African continent, with a catchment area of 3,007,000 km^2, which is shared by eight countries: Egypt, Sudan, Ethiopia, Uganda, Kenya, Tanzania, Rwanda, and Zaire. Its main sources are found in Ethiopia and the countries around Lake Victoria.

All along the Nile's course from its most remote source, the Cagier River in Central Africa, to the Mediterranean, people are affected to some extent by the river or its water. With a few exceptions, the water resources in the headwater areas of the system are not yet much developed. The main development has taken place in the countries situated in the semi-arid and arid zones such as Sudan and Egypt. The upstream countries, however, are now considering Nile resource-development projects in their territories.

The hydrographic and hydrological characteristics vary greatly over the basin. Rainfall in the headwater areas is abundant though seasonal. On the other hand, from about Sudan the river runs through arid country.

The river system has two main sources of water: the Ethiopian highlands and the equatorial region around Lake Victoria. More than 60% of the river flow arriving in Egypt originates in the Ethiopian highlands by way of the Sobat, Blue Nile, and Atbara Rivers, with the bulk of this water coming down during the summer. The remainder of the flow arrives by way of the White Nile, which has its most remote source in Burundi. This source is a tributary of the Kagera, which enters Lake Victoria near the border between Uganda and Tanzania. In the equatorial region, the Nile system consists of a number of great lakes, connected either by rocky sections or swamps. The White Nile, called Bahr el-Jebel after leaving the lake area, enters Sudan through rocky gorges and then flows through a large swamp area (the Sudd region) in southern Sudan, where it is joined by the Sobat from the east and the Bahr el-Ghazal, which occasionally receives water from Lake Chad from the west. In the Sudd region a huge quantity of water evaporates or is transpired from aquatic vegetation. Only a small part of the Bahr el-Ghazal flow ever reaches the Bahr el-Jebel, and practically all of its water disappears in the swamps. Although the contribution of the White Nile to the total annual flow at Aswan is only 30%, it is most important because of its timing: during the dry season from February to June its flow is large compared with that of the Blue Nile.

2.4.2 Hydrology

The Nile flows for half of its course through country with no effective rainfall. The rainfall of the Nile basin indeed is scanty compared with other major rivers in Africa such as the Zaire, Niger, and Orange Rivers. For the size of the Nile basin with its catchment area of $3{,}007{,}000$ km^2, the annual discharge is as small as 99.5×10^9 m^3, which is equivalent to 4.3% of the annual run-off. Rainfall is heavy in the headwater areas. The annual average rainfall in the lake plateau basin is about 750 mm (50 inches). The heaviest rainfall occurs at Kalungala on the island of Bugola, where it averages 2,250 mm (90 inches) per year. Other places of high rainfall are Bukoba on Lake Victoria and Gore in Ethiopia, where the average is about 2,000 mm (80 inches) per year. The distribution of rainfall is shown on the map in fig. 2.20.

The dependence of Egypt on the Nile has led to intensive studies of quantities of water carried by the main stream and its tributaries throughout the year. The long-term record of the annual flow discharge at Aswan from 1871 to 1965 is shown in fig. 2.21. The annual average for the 95 years is estimated to be 91.2×10^9 m^3, which was the basis of design for the year-to-year storage at the Aswan high dam.

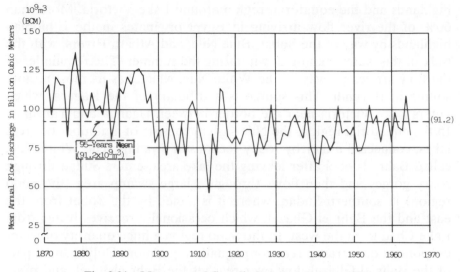

Fig. 2.21   **Mean annual flow discharge at Aswan, 1871–1965**

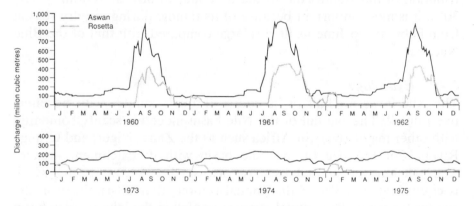

Fig. 2.22   **Mean annual flow discharge at Aswan and Rosetta, before and after construction of the Aswan high dam** (Source: Beaumont et al. 1988)

The change in the patterns of flow of the main Nile at Aswan and Rosetta before and after the construction of the Aswan dam are indicated in fig. 2.22. The upper graph in fig. 2.23 shows the average discharge of the main Nile at Aswan unaffected by reservoirs, the top line showing the discharge of the main river and other lines the component discharges. The peak discharge of 712 million m³ per day, recorded on 8 September, was made up as follows:
— from the White Nile, 70 million m³ (10%),

58

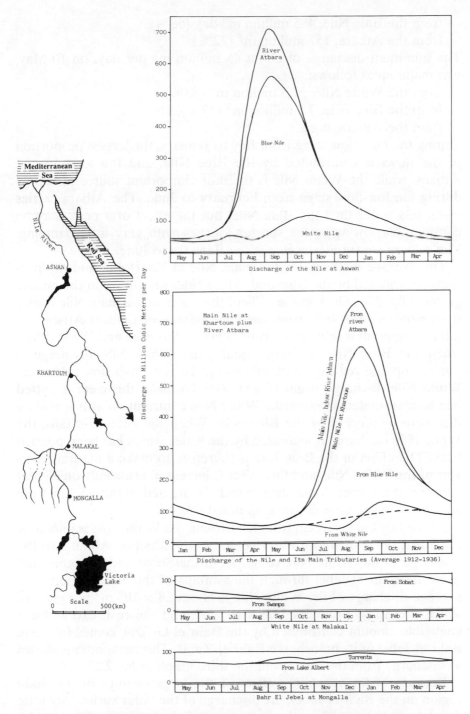

Fig. 2.23 **Flow diagram of the main Nile at Aswan and Khartoum** (Source: Hurst 1952)

— from the Blue Nile, 485 million m^3 day (68%),
— from the Atbara, 157 million m^3 (22%).
The minimum discharge of about 45 million m^3 per day, on 10 May, was made up as follows:
— from the White Nile, 37.5 million m^3 (83%),
— from the Blue Nile, 7.5 million m^3 (17%),
— from the Atbara, none.
During the high-flow stage from July to January, the largest proportion of the flows is contributed by the Blue Nile, and the least by the Atbara, while the White Nile is the more important source of supply during the low-flow stage from February to June. The Atbara carries much less water than the Blue Nile, but the effect of a peak may be considerable, owing to the shorter journey with very little damping. The Atbara contributes nothing from January to June.

The average discharge of the main Nile at Khartoum and the portions contributed by the Blue and White Niles are shown in the middle graph in fig. 2.23. On average 84% of the water of the main Nile comes from Ethiopia and 16% from the lake plateau of Central Africa. An interesting point is seen at the confluence of the Blue and White Niles: when the Blue Nile is rising rapidly, the White Nile discharge is ponded up and reduced, and only when the rise slows down does the White Nile discharge begin to increase. To make this clear a dotted line is interpolated showing the White Nile contribution as it would be if it were unaffected by the Blue Nile. When the Blue Nile falls, the White Nile discharge is increased by the water which has been ponded back. The effect of the Blue Nile is therefore to make a natural reservoir of the White Nile, and this effect is increased artificially on a great scale by the Gebel Aulia dam, which is situated about 45 km from Khartoum, some little distance up the White Nile.

About 800 km upstream from Khartoum, the White Nile is joined by the Sobat, 90% of whose water comes from Ethiopia. About half the discharge of the White Nile comes from the Sobat and the other half from the Bahr el-Jebel through the swamps of the Sudd region. The average discharge of the White Nile is about 28×10^9 m^3 per year, of which the Sobat produces 13.5×10^9 m^3, and the rest, except for a negligible amount contributed by the Bahr el-Ghazal, comes from the Bahr el-Jebel or its branch, the Bahr el-Zeraf. This remainder is shown as discharge from the swamps in the third graph in fig. 2.23.

Because of the regulating effect of the large swamps of the Sudd region on the Bahr el-Jebel, the discharge of the latter varies very little throughout the year (see the bottom graph in fig. 2.23). When a rise occurs upstream, most of the water flows out of the river into the swamps, and only a very small part of the increase is felt in the stream below. When the river falls, there is a tendency for the marshes to drain back into the river, but large areas are below river level and cannot drain back. The water that enters is lost by evaporation and by transpiration from the luxuriant vegetation, and in fact very little returns to the river, with the result that the Bahr el-Jebel loses nearly half its water in the swamps.

The heavy evaporation and general dryness of the climate in Egypt and most of Sudan have various implications, including a substantial evaporation loss from the surface of large reservoirs. The evaporation loss from Lake Nasser (the Aswan high dam reservoir) is estimated to be about 10×10^9 m^3 per year, which is about 10% of the net storage volume of 90×10^9 m^3. In Egypt evaporation is at a maximum in

Table 2.2 **Mean daily potential evaporation at selected points in the Nile basin**

	Potential evaporation (mm/day)	
	Piche	Open water
Mediterranean coast	6.1	3.0
Nile delta	4.6	2.3
Cairo and neighbourhood	5.5	2.8
Fayum	7.9	4.0
Oases	13.0	6.5
Upper Egypt	9.0	4.5
Northern Sudan (Halfa Atbara)	15.1	7.6
Khartoum and neighbourhood	15.5	7.8
Central Sudan (Dueim to Roseires)	12.6	6.3
Southern Sudan (Malakal and south swamp)	6.8	3.4
Lake Albert		3.9
Lake Edward		3.9
Lake Victoria		3.8

Source: Hurst 1952.

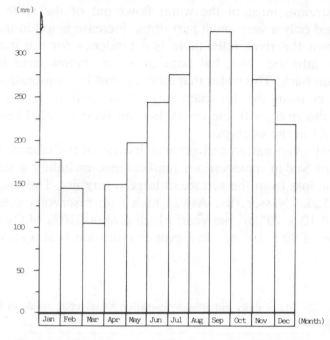

Fig. 2.24 **Monthly evaporation rates for Lake Nasser**
(Source: Hurst 1952)

June and a minimum in December and January. In northern Sudan it
is the same, but May has practically the same evaporation as June. In
the vicinity of Khartoum the maximum is in April and May, owing to
the reduction later caused by monsoon rains, of which this area is on
the fringe. In southern Sudan the minimum evaporation is in the
months of July and August, at the height of the rains. The evaporation
in Egypt and Sudan, on the whole, follows the temperature. Potential
evaporation at selected points in the Nile basin is shown in table 2.2
and the estimated monthly evaporation from Lake Nasser in fig. 2.24.

2.4.3 Water-resource development of the Nile system
The national-economy and social objectives of developing Nile
resources may vary from country to country. Certain Nile projects in
the upper parts of the basin could be also advantageous for the more
downstream countries. The timing of such projects could have a significant effect on the development of the resources of the basin as a
whole.

The Nile is a geographical unit, and projects for its full development

Table 2.3 **Existing dams in the Nile basin**

| Dam | Location | | Storage capacity (10^9 m^3) | Installed capacity (MW) | Evaporation loss (10^9 m^3) |
	Country	River			
Owen Falls	Uganda	Victoria Nile	—[a]	120	
Jebel Aulia	Sudan	Bahr el-Jebel	3.6		2.8
Tis Abbay	Ethiopia	Blue Nile	—[a]	9.6	
Roseires	Sudan	Blue Nile	2.7[b]	15	0.45
Khashm el-Girba	Sudan	Atbara	1.1	7	0.06
High Aswan	Egypt	main Nile	90[b]	1,815	10
Aswan	Egypt	main Nile	5	5	
Isna	Egypt	main Nile	—[c]		
Nag Hammadi	Egypt	main Nile	—[c]		
Assyut	Egypt	main Nile	—[c]		
Delta	Egypt	main Nile	—[c]		
Zifta	Egypt	main Nile	—[c]		
Edfina	Egypt	main Nile	—[c]		

Source: Deekker 1972.

a. Outflow regulation with lake storage, or run of the river.
b. Net.
c. Barrage for irrigation intake.

must also form a unity, the parts of which must work together. The basic idea of a 1950s scheme, an account of which follows, was year-to-year storage, or "century storage" in Hurst's (1952) terminology. The key projects in Hurst's master plan were the Owen Falls dam, Lake Kioga barrage, Lake Albert dam, Jonglei diversion canal, Lake Tana dam, Fourth Cataract dam, Aswan high dam, and Wadi Rayan reservoir (see table 2.3). The hydraulic works in the Nile basin are shown on the map in fig. 2.25.

A major step in achieving collaboration among the Nile basin states was initiated in 1967 when the five countries Kenya, Tanzania, Uganda, Sudan, and Egypt started a hydro-meteorological survey of the basins of Lakes Victoria, Kyoga, and Albert, with the assistance of the UN Development Programme.

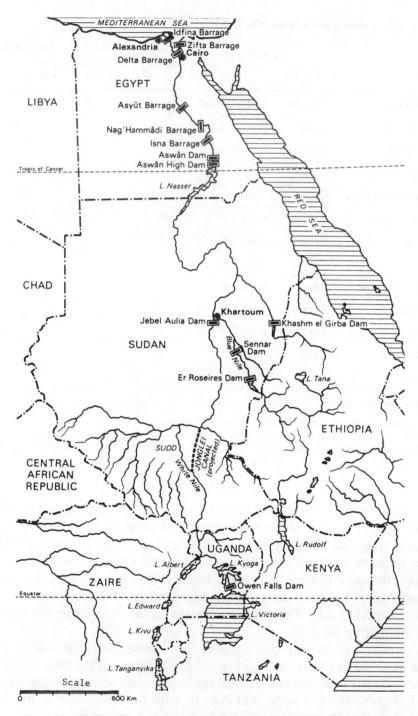

Fig. 2.25 **Hydraulic works of the Nile basin** (Source: Beaumont et al. 1988)

2.4.4 Jonglei diversion canal project

The Jonglei canal scheme to divert water from the Bahr el-Jebel above the Sudd region to a point farther down the White Nile, bypassing the swamps (see fig. 2.25), first studied by the government of Sudan in 1946, would make significantly more water available for use downstream. Plans were developed in 1954–59, and work on the project began in the 1970s, but it has been held up for many years by political instability in Sudan (Collins 1988).

The original plans could now be reviewed, taking into account the completion in 1970 of the Aswan high dam, with its gross storage capacity of 168.9×10^9 m^3 and maximum spillway capacity of 11,000 m^3/sec, and our present increased knowledge of the hydrology of the Blue Nile and the hydro-meteorology of the Albert-Victoria catchment. The water from the south-western tributaries (the Bahr el-Ghazal system) for all practical purposes does not reach the main river and is lost through evaporation and transpiration in the swamps. It should be possible to reduce these losses and to lead at least a part of the water to the main river. This procedure would require international collaboration, because storage and regulation would become necessary in Lake Albert to reduce flood levels in Sudan. Furthermore, storage would probably be needed on the Blue Nile in Ethiopia because the reservoir of the Aswan high dam by itself would not be large enough to regulate the combined floods of the Bahr el-Ghazal, Bahr el-Jebel, and Blue Nile. It is estimated that the Jonglei canal project would produce 4.8×10^9 m^3 of water per year, including 2.4×10^9 m^3 for the first-stage project and 2.4×10^9 m^3 for the second-stage project. There are, however, complex environmental and social issues involved, which may limit the scope of the project in practical terms.

2.4.5 Hydro-power potential

The hydro-potential of the Nile system is enormous, but the energy demand in the Nile basin countries is still small at present, with the exception of Egypt. According to the Ministry of Information of Ethiopia in 1966, the hydro-potential of the whole Nile system was preliminarily estimated to be about 8,000 MW (Deekker 1972). The most promising river for hydroelectric power development is the Victoria Nile, of which the hydro-potential is preliminarily estimated to be 1,843 MW in total, including six potential stations such as Bujagali (180 MW), Busowoko (150 MW), Kalagala (125 MW), Kamdinia (234 MW), Aingo (490 MW), and Murchison (664 MW) (Deekker 1972).

2.4.6 The Aswan high dam

The importance of energy production at the Aswan high dam to the Egyptian economy is perhaps about equal to that of making more water available for irrigation, taking into account the huge saving in crude oil for energy production.

The construction of the Aswan high dam has affected the entire economy of Egypt, allowing reliable irrigation throughout the year and satisfying about 40% or less of the country's energy demands. The flow of the Nile River below the Aswan high dam is fully regulated. Releases from the dam are authorized by the Ministry of Irrigation and are based on seasonal irrigation needs in the Nile delta. The nature of Egypt's climate, as well as the established cropping patterns, require a very high release in the summer months when agricultural production is at its peak. Monthly irrigation release requirements are shown in table 2.4. Hydro-power generation at the dam has always been viewed as a residual benefit since the potential varies extensively between summer and winter months because of the uneven distribution of downstream irrigation requirements.

Egypt's irrigation practices require nearly 55×10^9 m^3 of water from the Nile every year, which is the amount allotted to Egypt by the 1959 Nile Waters Agreement with Sudan. Sudan was allotted 18.5×10^9 m^3 by the same agreement but has been using only 16.5×10^9 m^3 per year in the 1970s. Monthly flows at various points along the Nile River have been recorded since the late 1800s. From 1871 to 1976 the flow records at Station Aswan were adjusted to account for Sudanese abstractions and evaporation losses.

The water stored in the upper rule storage zone is considered to be live storage and can be released to meet irrigation demands or to prevent flooding. Reservoir storage is discretized into 18 states, varying from a maximum of 168.9×10^9 m^3 (183-m elevation) to 89.2×10^9 m^3 (168-m elevation).

According to an inventory of the world's hydro-power in 1989, the

Table 2.4 Monthly irrigation release requirements (10^9 m^3) from the Aswan high dam

Jan	3.5	Apr	4.0	Jul	7.0	Oct	3.7
Feb	4.0	May	5.3	Aug	6.3	Nov	3.6
Mar	4.2	Jun	6.5	Sep	4.3	Dec	3.0
TOTAL							55.3

Source: Thompson and Marks 1982.

power station at Aswan has a rated capacity of 1,815 MW with an installed capacity of 2,100 MW, which accounts for about 40% of the national power supply (Mermel 1989).

2.4.7 *Waterlogging and salinization problems of the Nile delta*

Before the implementation of year-to-year storage at the Aswan high dam, the Nile floods brought silt to the fields of Egypt containing potassium and phosphorous and could also leach away accumulated salts.

The fine-grained alluvial soils of the Nile valley do not drain easily and need artificial drainage. Because of the hot-arid climate, irrigation water evaporates quickly, leaving behind salt which causes primary salinization. Consequently, farmers had to apply more water to wash the accumulated salts into the ground below the root zone. Deep percolation thus caused a rise in the water table to a few decimetres below the surface level soon after the change to perennial irrigation. The soil then became waterlogged. When the water table is less than two metres deep, capillary forces lift it to the surface, where the salts accumulate after evaporation. This is known as secondary salinization. Thus, to avoid primary salinization it is essential to ensure quick infiltration of irrigated water, and to avoid secondary salinization the water table must be kept low.

In 1982 almost all the irrigated area in Egypt was potentially affected by salt, and at least half of the area (12,000 km^2) is already more or less affected. Egypt's agriculture potential and Nile delta salinity are mapped in figs. 2.26 and 2.27. About 400 km^2 are provided with drainage systems each year at a cost of US$200 per hectare. Nevertheless, this is not sufficient to stop salinization. Farmers are unwilling to make this investment, and the government authorities have difficulty in keeping open the drainage channels that are essential for proper functioning of the tile drainage underneath the farmlands (Meybeck et al. 1989; Beaumont et al. 1988).

Regulating the flow of the Nile at the Aswan high dam has immensely increased the costs of agriculture for the irrigated lands on the Nile delta by requiring artificial fertilization, drainage systems, and water lifting. On the other hand, some costs have been reduced, such as those for clearing the irrigation channels of silt.

2.4.8 *Egypt's water crisis and the Aswan high dam*

Until high flows on the Blue Nile in 1990 saved the situation, Egypt was facing a national crisis as a result of nine years of falling water levels in the Nile and Lake Nasser. Countermeasures taken to avert

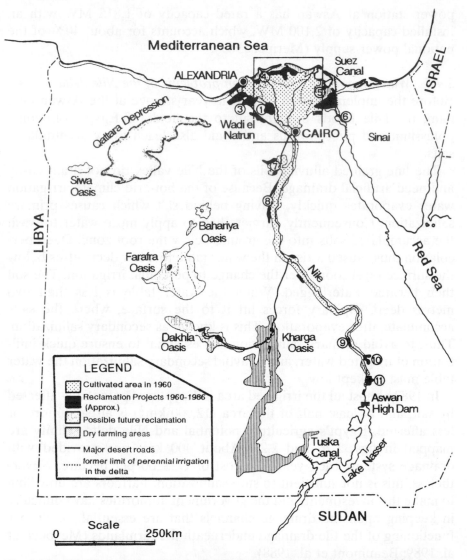

Fig. 2.26 **Egypt's agricultural potential.** Irrigation schemes: (1) Tahrir, (2) Maryut, (3) Nubariya desert, (4) northern delta, (5) south of Lake Manzala, (6) western Sinai, (7) Faiyum depression, (8) El-Minya, (9) Kena, (10) Radesia Wadi Abbady, (11) Kom Ombo. (Source: Beaumont et al. 1988)

the water crisis comprised the following three strategies (WPDC 1988):

≫ *rationalization*—improving irrigation systems to save 86 million m^3 of water per year, and recycling agricultural drainage to recover 196 million m^3 of water per year;

≫ *river development*—building a major new dam on the Nile at

68

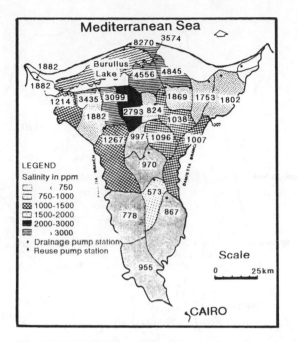

Fig. 2.27 **Nile delta salinity** (map area indicated
by box in fig. 2.26) (Source: Ab-Zeid and Biswas
1990)

Rashid, near Alexandria, to reduce the Nile's flow into the Mediterranean;
≫ *groundwater development*—exploiting underground reservoirs to
develop non-renewable groundwater in the deep sandstone aquifers.

Details of the groundwater development plan for the deep sandstone aquifers in the New Valley are given in section 2.7.4.

2.5 The Jordan River

Owing to the general aridity of the region, a very large portion of the
total area consists of endoreic or inland drainage. The Jordan River,
the third largest perennial river in the Middle East, receives most of its
discharge from precipitation on the southern part of the Anti-Lebanon
range.

The Jordan is a multinational river, flowing southwards for a total
length of 228 km through Lebanon, Syria, Israel, and Jordan (figs. 2.28
and 2.29). It is already overdeveloped except for a winter flow in its
largest tributary, the Yarmouk River, which forms the present boun-

69

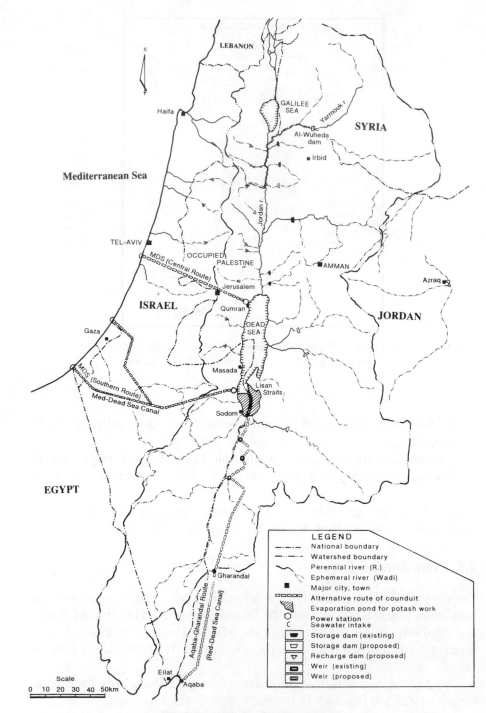

Fig. 2.28 **The Jordan River basin**

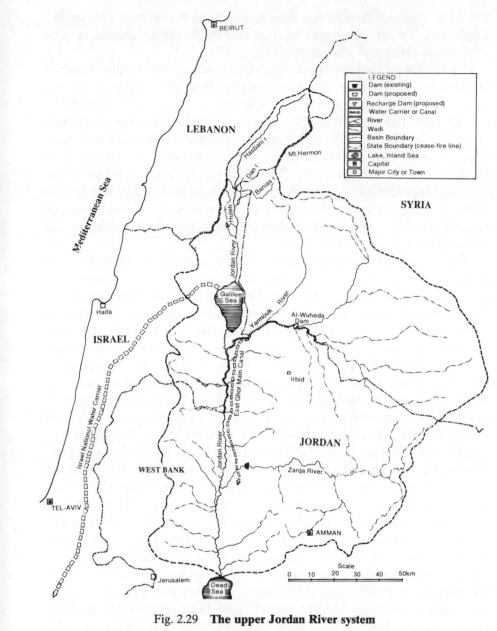

LEGEND

Dam (existing)	
Dam (proposed)	
Recharge Dam (proposed)	
Water Carrier or Canal	
River	
Wadi	
Basin Boundary	
State Boundary (cease-fire line)	
Lake, Inland Sea	
Capital	
Major City or Town	

Fig. 2.29 **The upper Jordan River system**

dary between Syria and Jordan for 40 km before becoming the border between Israel and Jordan.

In the absence of irrigation extraction, the Jordan system delivers an average annual flow of 1.85×10^9 m^3 to the Dead Sea, equivalent to

71

2% of the annual flow of the Nile and 7% of the annual flow of the Euphrates. Twenty-three per cent of this discharge originates in pre-1967 Israel (Naff and Matson 1984).

The discharge that feeds into the upper part of the Jordan River is derived principally from groundwater flow through a group of karstic springs on the western and southern slopes of Mount Hermon (Jabel esh-Sheikh). There are three rivers in the headwaters of the north fork of the Jordan River: the Dan River, the Hasbani River, and the Banias River, of which the quality of water is excellent, with salinity less than 15–20 mg of chlorine per litre. The flow in the lower reaches of the system is supplemented by springs, but much of their contribution is so saline that they degrade the quality of the river flow, to the extent of several thousand parts per million of total dissolved solids at the Allenby Bridge near Jericho.

Few regions of the planet offer a more varied physiography or a richer mix of ethnicities, religions, languages, societies, cultures, and politics than the Middle East. At the same time, no segment of the globe presents its diverse aspects in such an amalgam of conflicts and complexities. Out of this compound, one issue emerges as the most conspicuous, cross-cutting, and problematic: water. Its scarcity and rapid diminution happen to occur in some of the driest sectors of an area where there are also some of the fiercest national animosities. River waters in the Middle East are thus a conflict-laden determinant of both the domestic and external policies of the region's principal actors. Equally, though, they could be a catalyst for lasting peace.

As water shortages occur and full utilization is reached, water policies tend to be framed more and more in zero-sum terms, adding to the probability of discord. The severity of Middle Eastern water problems will, unavoidably, increase significantly year by year. In an already over-heated atmosphere of political hostility, insufficient water to satisfy burgeoning human, developmental, and security needs among all nations of the Middle East heightens the ambient tensions. By the end of the 1990s, Israel, Jordan, and the West Bank will have depleted virtually all of their renewable sources of fresh water if current patterns of consumption are not quickly and radically altered. In these circumstances, the Jordan River system, which includes the Al-Wuheda dam scheme on the Yarmouk River, unquestionably holds the greatest potential for conflict.

Despite the endless political complications in the Middle East, there is a recent history of tacit, although limited, cooperation over multinational river development even among the bitterest opponents. Israel, before its invasion of Lebanon and its troublesome stand on clearing out obstructions to the intake of Jordan's East Ghor canal, had more or less agreed informally to share the Jordan River system within the framework of the 1955 Johnston Plan.

The largest water-resource development project in Israel has been the National Water Carrier, which is a huge aqueduct and pipeline network carrying water from the Jordan southwards along the coastal region. The water is pumped from the En-Sheva intake in the north-west of Lake Tiberias at an elevation of 210 m below sea level to a height from which it flows by gravity to a reservoir at Rasalom. The installed capacity of the En-Sheva pumping station was 360 million m^3 per year in 1968, and it could conceivably be increased to a maximum level of 500 million m^3 per year, which is 90% of the Jordan's inflow of 544 million m^3 per year at the inlet to Lake Tiberias (Beaumont et al. 1988). Such cutting of fresh-water flows in the upper Jordan River would, however, have seriously adverse effects on the quality of Lake Tiberias and its lower reaches by increasing salinity. The Medi-terranean–Dead Sea canal and pumped-storage schemes in Lake Tiberias and the Dead Sea, described in chapter 5, are the key techno-political alternatives.

Israel currently uses as much as 90% or more of the stream water from the upper Jordan River. Jordan's water problems have undoubt-edly been exacerbated by Israel's actions to deny it the right to develop fully the water resources of the Jordan River within its bor-ders. The problem is particularly acute over the postponement of con-struction of the Al-Wuheda dam on the Yarmouk River. The upper Jordan has already been developed to a maximum capacity. The Al-Wuheda dam would complete development of the Yarmouk.

There have been several changes in the Israel-Arab situation since the Iraqi invasion of Kuwait in 1990. From integrated hydrological studies on the Jordan River system, it is now possible to conceive a comprehensive development plan that will be not only technically and economically feasible but also politically desirable and urgent. The Mediterranean–Dead Sea conduit scheme and the Al-Wuheda dam project could now be discussed simultaneously without threatening new political conflicts but rather to promote peace and economic development for the Palestinians. Discussion can now be based on a sense of the water cycle, in the context of hydrology, energy, and politics.

The following section describes the hydrology and water resources of the Jordan River system. Discussion of opportunities for integrated

73

planning for comprehensive water-resource development is given in chapter 5.

2.5.1 The river basin

The catchment of the Jordan River, excluding its upper basin, is an integral part of the arid to semi-arid region (see fig. 2.28). There is a marked spatial variation in the distribution of precipitation over the catchment since the recharge area is confined to the mountainous areas of the Anti-Lebanon range, where the mean annual precipitation amounts to 1,400 mm, and the climate in the lower reaches of the Jordan in the Rift valley is arid to hyper-arid, with an annual mean precipitation of less than 50–200 mm.

The Jordan originates in the south-western Anti-Lebanon range, on the slopes of Mount Hermon, which is covered with snow in winter. It then flows through Lebanon, Syria, Israel, and Jordan for a total distance of 228 km along the bottom of a longitudinal graben known as the Rift valley, or Ghor, before emptying into the Dead Sea. Its principal tributary, the Yarmouk, forms the border between Syria and Jordan and divides Israel from Jordan in the Yarmouk triangle. The lower reaches of the Jordan River border on part of the Israeli-occupied West Bank to the west and Jordan to the east for a distance of about 80 km.

The catchment area of the Jordan is 18,300 km² in total, of which 3% lies in pre-1967 Israel. The lower Jordan River between Lake Tiberias and the Dead Sea has a catchment area of 1,050 km².

The Jordan River system may be classified on the basis of hydrology, hydrogeology, and water use into three sections: (1) the upper Jordan—headwaters, the Huleh valley, and Lake Tiberias; (2) the Yarmouk River; and (3) the lower Jordan—the main stream and the Dead Sea.

2.5.2 The upper Jordan

The upper Jordan River system includes (1) the three major headwater streams, the Dan, Hasbani, and Banias, (2) the Huleh valley, and (3) Lake Tiberias, or the Sea of Galilee (see fig. 2.29).

THE DAN RIVER. The largest of the springs is the Dan spring, which rises from Jurassic carbonate rocks and supplies a large and relatively steady flow that responds only slowly to rainfall events. The average discharge of the spring is 245 million m³ per year, varying from 173 million to 285 million m³. The Dan typically accounts for 50% of the discharge of the upper Jordan.

THE HASBANI RIVER.   The Hasbani River derives most of its discharge from two springs, the Wazzani and the Haqzbieh, the latter being a group of springs on the uppermost Hasbani. All of these springs rise from subsurface conduits in cavernous Cretaceous carbonate rocks. Their combined discharge averages 138 million m^3 per year but the values vary over a greater range than those of the Dan spring; over a recent twenty-year period, the flow of the Hasbani varied from 52 million to 236 million m^3 per year. The Hasbani discharge responds much more rapidly to rainfall than does that of the Dan spring.

THE BANIAS RIVER.   The Banias River is fed primarily from Hermon springs that issue from the contact of Quaternary sediments over Jurassic limestone in the extreme north-east of the Jordan valley. The average discharge of the Hermon springs is 121 million m^3 per year; during a recent twenty-year period it varied from 63 million to 190 million m^3.

The Dan spring, the largest of the sources of the upper Jordan, lies wholly within Israel close to the border with Syria. The spring sources of the Hasbani River lie entirely within Lebanon. The spring source of the Banias River is in Syria. These three small streams unite 6 km inside Israel at about 70 m above sea level to form the upper Jordan River.

Together the springs provide more water than can be accounted for as a result of rainfall over their immediate watersheds; thus, it is surmised that they represent the outflow of a large regional aquifer. The combined outflow of the springs and the precipitation that falls on the surface watershed of the upper Jordan is of the order of 500 million m^3 per year. In a typical year, these karstic springs provide 50% of the

Table 2.5   **Annual discharge of the headwater rivers of the upper Jordan**

River	Riparian states	Flow (million m^3)	
		Mean	Range
Dan	Israel	245	173–285
Hasbani	Lebanon	138	52–236
Banias	Syria/Israel	121	63–190
TOTAL		504	298–711

Source: Naff and Matson 1984.

75

Table 2.6   **Water budget of the Huleh valley**

	Million m^3
Inflow into valley	504
Plus local run-off from Huleh to Jisr Banat Yaqub	140
Minus irrigation in valley	−100
Outflow into Lake Tiberias	544

Source: Naff and Matson 1984.

discharge of the upper Jordan River; the rest is derived from surface run-off directly after the winter rainfalls. In dry years, spring outflow may make up as much as 70% of the flow of the upper Jordan. Table 2.5 summarizes the mean annual discharges of the three rivers.

HULEH VALLEY.   The flow of the upper Jordan enters the Huleh valley (formerly Lake Huleh), where it is augmented by the flow of sub-lacustrine springs. Among the minor springs and seasonal water-courses contributing the flow of the upper Jordan, the most important is the Wadi Bareighhit. The water budget of the Huleh valley is shown in table 2.6.

LAKE TIBERIAS.   Beyond the Huleh valley, the north fork of the Jordan falls 200 m to Lake Tiberias (the Sea of Galilee), which lies 210 m below sea level. The upper Jordan contributes an average of 660 million m^3 per year to the lake, or 40% of Israel's total identified renewable water resources. An additional 130 million m^3 per year enters the lake as winter run-off from various wadis and in the form of discharge from sublacustrine springs that contain high salinity. Table 2.7 summarizes the water budget of Lake Tiberias.

Lake Tiberias has a volume of 4×10^9 m^3, which is 6.5 times the annual inflow from the upper Jordan and 8 times the annual outflow. The water depth is 26 m on average, with a maximum of 43 m. The surface area is 170 km^2, which loses about 270 million m^3 of water per year by direct evaporation. The salinity of the lake varies from a low of 260 mg to a high of 400 mg of chlorine per litre; this variation depends primarily on the flow of the upper Jordan, in which salinity does not exceed 15–20 mg of chlorine per litre (Naff and Matson 1984). About 500 million m^3 leaves Lake Tiberias per year via its outlet and flows south along the floor of the Dead Sea Rift for about 10 km to the confluence with the Yarmouk River.

Table 2.7 **Water budget of Lake Tiberias**

	Million m³
Inflow into lake	544
Plus rainfall over lake	65
Plus local run-off	70
Plus springs in and around lake	65
Minus evaporation from lake surface	−270
Outflow to lower Jordan	474

Source: Naff and Matson 1984

2.5.3 The Yarmouk

The Yarmouk River originates on the south-eastern slopes of Mount Hermon in a complex of wadis developed in Quaternary volcanic rocks. The main trunk of the Yarmouk forms the present boundary between Syria and Jordan for 40 km before it becomes the border between Jordan and Israel. Where it enters the Jordan River 10 km below Lake Tiberias, the Yarmouk contributes about 400 million m³ per year (Huang and Banerjee 1984).

There is no flow contribution from the part of the valley where Israel is a riparian. Of the 7,242 km² of the Yarmouk basin, 1,424 km² lie within Jordan and 5,252 km² within Syria. The flow of the Yarmouk is derived from winter precipitation that averages 364 mm per year over the basin (Naff and Matson 1984). The stream flow is supplemented by spring discharges from highly permeable zones in the lavas; some further spring discharges may be channelled to the surface on wadi floors via solution pathways in the underlying limestones.

The mean annual flow discharge is 400 million m³, which is 65% of the total discharge of 607 million m³ per year from the Jordan's East Bank. The flow is largely influenced by the rainfall pattern in the Mediterranean climate, indicating a maximum monthly discharge of 101 million m³ in February and a minimum of 19 million m³ in September (Huang and Banerjee 1984).

The salinity of the Yarmouk River is quite low, being between 280 and 480 mg of total dissolved solids per litre.

EAST GHOR MAIN CANAL PROJECT. The Yarmouk's mean annual discharge of 400 million m³ provides almost half of the surface water resources of the Jordan River. After allowing for some 17 million m³ per year for downstream users in neighbouring countries, this water is

77

diverted through the East Ghor Main Canal, an irrigation canal running along the Jordan River, to provide for agricultural water needs in the Jordan valley (fig. 2.29). The upper phase of the canal was completed in 1964, and by 1979 it had reached a length of 100 km, which could permit the irrigation of 22,000 ha (Beaumont 1988).

AL-WUHEDA (MAQARIN) STORAGE DAM SCHEME. The Al-Wuheda dam, first conceived in 1956, would be built in the northern part of Maqarin, about 20 km north of Irbid, to store the waters of the Yarmouk River. The estimated stream flow at the Maqarin gauging station is 273 million m^3 per year on average, which includes flood waters being discharged to waste. On the basis of a bilateral riparian agreement between Syria and Jordan in 1988, preliminary work for opening an 800-metre-long diversion tunnel was completed by the end of 1989. The dam reservoir would have a gross capacity of 225 million m^3, with effective storage of 195 million m^3 annually. The water would irrigate an additional 3,500 ha in the Jordan valley, and supply 50 million m^3 of water a year to the Greater Amman area and the eastern heights. It would also generate an average of 18,800 MWh of electricity a year. Syria would use part of the water and 75% of the total hydroelectric power generated by a power station near the dam. However, this project was stopped by Israeli opposition over water-allocation problems.

2.5.4 The lower Jordan River and the Dead Sea

South of its confluence with the Yarmouk, the Jordan flows over late Tertiary rocks that partially fill the Rift valley. For the first 40 km the river forms the international boundary between Israel and Jordan; south of that reach, it abuts the Israeli-occupied West Bank of the Jordan, where it forms the present cease-fire line. The Jordan here flows through the deepest portion of the Rift valley to enter the Dead Sea at 401 m below sea level, the lowest point on earth.

Run-off from winter rainfall within the valley is carried to the Jordan River via steep, intermittent tributary wadis incised in the wall of the Jordan valley, primarily on the East Bank. This source represents an additional 523 million m^3 per year, of which only 20% originates in Israel; 286 million m^3 is derived from perennial spring flow, while 237 million m^3 is provided by winter rainfall (Naff and Matson 1984). The main tributaries on the East Bank, including the Zarqa River and Wadis Arab, Ziqlab, Jurm, Ubis, Kafrain, Rajib, Shueib, and Hisban are described in chapter 4.

The quality of the lower Jordan is influenced both by rainfall patterns and by the amount of base flow extracted upstream. Water salinity is about 350 mg of total dissolved solids per litre in the rainy season, while it rises to 2,000–4,000 mg per litre in the dry season at Allenby Bridge near Jericho. Finally, the salinity of the system reaches 250,000 mg of total dissolved solids per litre in the Dead Sea, a level approximately seven times as high as that of the ocean. This salinity level is too high to sustain life, but certain minerals such as potash and bromines can be extracted by solar evaporative processes.

The Dead Sea covers an area of over 1,000 km² at a surface elevation of 400 m below mean sea level. It has two basins, separated by the Lisan Straits, the northern basin with an area of 230 km² and the southern basin with an area of 720 km². The catchment area is 40,000 km², including parts of Israel, Jordan, and Syria. The shortest distance between the Dead Sea and the Mediterranean Sea is 72 km (fig. 2.28).

The Dead Sea is a closed sea with no outlet except by evaporation, which is very high, amounting to 1,600 mm per year. In the past, the evaporation losses were replenished by an inflow of fresh water from the Jordan River and its tributaries, as well as other sources such as wadi floods, springs, and rainfall. The mean volume of water flowing into the sea before 1930 was about 1.6×10^9 m³ per year, of which 1.1×10^9 m³ were carried by the Jordan (Weiner and Ben-Zvi 1982). Under these conditions, the sea had reached an equilibrium level at a height around 393 m below sea level, with some seasonal and annual fluctuation due to variations in the amount of rainfall. However, since the early 1950s, Israel and later Jordan have taken steps to utilize the fresh water flowing into the Dead Sea for intensified irrigation and other purposes, which has reduced the amount of water entering the sea by 1×10^9 m³ per year. Consequently, the water level has declined in recent years to 403 m below sea level today, almost 10 m lower than its historical equilibrium level. The surface area of the Dead Sea and the volume evaporated from the surface vary only by a few percentage points between elevations from -402 to -390 m, while the water levels fluctuate considerably.

2.5.5 Water allocation problems and international riparian agreements

In 1953 the four countries Lebanon, Syria, Israel, and Jordan agreed in principle on the priority use of Jordan River waters, in the so-called Johnston Agreement, which provided for priority use of the main stem of the Jordan River by Israel and Lebanon, while the biggest tributary, the Yarmouk, running along the national boundary, was to be exclusively used by Syria and Jordan. This established a water allocation of the usable Jordan River estimated at 1.38×10^9 m^3 per year in total: 52% (720 million m^3) to Jordan, 32% (440 million m^3) to Israel, 13% (180 million m^3) to Syria, and 3% (40 million m^3) to Lebanon (Naff and Matson 1984). It is widely assumed that the technical experts of each country involved in this discussion agreed on the details of this plan, although soon afterwards the governments rejected it for political reasons.

With the failure of these negotiations, both Israel and Jordan decided to proceed with water projects situated entirely within their own boundaries. As a result, Israel began work in 1958 on the National Water Carrier, which is currently abstracting 90% or more of the flow from the upper Jordan River through their intake in the north-west of Lake Tiberias.

Syria continued implementation of small-to-medium size dam development schemes for the upper Yarmouk. These plans could lead to increased salinity levels in the lower Yarmouk and lower Jordan Rivers, lower water levels in the Dead Sea, and reduced irrigation water for Jordan's East Ghor development project. From a strategic point of view, this long-term Syrian effort could reduce Jordanian access to the Yarmouk, on which Jordan relies to irrigate the Jordan valley, and may affect downstream availabilities for Israel. Ultimately, the possibility of heightened tension or even armed conflict among the riparians might increase (Starr and Stoll 1987).

The 1988 protocol of understanding between Jordan and Syria paving the way to renewing work on the Al-Wuheda dam project as part of a multinational master plan for development of the water resources of the region is described in chapters 4 and 5.

2.6 The Colorado River

Increasing salinity is one of the most significant forms of groundwater and/or stream-flow pollution and certainly the most widespread. The most important causes are an increase in the salinity of groundwater from the effects of irrigation, and the intrusion of saline water (seawater), mainly in basins of internal drainage, islands, and coastal areas.

In arid climates, infiltration from rainfall may be negligible and leaching is not effective in diluting soil salt solutions enriched by evaporation. Any infiltration that does reach the groundwater table will be relatively highly mineralized. In poor drainage areas, particularly basins of internal drainage which are groundwater discharge areas, evaporation can produce significant increases in salinity.

Changes in the salinity of rivers along their courses and with time are mainly the result of return flows from subsurface drainage water. The effect of irrigation returns on river salinity has been experienced in various arid regions in advanced countries, including the upper Rio Grande in Texas and the Colorado River in Arizona, both in the United States of America, and the Murray River in Australia (Meybeck et al. 1989).

As a case study in the control of river salinity problems, this section discusses the world's largest desalting facility, built to salvage about 72.4 million gallons (274,000 m^3) of brackish water per day from irrigation drainage in the Colorado River valley in the state of Arizona. The reverse-osmosis desalination project, located at Yuma in the south-western corner of Arizona, is intended to control the quality of the Colorado River where it crosses the border between the United States and Mexico.

2.6.1 Background

The Colorado River is one of the world's most regulated rivers. But the regulation necessary to ensure a sufficient quantity of water for users has also exacted a price in the quality of the water available. As the south-western United States was being developed during the early part of this century, the big question was whether there would be enough water. Today people also ask how good the available water will be. Under a 1944 treaty with the United States, Mexico has a guaranteed allotment of 1.85×10^9 m^3 of water per year. Between 1945 and 1961 there were no major problems resulting from the treaty, as the salinity of the water crossing the border into Mexico was generally within 400 mg/l at Imperial dam, the last major diversion for users in the United States.

Regulation of the Colorado by a series of large dams (fig. 2.30) has substantially increased stream salinity by two processes: the tremendously increased evaporation surface, and contaminated irrigation return flows. The stream salinity at the Mexican border has been doubled, from 400 mg of total dissolved solids (TDS) per litre in the early 1900s to 800 mg in the 1950s. In 1961 Mexico began complaining that the increased salinity was harming crops in the Mexicali valley. In 1973 the United States agreed, in Minute No. 242 of the International Boundary and Water Commission, to a salinity level for water being delivered to Mexico at Morelos dam.

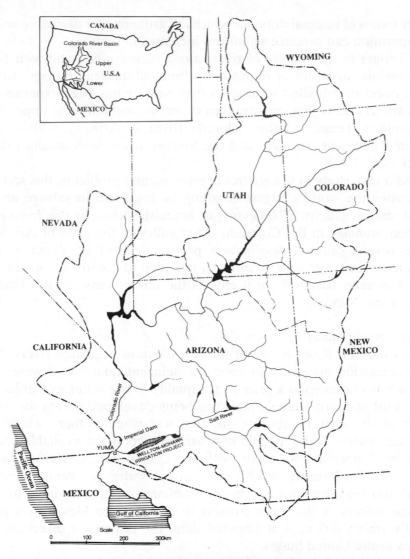

Fig. 2.30 **The Colorado River basin**

This agreed-upon salinity level has had to be achieved by constructing a massive desalination plant. Enough of the salts have to be removed from irrigation return flows to make the water acceptable for discharge into the river and later delivery to Mexico. The plant, completed in 1992, is the world's largest reverse-osmosis desalting facility with an installed capacity of 274,000 m³ per day. It salvages most of the irrigation return flows of 98 million m³ per year which were formerly diverted to the Gulf of California (Applegate 1986).

2.6.2   The river basin

The Colorado River is an international drainage system that drains an area of approximately 583,000 km² and flows through seven states of the United States and the Republic of Mexico.

The average annual natural flow of the river at Lees Ferry, Arizona, the dividing point between the upper and lower river basins, has been estimated at about 18×10^9 m³ per year, which also approximates the present consumptive use within the basin plus deliveries to Mexico. The total annual salt load at Lees Ferry is 7.4 million metric tons, of which irrigated agriculture is estimated to contribute a further 1.8–3 million metric tons. Eighty-eight per cent of the total salt load from irrigated agriculture in the entire basin is estimated to originate in the upper basin (Worthington 1977).

2.6.3   Salinity problems of the Colorado River

Salinity is a naturally occurring phenomenon in almost all rivers in the arid zone. The salinity of the Colorado River water at its headwaters in the Rocky Mountains is about 50 mg of TDS per litre, but where the river crosses the border into Mexico, it was already about 400 mg/l in the early 1900s. Owing to the tremendously increased evaporative surfaces in over 20 reservoirs and numerous irrigation systems in arid terrain, the salinity of the river water at the border reached an unacceptable level.

The Wellton-Mohawk Irrigation and Drainage District in southwestern Arizona, east of Yuma (fig. 2.30), established in the early 1950s, was one of the last districts to be developed. The project included a system of drainage wells, the discharge from which included a substantial amount of highly saline groundwater that had been concentrated through re-use during the previous 50 years. Initially it had a salinity of 6,000 mg/l. This resulted in a sharp increase in the salinity of the water crossing the border into Mexico, from around 850 mg/l in 1960 to more than 1,500 mg/l in 1962. At about the same time, releases into Mexico were greatly reduced in anticipation of storage behind the newly constructed Glen Canyon dam. This loss of dilution water is illustrated by the fact that from 1951 to 1960 the average delivery to Mexico was 5.2×10^9 m³ per year, while from 1961 to 1970, the flow averaged only 1.9×10^9 m³ per year. Mexico raised strenuous objections (Worthington 1977).

As a result of Minute 242 of 1973, the salinity of water as it enters Mexico at Morelos dam now averages no more than 115 mg/l plus or minus 30 mg/l over the average annual salinity of waters arriving at Imperial dam (Worthington 1977).

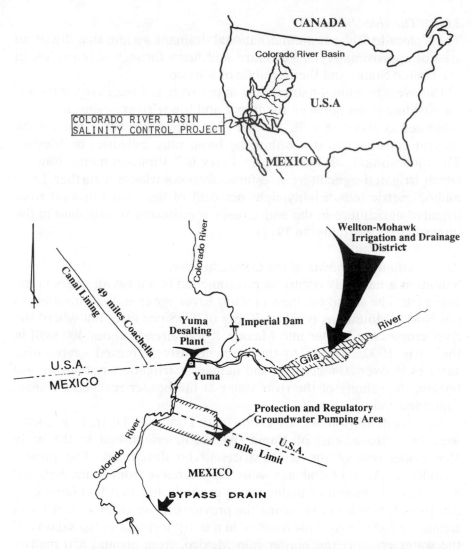

Fig. 2.31 **Colorado River basin salinity-control project** (Source: US Bureau of Reclamation 1980)

2.6.4 *Countermeasures to control river salinity*

To comply with Minute 242, the United States has been undertaking the following works (fig. 2.31):

— the Yuma desalting plant for Wellton-Mohawk drainage waters,
— extension of the Wellton-Mohawk drain by 85 km to the Gulf of California,

— lining or construction of a new Coachella canal in California,
— reduction in the Wellton-Mohawk district acreage and improved irrigation efficiency,
— construction of a wellfield on the US side of the international boundary to balance wellfields recently installed by Mexico near the border.

All of the costs in money or water to satisfy Minute 242 are to be borne by the United States, at a cost of several hundred million dollars annually. Both the United States and Mexico will receive tangible benefits. The US Bureau of Reclamation estimates that an increase of one mg/l in salinity at Imperial dam results in a cost of US$240,000 per year to water users in Arizona, California, and Nevada. In the absence of any measures to control salinity, the total impact of salinity increases on users in the three lower-basin states was predicted to be about US$80 million per year by the year 2000 (Worthington 1977). The dollar values of detriments to users in Mexico would be additional, but have not been estimated.

Authorization to begin the salinity control work was provided by the Colorado River Basin Salinity Control Act, passed by Congress in June 1974. This legislation was in two parts: one for salinity-control measures downstream of the Imperial dam, and one for salinity-control measures in the seven Colorado River basin states upstream of Imperial dam.

2.6.5 *Salinity control by the world's largest RO desalting facilities*
The agreed-upon salinity level is being achieved by desalination. Enough of the salts are removed from irrigation return flows to make the water acceptable for discharge into the river and later delivery to Mexico. While the desalination plant was being completed, drainage water from the farmlands east of Yuma were bypassed around Mexico's diversion point at Morelos dam and carried in a concrete-lined drain to the Santa Clara slough at the Gulf of California (Wagner 1989). At the same time, these bypassed flows were replaced by water from upstream storage to fully meet the quantity of 1.5 million acre-feet (1.85×10^9 m^3) of water owed to Mexico. When the desalting plant was completed, the irrigation return flows that were being diverted could be salvaged.

The Yuma desalting plant provides for salinity-control measures downstream of Imperial dam. Approximately 100 million gallons of saline irrigation drainage per day (138 million m^3 per year) from the Wellton-Mohawk farmland is delivered to the plant via an existing

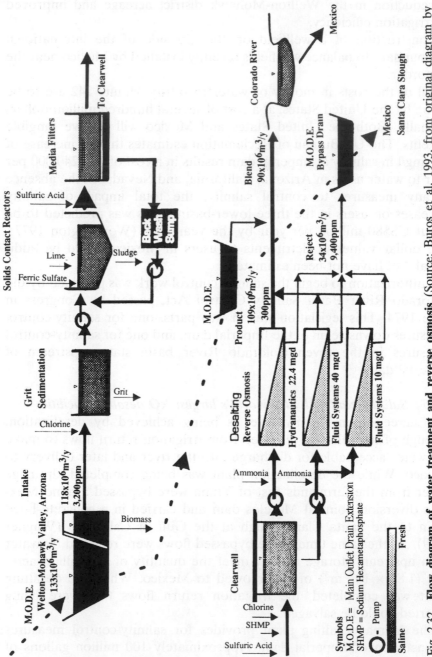

Fig. 2.32 **Flow diagram of water treatment and reverse osmosis** (Source: Buros et al. 1993, from original diagram by Wagener)

concrete-lined drain. The plant has an installed design capacity of about 72 million gallons (274,000 m³) per day, which can be expanded to 96 million gallons (365,000 m³) per day. A flow diagram of the treatment system is shown in fig. 2.32.

PRE-TREATMENT. Before being desalted, the water passes through three pre-treatment steps to remove all solids that would quickly clog the expensive desalting membranes if not removed. Pre-treating the water will ensure a membrane life of three to five years.

As the water flows into the plant, chlorine is added to prevent the growth of algae and other organisms. The water first goes through a grit sedimentation basin to remove heavy grit, sediment, and sand suspended in the water. The water is also softened by removing some of the calcium. Lime and ferric sulphate are both used in solid contact reactors. The last step in the pre-treatment process is dual media filters, which remove any fine particles or organisms remaining in the water.

PROCESSING. Reverse osmosis is the separation of one component of a solution from another (in this case, salt from the water) by means of pressure exerted on a semi-impermeable plastic membrane. A total of about 9,000 membrane elements, inserted into fibreglass pressure vessels desalt the water. While the pressure tubes are all 6 m (20 feet) long, some membranes have a diameter of 30 cm (12 inches) while the diameter of others is 20 cm (8 inches). The element is made up of a number of sheets rolled into a spiral-wound membrane.

Separation of salts from the product water is both a chemical process and a physical diffusion process. The water is forced through the walls of the cellulose acetate membranes by applying pressure at about 30 kg/cm² (about 400 pounds per square inch), allowing only the freshly desalted water to pass through. This process removes about 97% of the salts from the water. The fresh water is forced by the pressure down towards the centre tube.

WATER CONTROL AND MANAGEMENT. After desalination, the product water (with a salinity level of 285 mg of TDS per litre) is collected and combined with untreated drainage water (with salinity around 3,000 mg/l) to achieve the desired salinity level of about 700 mg/l. The salvaged water is then conveyed in a concrete channel to the Colorado River. Brine (with 10,000 mg/l salinity) is piped to the existing bypass drain, where it mixes with excess untreated Wellton-Mohawk drain-

Table 2.8 **Anticipated performance of Yuma desalting plant**

Constituent	Feed water (mg/l)	Reject water (mg/l)	Product water (mg/l)
Ca	145	477	
Mg	85	279	2
Na	739	2,246	93
K	9	27	1
HCO_3	19	15	<1
SO_4	1,011	3,380	11
Cl	870	2,563	145
NO_3	1	3	<1
SiO_2	23	63	6
TDS	2,987	9,047	261

Source: US Bureau of Reclamation, Yuma Desalting Office.

age. The anticipated performance of the reverse-osmosis desalination is shown in table 2.8. This effluent/drainage flow then travels to the Santa Clara slough above the Gulf of California, where it combines harmlessly with 30,000 mg/l salinity ocean water (Applegate 1986). No adverse effect on the water environment in the Gulf of California is foreseen.

COST. The US Bureau of Reclamation estimated the project cost of the Yuma desalting plant in 1975 at US$149,446,000, including:
— pre-treatment, US$56,000,000,
— desalting plant, US$70,300,000,
— control and operating system, US$5,300,000,
— appurtenant works, US$17,860,000.
The annual cost was estimated to be US$8,988,500 in financing costs plus US$11,520,000 for operation and maintenance for a design output of 126.6 million m^3 of product water per year with a salinity of 386 mg of TDS per litre. The unit cost of the product water was estimated to be US$0.16/m^3, based on 1975 prices without interest during construction. A recent cost study of the project estimated the unit cost of the product water with salinity at 285 mg/l and an output of 85 million m^3 per year to be US$0.48/m^3, with a construction period of three years

Table 2.9   **Unit costs of reclaimed water from various water-processing facilities**

	Salinity of source water (TDS mg/l)	Unit water cost (UN$/m³)
Seawater desalination (Kuwait)		
multi-stage flash evaporation[a]	45,000	2.70
reverse osmosis	45,000	1.60
Brackish-groundwater desalination		
Yuma	3,000	0.46
Orange County	1,000	0.14
Advanced waste-water treatment (Orange County)	<500	0.17

a. Using waste heat from steam-driven power plant.

and an interest rate of 8%. The project cost of the plant based on 1990 prices was estimated to be as follows:
— capital cost, US$211,518,000,
— design and construction management, US$52,911,000,
— financial expenditure, US$68,672,000,
— annual operation and maintenance cost, US$20,551,000.

A comparison with the unit water costs of various other projects— desalination of seawater by multi-stage flash evaporation and by reverse osmosis in Kuwait (Darwish and Jawad 1989), and desalination of brackish water and advanced waste-water treatment at a facility in Orange County, Calif., USA—is shown in table 2.9.

The operation and maintenance costs of reverse-osmosis desalination is likely to be reduced in the future by the introduction of low-pressure membrane modules.

2.6.6 *Remarks on the Colorado River salinity control and water resources management*

The product water from the desalting plant is being mixed with raw drainage water to develop a total of 89 million m³ of blended water per year to be delivered to the Colorado River. Salinity control of the river by the desalting facility is not only to protect the water-quality environment but also to sustain arid-land agriculture in both the United States and Mexico. The Colorado River salinity control programme, of which the Yuma desalting plant is a key element, may be a significant development in water-resources management of the river.

Such large-scale reverse-osmosis desalination will be applicable, however, only in countries where plant operational skills are already at a high level. The US Bureau of Reclamation and the National Water Supply Improvement Association jointly held a seminar and workshop on design, operational, legislative, and educational issues impacting large-scale desalting plants, including technical transfer to the developing countries in August 1993 (Buros et al. 1993).

2.7   Non-renewable groundwater development in the Middle East

It is possible to distinguish two major types of aquifers in the Middle East. Along river valleys and beneath alluvial fans and plains, there are shallow alluvial aquifers. These are generally unconfined, small in area, and have water tables that respond rapidly to local precipitation conditions. The second type are deep rock aquifers of sedimentary origin, usually sandstone and limestone. These are often confined systems, sometimes of considerable areal extent, and store water that can in part be many thousands of years old.

The deep rock aquifers often extend over many thousands of square kilometres in area, with natural recharge occurring in upland and foothill zones where the rocks have surface outcrops. There is still considerable uncertainty as to the degree to which recharge is taking place in these large rock aquifers at the present day, partly because little is known about how much run-off is generated during the rare, but often intense, local storms.

The potential for conventional water resources such as river water and renewable groundwater is extremely limited in the Arabian peninsula and North Africa, excluding minor areas in the mountain ranges where annual rainfall exceeds 10 inches, or 250 mm. By over-exploiting major rivers such as the Nile, Jordan, Tigris, and Euphrates, groundwater resources in deep sandstone aquifers, such as the Nubian sandstone aquifers and equivalent formations, could have been conceived as a major source of water for development in the Middle East and North Africa in the 1980s. Groundwater in the deep sandstone aquifers, however, is non-renewable or "fossil" water which may offer an opportunity for short-term and emergency uses. Large-scale deep sandstone aquifer development projects in Saudi Arabia, Libya, and Egypt are discussed in this section.

2.7.1   Groundwater resources in deep sandstone aquifers

NUBIAN SANDSTONES.   Sandstones of Nubian facies underlie most of the Arabian peninsula and the Sahara, and represent one of the most extensive artesian groundwater basins of the world. Nubian sandstones derive from the Precambrian and from reworked sandy Palaeozoic deposits and have not been altered by metamorphic processes.

The sediments, as a rule, are deposited either in flood facies represented by poorly sorted, coarse- to medium-grained, commonly cross-bedded, brownish sandstones containing mud flakes and quartz pebbles, or in lacustrine facies consisting of clay banks and sandstone tongues and reaching a maximum thickness of 3,500 m. Rapid facies changes are typical and marine incursions common, particularly over the less stable parts of the platform.

The age of the Nubian sandstones is poorly defined. In Libya, Late Jurassic to Early Cretaceous age is indicated, while the formation extends into the Palaeocene in Egypt. It seems that the name "Nubian sandstones" is best regarded as a purely litho-stratigraphic unit that does not easily fit into a chrono-stratigraphic system.

GROUNDWATER BASINS IN THE SAHARA.   The groundwater of the Sahara is to be found mainly in the following seven major basins: the Great Western Erg and Great Eastern Erg in the north, Fezzan and Tonezroft in the central region, the Western desert of Egypt in the east, and Chad and Niger in the south (fig. 2.33). A very large groundwater reservoir of fresh water is found in the Libyan part of the Sahara up to a depth of approximately 3,000 m. The water in the aquifers of Nubian sandstone correlates with the "continental intercalaire" in the western Sahara and is normally of good quality with the total dissolved solids content being usually less than 500 mg/l (Gishler 1979). The Nubian aquifer system of the north-eastern Sahara, which is one of the largest groundwater systems of the Sahara, covers an area of about 2 million km² and has two principal basins: the Kufra basin in Libya, north-eastern Chad, and north-western Sudan, and the Dakhla basin of Egypt (fig. 2.34).

RECHARGE.   Despite the hyper-arid climate, huge reserves of fresh groundwater are contained in Nubian sandstone in several thousand metres of saturated rock. The average rainfall is less than 5 mm per year, from which it is obvious that there has been no recent groundwater recharge in most of the system. For the occurrence of the

91

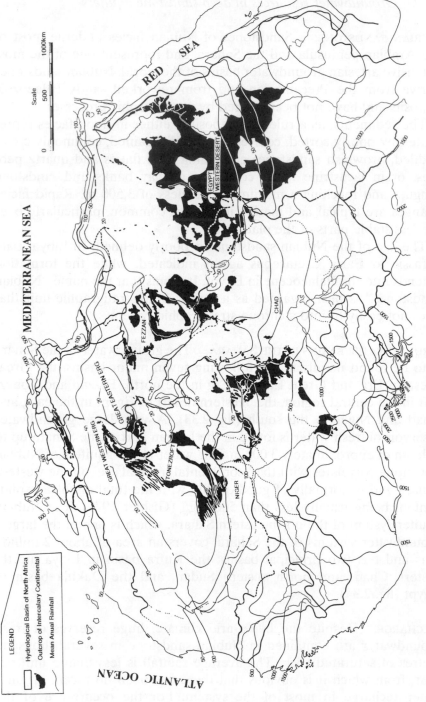

Fig. 2.33 **Major groundwater basins in North Africa** (Source: Gischler 1979)

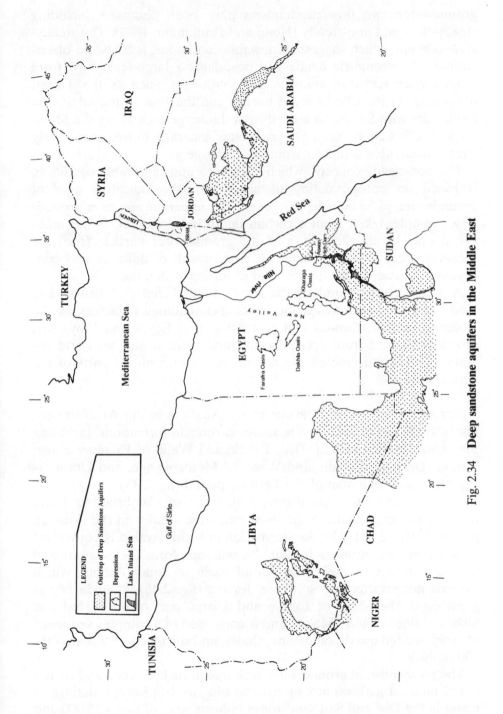

Fig. 2.34 Deep sandstone aquifers in the Middle East

LEGEND

Outcrop of Deep Sandstone Aquifers

Depression

Lake, Inland Sea

TURKEY

Mediterranean Sea

SYRIA

IRAQ

LEBANON

ISRAEL

JORDAN

SAUDI ARABIA

Red Sea

EGYPT

Nile river

New Valley

Farafra Oasis

Dakhla Oasis

Kharaga Oasis

Aswan
High Dam

SUDAN

LIBYA

Gulf of Sirte

TUNISIA

NIGER

CHAD

groundwater, two flow mechanisms have been discussed, including steady-state and non-steady (Heinl and Brinkmann 1989). The steady-state concept, which suggests renewable conditions, is based on obser-vations of piezometric heads and postulates a large-scale flow from mountainous recharge areas in the south-west, such as the Tibesti mountains on the Chad/Libyan border and the Ennedi mountains on the border with Sudan, to a north-east discharge area along the Medi-terranean Sea coast. Such artesian water generally moves very slowly over considerable distances from the recharge area.

The non-steady concept, which suggests a non-renewable condition, is based on isotope dating of water samples, indicating ages of groundwater of 25,000–40,000 years. The apparent age of a ground-water sample, taken from a certain depth in an aquifer, is not influ-enced only by the flow time of the groundwater particle from the recharge area; to a large extent it is the result of diffusive and con-vective processes in the aquifer and of mixing within the well.

A recent model simulation study in 1989 (Heinl and Brinkmann 1989), which took into account palaeo-climatological factors in the Holocene period, showed that groundwater in Egypt and Libya was probably derived from precipitation during humid and semi-arid cli-matic periods and entered the aquifer in the unconfined parts of the aquifer.

AQUIFERS IN THE ARABIAN PENINSULA. Aquifers in the Arabian pen-insula are found in arenaceous and/or carbonate formations, including the major formations Saq, Disi, Tabuk, and Wajid of Palaeozoic age; Minjur, Dhruma, Biyadh, and Wasia of Mesozoic age; and Umm er-Radhuma and Damman of the Tertiary period (fig. 2.35).

The Saq and Disi sandstones, which are of Cambrian to Early Ordovician age, constitute the most extensive aquifer in the Arabian peninsula (fig. 2.34). The Saq formation in Saudi Arabia is equivalent to the Disi formation in Jordan. Its outcrops form the western and southern fringes of the Great Nafud basin of Saudi Arabia, which extends northwards into southern Jordan (fig. 2.36). It underlies at great depth the whole of Jordan and a large part of the Nafud and Sirhan basins in Saudi Arabia, and is composed of a complex sequence of cross-bedded quartz sandstone, shales, and siltstone more than 600–900 m thick.

The mechanism of groundwater recharge in such a hyper-arid region is still under discussion among hydrogeologists, but isotope datings of water in the Disi and Saq sandstones indicate ages of up to 35,000 and 20,000 years respectively (NRAJ 1986). The current hypothesis is that

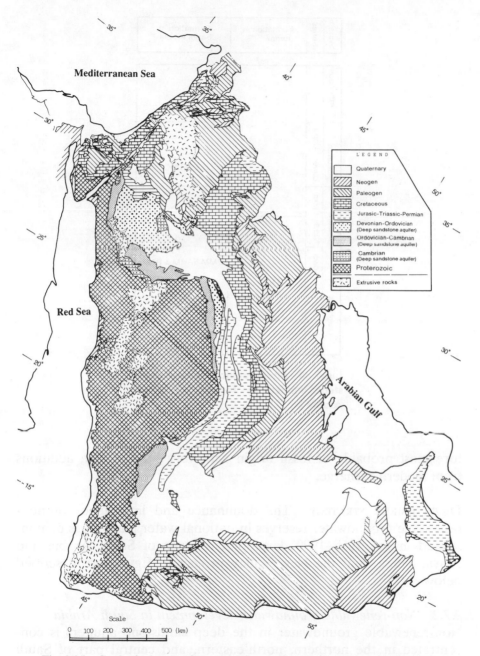

Fig. 2.35 **Geological map of the Arabian peninsula** (Source: AOMR 1987)

the observed hydraulic gradients cannot be attributed to replenishment and must be the result of dewatering of an ancient recharge area at outcrops. Groundwater reserves in the Disi/Saq aquifer are there-

95

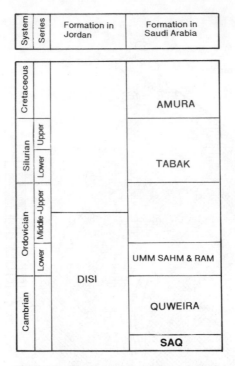

Fig. 2.36 **Stratigraphic section of sand-stone aquifers in Jordan and Saudi Arabia**

fore most probably of fossil origin with very little, if any, additions from modern recharge.

DEVELOPMENT STRATEGY. The dominance and importance of non-renewable groundwater reserves in national water planning is demonstrated in the 1985–1990 development plans of Saudi Arabia and Libya. These, and the New Valley project in Egypt, are described below.

2.7.2   Non-renewable groundwater development in Saudi Arabia
Non-renewable groundwater in the deep sandstone aquifers is concentrated in the northern, north-eastern, and central part of Saudi Arabia. The surface water and renewable groundwater is generally concentrated in the west and south-west, near the Hijaz and Assir mountains, while non-renewable groundwater with brackish quality in the Mesozoic to Neogene aquifers is found in extensive areas in the north-eastern part of the country, as shown in fig. 2.37.

96

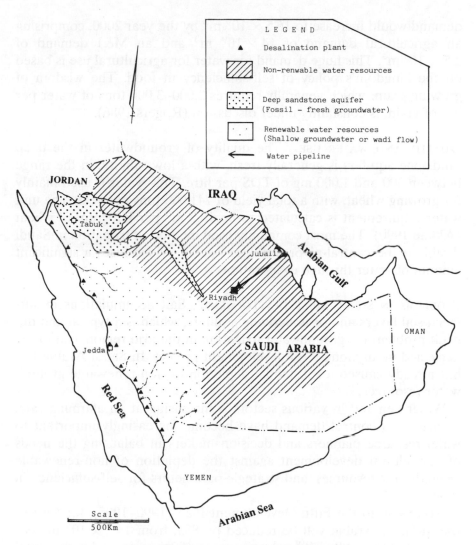

L E G E N D

▲ Desalination plant

▨ Non-renwable water resources

⋮ Deep sandstone aquifer
(Fossil – fresh groundwater)

· Renewable water resources
(Shallow groundwater or wadi flow)

← Water pipeline

JORDAN

IRAQ

Tabuk

Jubail

Arabian Gulf

Riyadh

OMAN

SAUDI ARABIA

Jedda

Red Sea

YEMEN

Scale
500Km

Arabian Sea

Fig. 2.37 **Water resources of Saudi Arabia**

Saudi Arabia today is one of the world's leaders in the production of wheat for self-sufficiency in food. The production of wheat, however, is dependent almost wholly on the mining of non-renewable ground-water resources.

According to the Fourth Development Plan (1985–1990) of the Ministry of Agriculture and Water, agricultural water demand in Saudi Arabia in 1985 amounted to 8×10^9 m^3 per year, while the demand for water for urban, rural, and industrial (M&I) use was 1.6×10^9 m^3 per year (MAWSA 1985). It was estimated that the total annual

97

demand would increase to 16.5×10^9 m^3 by the year 2000, comprising an agricultural demand of 14×10^9 m^3 and an M&I demand of 2.5×10^9 m^3. This huge demand for water for agricultural use is based on the kingdom's policy of self-sufficiency in food. The wisdom of growing grain, which generally requires 2,000–3,000 tons of water per ton of grain, is constantly under discussion (Rogers 1986).

QUALITY AND WATER USE. The quality of groundwater in the deep sandstone aquifers is generally fresh, with a low salinity, in the range between 300 and 1,000 mg of TDS per litre. This water is used mainly for growing wheat, with a total yield of 741,000 tons per year. The unit water requirement is calculated to be 10.8 m^3 per kilogram of wheat (Akkad 1990). The most commonly used method of irrigation in Saudi Arabia is the central-pivot sprinkler system, which loses a significant amount of water through evaporation.

PROBLEMS IN SUSTAINABLE DEVELOPMENT. Salt accumulations in surfacial soil layers and/or underlying aquifers, which is a typical and difficult problem for groundwater irrigation in the arid region, cannot be neglected in any long-term development project. In Saudi Arabia this has already caused a substantial depletion of non-renewable groundwater resources.

Water demand in various sectors is increasing at an alarming rate. Measures to control demand have become increasingly important to water-resource planners and decision makers in balancing the needs of agricultural development against the depletion of non-renewable groundwater resources, and strategic parameters for self-sufficiency in food.

According to the Fifth Development Plan (1990–1995), total water use in Saudi Arabia will be reduced by 8%, from 16.2×10^9 m^3 per year in 1990 to 14.9×10^9 m^3 per year in 1995, compared with a total increase of 89% during the Fourth Plan period. The reduction in water consumption will be the result of a projected decline in annual agricultural consumption from 14.6×10^9 m^3 at the beginning of the period to 12.7×10^9 m^3 at the end. This change in the consumption rate is expected to take place through changing crop patterns, the intensification of water-saving techniques, and other appropriate measures, all of which will not affect the desirable growth rate of agricultural production or its value added. This 8% of reduction in the national water supply may be the world's first initiative to conserve non-renewable groundwater resources (MAWSA 1990). Many countries in the Middle

East must consider such a conservation policy for sustainable development, including the reduction of national water supply.

2.7.3 The Great Man-Made River project in Libya

SAHARA/LIBYAN DESERT.   Libya is located in the northern part of the Sahara desert in Africa, and extends from 19° to 33° north latitude and from 9° to 25° east longitude, with a land area of 1,759,540 km² (see fig. 2.34). Except for the Mediterranean coastal belt, the country consists of barren rock deserts, undulating sand seas, salt-marsh depressions, and mountains that rise to 1,200 m in the south-west and 1,800 m in the south-east. Climatically Libya is influenced by both the Mediterranean and the Sahara. The coastal region has a Mediterranean climate: winters are mild with 250 400 mm of rain, and summers are hot and dry. Conditions in the desert interior are extremely hot and arid, with an annual rainfall of 0–120 mm.

Hydro-meteorologically Libya is a desert in which the surface hydrology is of no direct practical importance, while huge amounts of fossil groundwater are stored in the Nubian sandstones that underlie wide areas of the Libyan desert. Groundwater development and/or mining of the Nubian sandstones in the inland desert depressions, named the "Great Man-Made River project," is the key to the nation's development strategy.

GREAT MAN-MADE RIVER PROJECT.   A vast aquifer estimated to hold an amount of fresh water equivalent to the total flow of the Nile River over a 200-year period was discovered accidentally by an American geologist during crude-oil exploration in the Sahara desert in the early 1960s. The Libyan government saw an opportunity to pump the water, at a rate of 5.7 million m³ per day (66 m³/sec), then convey it over 600 km north to farms on the Libyan coast. The total length of the water pipeline is estimated at 4,000 km, which will be the world's largest water pipeline system (fig. 2.38).

Some agricultural development has already begun around the desert oasis of Kufra, using the self-flowing artesian wells in the depression. Acres of wheat, barley, and alfalfa grow where there were only desert and gravel plains before. According to an article in the British journal *New Scientist*, the amount of sustained yield of groundwater resources is in some doubt; Professor Ahmad, a hydrogeologist at the University of Ohio, says that water is moving into the two aquifers that are to be tapped at a rate of 80 m³/sec, whereas Dr. E. Wright of the British

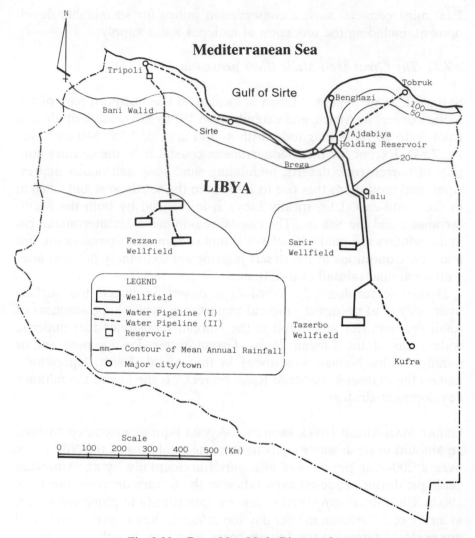

Fig. 2.38 **Great Man-Made River project**

Geological Survey says that the figure is closer to 5 m³/sec. The life of the Nubian sandstone aquifer is estimated to be between 20 and 200 years, owing to the lack of data for estimating groundwater recharge through the wadi beds and/or the depressions during occasional and temporary flash floods. The total pipeline system is therefore designed on the assumption of an aquifer life of 50 years.

In 1984 the Libyan government began the first phase of construction for the Great Man-Made River project. This comprises a 2 million m³ per day twin pipeline in eastern Libya, leading from wellfields in the Tazerbo and Sarir regions, deep in the desert, to the small coastal town of Agedabia. The trunk main is 667 km long. The line splits into two spurs, one a 150-km link to Benghazi, the other going south-west to Marsa el-Brege. From there the line will extend west to Sirte. By the end of 1992 Libya had spent more than US\$5 × 10^9 of the initial US\$14 × 10^9 allocated to the project, and the first section had been completed (Bulloch and Darwish 1993).

The second phase, consisting of a 600-km-long prestressed concrete pipeline to convey 2 million m^3 per day from beneath the western deserts to the Tripoli area on the coast, began in 1986.

The constant increase in the price of the total scheme will have to be taken into account when figures are worked out for the cost of growing the wheat to be irrigated. The whole idea of using this valuable resource for agriculture is very much open to question, in which the groundwater irrigation accumulates substantial salts in the irrigated land. The total cost was estimated in 1990 at US\$27 × 10^9, but that figure is likely to rise further: in 1985 the total cost was expected to be US\$20 × 10^9 and in 1980, US\$14 × 10^9 (Bulloch and Darwish 1993).

2.7.4   New Valley project in Egypt

THE SAHARA DESERT IN EGYPT.   Egypt is located in north-eastern Africa, extending from 22° to 31.5° north latitude and from 25°–36° east longitude, with a land area of 1,002,000 km^2 (fig. 2.34). About 96% of Egypt is desert. The area west of the Nile is an arid plateau some 200 m high, crossed by belts of sand dunes in the centre and west. The Nile is Egypt's most important feature. It divides 25 km north of Cairo into the Rashid and Dumyat, the two main channels of the 22,000-km^2 delta. Rainfall is minimal: Cairo receives only 60 mm annually, while the desert often has no rain at all. A narrow stretch of the Mediterranean coast is milder and wetter, with 250 mm of rain a year.

Hydro-meteorologically Egypt is a desert, however, in which the surface hydrology of the Nile River is of direct practical importance. The Nile is the basic source of water and, with the aid of dams and barrages, supplies an extensive network of distributary canals. West of the Nile, Nubian sandstones that store a huge amount of fossil to semi-fossil water underlie the desert. Groundwater development in the depressions, where the saturated Nubian sandstone aquifer underlies, is the worthy complement of the green revolution in western Egypt.

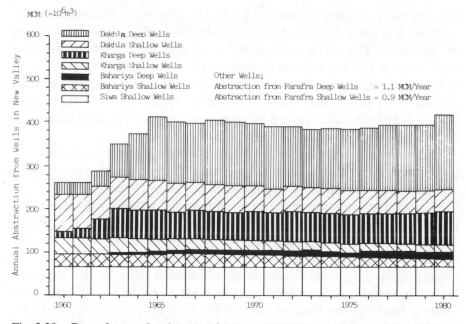

Fig. 2.39 **Groundwater development in the New Valley project in Egypt** (Source: Shahin 1987)

THE KHARGA AND DAKHLA OASES IN THE WESTERN DESERT. In 1950 about 24 km² out of a total of 4,000 km² in the Kharga oasis was cultivated. Abstraction of groundwater from shallow wells amounted to 38.7 million m³ per year in the Kharga oasis and 92.7 million m³ per year in the Dakhla oasis (fig. 2.39). Seven deep boreholes drilled between 1938 and 1952, with depths varying between 342.5 and 509.3 m, encountered artesian flow. The yield of these deep wells was 20.6 million m³ per year in total; however, the yields decreased after a few years of operation by not less than 40% of their initial values.

GROUNDWATER DEVELOPMENT IN THE NEW VALLEY PROJECT. Extensive deep production wells were drilled in the mid-1950s, to correspond with the New Valley project which aims to expand the cultivated area in the Kharga and Dakhla oases. At first, much of the water was self-flowing under artesian conditions. The pressure quickly fell, however, and an increasing use of water required ever greater amounts of pumping. Saline water began to contaminate some wells, limiting the crops which could be grown. In 1963 the combined discharge of shallow wells and deep production wells in el-Kharga amounted to about 117 million m³ per year, but this had dropped to a level of 80 million

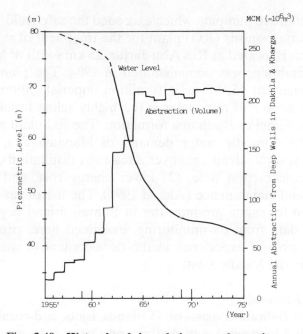

Fig. 2.40 **Water head in relation to abstractions from deep wells in the Dakhla and Kharga oases**

m^3 by the end of 1967. The construction of deep production wells in the Dakhla oasis, completed by 1966, increased the combined yield of the shallow and deep systems up to 190 million m^3 per year, but this had decreased to a level of 159 million m^3 by the end of 1969. The response of the head of water to the growing abstractions from the deep production wells in Kharga and Dakhla oases from 1956 to 1975 is shown in fig. 2.40. The Egyptian authorities are planning to augment extraction until it reaches 2.4×10^9 m^3 per year by the year 2000 (Shahin 1987). Extraction of the target volume will lead to a further decline in the piezometric head to cease the artesian flow. Another problem of the development project is the human problem that many of the managerial staff do not like living in such isolated areas. Overall, the project cannot be considered a success (Beaumont et al. 1988).

2.8 Brackish-groundwater reverse-osmosis desalination in Bahrain

Groundwater in the Damman aquifer on Bahrain island has been seriously contaminated by seawater intrusion or upward leakage from the underlying saline aquifer of Umm er-Radhuma since the 1960s,

103

owing to intensive pumping which exceeded the safe yield. The world's largest reverse-osmosis (RO) plant for the treatment of saline ground-water, which is located at Ras Abu-Jarjur, 25 km south of Manama, the capital of Bahrain, was commissioned in 1984. The plant has an in-stalled capacity of 45,500 m³ (10 million imperial gallons [mig]) per day, whose source of raw water is the highly saline brackish ground-water in the Umm er-Radhuma formation. The RO plant was designed to meet the domestic water demand of Manama city, taking into account its several advantages over a seawater distillation (MSF) plant: (1) short construction time, (2) lower energy cost, and (3) ease of operation and maintenance (Akkad 1990). The use of reverse-osmosis desalination for saline groundwater in Bahrain island began in 1984–1986. The data from its monitoring, examined here, provide one of the key sources of experience in the development of marginal water resources in the Middle East.

2.8.1 Background
The state of Bahrain consists of 33 islands, islets, and coral reefs in the Arabian Gulf between Saudi Arabia and Qatar, between the latitudes 25°45′ and 26°27′ north and longitudes 50°25′ and 50°54′ east. The country has a land area of 662 km², of which the island of Bahrain itself, with its capital Manama, occupies 85% (fig. 2.41). The popula-tion was estimated at 427,271, with a growth rate of 4.2% per year in 1985 (Beaumont 1988).

The climate is arid to extremely arid. The mean monthly tem-perature varies from 17°C in January to 34°C in July and August. Owing to the surrounding Arabian Gulf, the humidity is generally high. Rainfall is confined to the period between November and April, with an annual average of 76 mm, which occurs essentially in a form of ephemeral thunder showers. There are no rivers, streams, or lakes.

The country is occupied by Tertiary sediments, which are rather gently folded on a regional scale into elongate domes or periclines of near north–south trend. Bahrain island is dominated by one such dome, developed principally in carbonate sediments of Cretaceous–Tertiary age, which dip gently outwards. The Bahrain dome is elongate (about 30 km × 30 km) and with slight asymmetry, as seen in fig. 2.41.

The sequence is composed of three formations: Damman, Rus, and Umm er-Radhuma, as seen in the schematic geological profile in fig. 2.42. The Damman formation, which consists of fossiliferous dolom-itized limestone, dolomitic marl, and dolomitic limestone, has two forms, known as Alat limestone and Khobar dolomite, from the Mid-

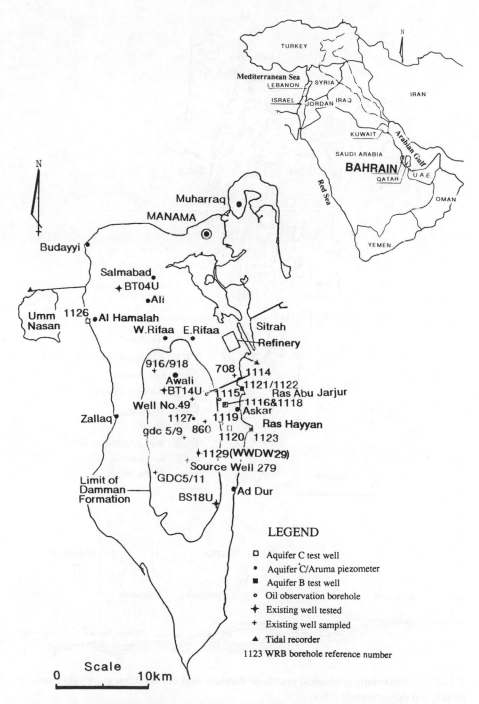

Fig. 2.41 **Bahrain island** (Source: Birch and Al-Arrayedh 1985)

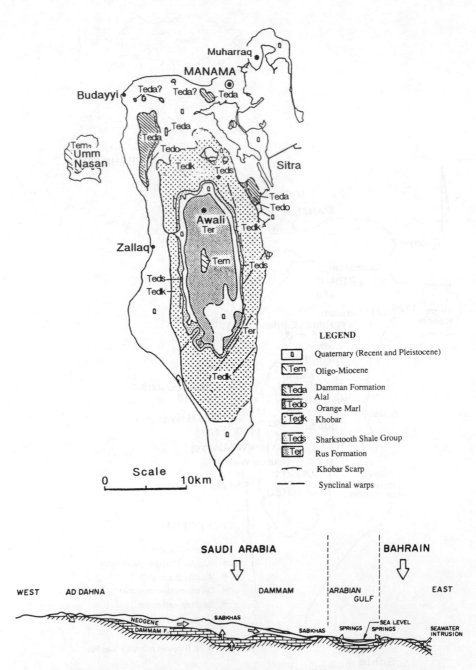

Fig. 2.42 Schematic geological profile of Bahrain and the Arabian peninsula (Source: Birch and Al-Arrayedh 1985)

dle Eocene. The Rus formation of the Lower Eocene consists of chalky dolomitic limestone, shale, gypsum, and anhydrite. The Umm er-Radhuma formation of the Palaeocene is composed of dolomitic limestone and calcarenite with some argillaceous and bituminous facies, which is underlain by shales, marls, and argillaceous limestone of the upper Arma formation of the Cretaceous. The geological sequence and aquifer characteristics are shown in fig. 2.43.

2.8.2 Water resources

Historically, Bahrain has utilized groundwater for both agriculture and municipal requirements. Natural fresh-water springs used to flow freely in the northern part of Bahrain, but, with increased demand, spring flow has decreased and pumped boreholes became the normal means of obtaining water. Before 1925, the water supply depended on free-flowing springs and some hand-dug wells, whose discharge was estimated to be 93 million m³ per year in total. With increased water demand after the exploration of offshore reservoirs of crude oil and gas in 1946, spring flow decreased and pumped boreholes became the normal means of procuring water. Groundwater use in Bahrain at that time was estimated to be 153 million m³ per year in total, which included 138 million m³ of tube-well abstraction, 8.1 million m³ of land springs, and 6.6 million m³ of marine springs (Mussayab 1988). During the 1980s, most of the springs ceased flowing, and further increase in water demand has caused deterioration in water quality, including the intrusion of seawater into the aquifer system.

Faced with rising demand and the contamination of the aquifers by seawater intrusion, Bahrain turned to desalination of seawater to provide for the increasing demand for M&I water supply. On the basis of a 1983 groundwater model study (Birch and Arrayedh 1985), which included the recommendation to reduce groundwater abstraction from the Damman aquifer to the level of 90 million m³ per year, the Ministry of Works, Power, and Water instigated a crash programme to increase Bahrain's desalinated water capacity from 22,730 m³ (5 mig) to 204,570 m³ (45 mig) per day. Production of water for M&I water supply was estimated to be 101 million m³ per year in 1987, including 53 million m³ of groundwater and 48 million m³ of desalinated water (Birch and Arrayedh 1985).

2.8.3 Hydrogeology and seawater intrusion

The principal aquifers are pervious limestone units in Palaeocene to Eocene sedimentary rocks. Damman and Umm er-Radhuma are the important aquifers in Bahrain.

107

ERA	PERIOD	FORMATION	MEMBER	APPROXIMATE THICKNESS (m)	LITHOLOGY	HYDROGEOLOGICAL SIGNIFICANCE
QUATERNARY	Recent	Superficial		5	Aeolian sand, bioclastic limestone, beach deposits	Unsaturated.
	Pleistocene	Superficial		10	Sand, sabkha deposits	Unsaturated.
TERTIARY	Oligocene-Miocene	Jabal Cap		33	Dolomitic bioclastic limestone, algal coral breccia	Forms cap to Jabal Dukhan.
		Neogene		10-60	Marl with subordinate sandy limestone	Confines Dammam aquifers. Basal limestone forms part of the 'A' aquifer.
	Eocene	Dammam	Alat Limestone	15-25	Fossiliferous dolomitised limestone	Main 'A' aquifer. Formerly sustained small artesian flows. Low productivity. Used in NE and W coast.
			Orange Marl	19-15	Orange-brown dolomitic marl	Confines Aquifer B when present
			Khobar Dolomite	30-39	Dolomitic limestone	Main 'B' aquifer, usually confined. Highly permeable in top 5-10m. Main source of freshwater.
			Khobar Marl	Discontinuous c. 10	Marl and shale	Forms part of the 'B' aquitard
			Alveolina Limestone		Friable brown dolarenite	
			Sharks Tooth Shale	8-20	Shale with silty dolomitic limestone	Aquitard
		Rus		60-150	Chalky dolomitic limestone, shale, gypsum and anhydrite	Part of 'C' aquifer. Aquitard if evaporites present.
	Paleocene	Umm Er Radhuma		115-350	Dolomitic limestone and calcarenite, often argillaceous and bituminous	'C' aquifer in upper UER and Rus. Salinity stratified. Lower UER saline with low permeability.
MESOZOIC	Cretaceous	Aruma		c. 400	Mainly shale in the upper part, limestone predominant below	Aruma shales form hydraulic base to Umm Er Radhuma.

Fig. 2.43 **Geological sequences of Bahrain** (Source: Birch and Al-Arrayedh 1985)

The Alat limestone in the upper Damman formation used to sustain small artesian flows or springs in the northern island. The Khobar dolomite in the lower Damman formation, a highly pervious unit, was the main productive aquifer to produce fresh groundwater, with a typical salinity of 2,500 mg of TDS per litre. Due to excessive abstraction, however, piezometric levels in the Khobar aquifer declined continuously with substantial increase in water salinity (figs. 2.44 and

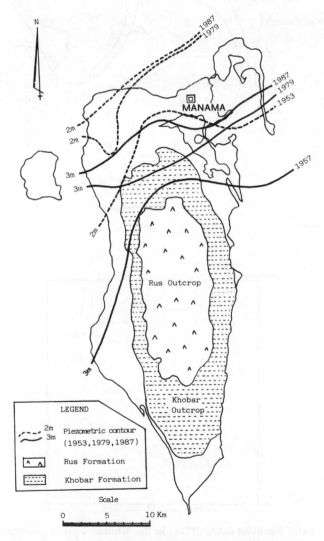

Fig. 2.44 **Piezometric-level changes in the Khobar aquifer in Bahrain** (Source: Birch and Al-Arrayedh 1985)

109

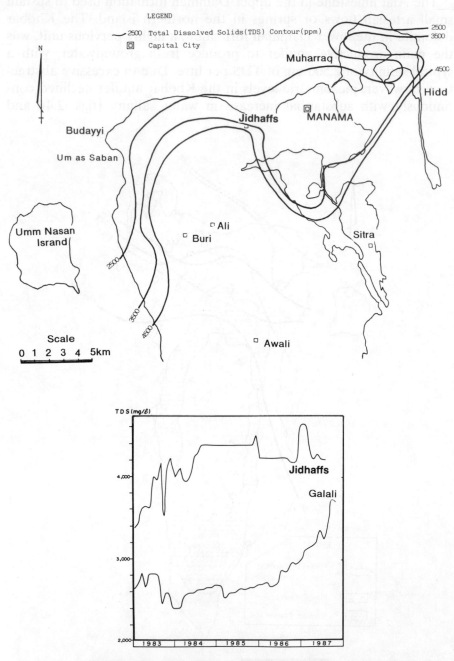

Fig. 2.45 **Total dissolved solids (TDS) in the Khobar aquifer** (Source: Birch and Al-Arrayedh 1985)

2.45). This aquifer has become saline in the Ali-Buri area, due to upward leakage of brackish water, and on Sitra, due to seawater intrusion (fig. 2.45). Significant upward leakage of brackish water from the underlying aquifer of Umm er-Radhuma occurs only in eastern and central Bahrain, where the evaporite layers in the Rus formation have been removed by solution.

The deeper aquifer of Umm er-Radhuma, composed of dolomitic limestone and calcarenite, is a salinity stratified aquifer with a total thickness of about 200 m. A further highly saline groundwater contains hydrogen sulphide and hydrocarbons from bitumens as specific contaminants.

2.8.4 Desalination

Since it has become the policy to curb the abstraction of groundwater resources in the Damman aquifer and to improve its quality, such as the salinity of domestic water supply, further development of water resources will undoubtedly be by means of desalination, either by a thermal process or reverse osmosis. The choice will depend on the site-specific conditions and economy or cost.

The first multi-stage flash (MSF) distillation plant was introduced in Bahrain in 1976. The total installed capacity of this plant was 22,730 m^3 (5 mig) per day in 1981, which was 15% of the total demand of 154,000 m^3 (34 mig) per day. The present installed capacity of desalination plants in Bahrain is 205,000 m^3 (45 mig) per day, including 160,000 m^3 (35 mig) of seawater distillation by MSF and 45,000 m^3 (10 mig) of desalination of brackish groundwater by RO. A further 45,000 m^3 per day of seawater desalination capacity by RO is under construction (Mussayab 1988).

2.8.5 Brackish-groundwater reverse-osmosis desalination

The RO desalination plant at Ras Abu Jarjur, 25 km south of Manama, with an installed capacity of 45,000 m^3 per day, the world's largest RO plant with seawater membranes in the 1980s, was commissioned in 1984 (Al-Arrayedh 1985). The raw water source is a highly saline groundwater (13,000 mg of TDS per litre) in the Umm er-Radhuma formation, containing hydrogen sulphide and hydrocarbons from oil as specific contaminants. It is predicted that the water quality will deteriorate with time, implying significant increases in the hydrocarbon concentration from a trace to 2 mg/l, the hydrogen sulphide concentration from about 2 mg/l initially to about 13 mg/l, and the total dissolved solids (TDS) from about 13,000 mg/l up to about 30,000 mg/l after

111

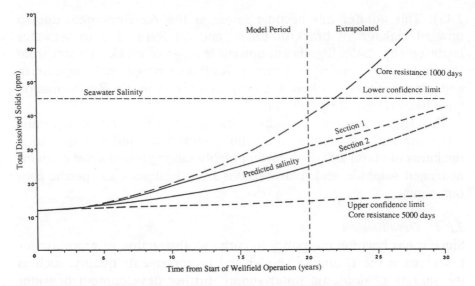

Fig. 2.46 Predicted range of feed-water salinity for RO desalination plant in Bahrain (Source: Birch and Al-Arrayedh 1985)

20 years' operation. The design TDS for the plant is 19,000 mg/l; it is predicted that this concentration will be reached after 10 years' operation. The predicted range in feed-water salinity is shown in fig. 2.46. The permeate is being produced from highly brackish well water at a conversion rate averaging 65%, of which the salinity averages as low as 210 mg of TDS per litre, well below the design criterion of 500 mg/l. The plant contains five basic systems: a well-water supply, pre-treatment, RO desalination, post-treatment, and product-water transfer systems, as shown in the process flow diagram in fig. 2.47.

WELL-WATER SUPPLY SYSTEM. Raw water is pumped from 15 bore-holes, which include 13 duty wells and 2 standby wells. Submersible pumps are designed to abstract an average of 3,200 m³ of brackish groundwater per hour from a group of boreholes. Four anti-surge tanks at the high and low points of the wellfield are installed to protect the collection pipes from sudden pressure surges. The anti-surge tanks are pressurized with nitrogen gas to prevent oxidation of hydrogen sulphide in the well water.

PRE-TREATMENT SYSTEM. To protect the RO system, well water entering the plant is filtered and chemically treated to remove silt, oil, and

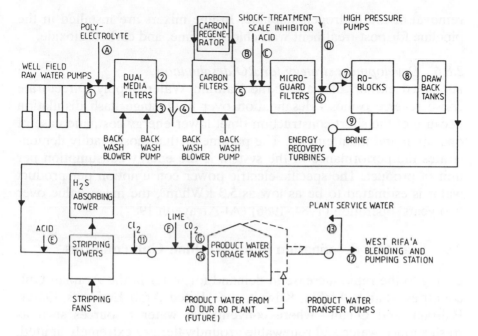

Fig. 2.47 **Flow scheme of RO system in Bahrain** (Source: Birch and Al-Arrayedh 1985)

other hydrocarbons. The raw water passes through a series of dual media filters and carbon filters. Sodium hexametaphosphate and sulphuric acid are then injected downstream of the carbon filters to prevent scaling of the system.

RO SYSTEM. Before entering the heart of the RO system, the water passes through eight micro-guard filters (10-micrometre) with polypropylene cartridge elements. Seven horizontal multi-stage diffuser-type high-pressure pumps are installed to feed water with an average pressure of 60 bar (maximum pressure 69 bar). Each pump is equipped with Pelton wheel impulse-type energy-recovery turbines. The RO membrane unit comprises a total of 2,100 permeators. The permeators are hollow fibre-type, such as DuPont B-10.

POST-TREATMENT. Since the well water contains a high level of hydrogen sulphide, the RO product water must pass through a series of stripping towers to remove the gas. Adjustment of the pH of the permeate with sulphuric acid is also needed before stripping for maximum

113

removal of the hydrogen sulphide. In-line mixers are installed in the pipeline for post-treatment with chlorine, lime, and carbon dioxide.

2.8.6 Development strategy for RO desalination

As stated earlier, officials of the Bahrain Water Supply Directorate chose reverse osmosis desalination over multi-stage flash distillation because of the short construction time, lower energy cost, and ease of operation and maintenance. The parameter that most readily demonstrates the performance of the system is the energy consumption per unit of product. The specific electric power consumption per product water is estimated to be as low as 5.3 kWh/m^3, the mean value over two years' operation (1984–1986) (Al-Arrayedh 1987).

2.9 Seawater desalination in the Arabian Gulf countries

Owing to the rapid increase in demand for water in the Arabian Gulf countries—Saudi Arabia, Kuwait, the United Arab Emirates, Qatar, Bahrain, and Oman—where conventional water resources such as fresh surface water and renewable groundwater are extremely limited, other alternatives such as waste-water reclamation and desalination have been adopted since the 1960s. Countries such as Saudi Arabia, Kuwait, Qatar, and Bahrain all use non-renewable groundwater resources in large quantity, causing depletion of these valuable resources and deterioration in the quality of water. Although conventional water resources such as renewable groundwater and surface run-off are available in countries like Oman, the United Arab Emirates, and Saudi Arabia, these resources still need to be properly developed in an integrated water-resources planning context.

In some of the more arid parts of the Middle East, in particular the Gulf states, where good quality water is not available or is extremely limited, desalination of seawater has been commonly used to solve the problems of water supply for municipal and industrial uses.

Kuwait was the first state to adopt seawater desalination, linking electricity generation to desalination. The co-generation station, as it is called, re-uses low pressure steam from the generator to provide energy for the desalination process. As a result, both energy and costs are minimized. Kuwait began desalinated water production in 1957, when 3.1 million m^3 were produced per year. By 1987 this figure had risen to 184 million m^3 per year.

In Qatar, too, an intensive programme of desalinated water production has been started, which should be supplying about 150 million m^3 of water per year by the year 2000. This is believed to be about three-quarters of the total water demand, with the rest to be supplied from groundwater sources, which are mostly brackish. About half of the country's demand will be generated in the urban/industrial centres.

Saudi Arabia entered the desalinated water field much later than Kuwait. The first plant was commissioned in 1970. It has, however, gone in for an ambitious programme of desalination plant construction on both the Red Sea and Gulf coasts. The Saline Water Conversion Corporation had installed 30 desalination plant projects by the end of the 1980s. The total production of desalinated water is estimated to be 2.16 million m^3 (572 million [US] gal.) per day including a facility at Al-Jubail producing 1 million m^3 per day, which is currently the world's largest distillation plant.

In spite of the high cost of seawater desalination, with unit water costs five to ten times as high as those of conventional water-resources development, a vast quantity has been produced to meet the increasing demand for domestic water in the Arabian Gulf countries. As in Kuwait, however, there is increasing government concern about the production cost of desalinated water, and every effort is being made to ensure that water use is as efficient as possible.

2.9.1 Installed capacity of desalination plants

There are about 1,483 desalination units operating in the Arabian Gulf countries, which account for 57.9% of the worldwide desalting plant capacity. The dominant plant type is multi-stage flash (MSF) which accounts for 86.7% of the desalting capacity, while the reverse osmosis accounts for only 10.7%. The installed capacity of desalination plants in the Arabian Gulf countries is estimated at 5.76 million m^3 per day in total, including 2.98 million m^3 in Saudi Arabia, which is approximately half of the total desalination capacity of the Gulf countries (Al-Mutaz 1989). The installed capacity with shares of each process are shown in table 2.10.

MSF desalting has proved to be the simplest, most reliable, and most commonly used seawater system in large capacities. It has reached maturity with very little improvement in sight. This maturity is expressed in reliable designs of large units up to 38,000 m^3 (10 million gal.) per day, long operation experience with high on-line stream factors (up to 95%), confidence in material selection, and very satisfactory water pre-treatment. However, there has been a recent trend towards the use of reverse osmosis in seawater desalination, both for new plants and in connection with the present MSF plants, taking into

115

Table 2.10 **Installed capacity of desalting plants and share by process type in the Arabian Gulf countries**

	No. of units	Capacity (1,000 m³/day)	Share by process type (%)				
			MSF	RO	ED	VC	MED
Saudi Arabia	874	2,980	80.7	16.2	2.6	0.5	—
Kuwait	279	1,090	95.5	1.8	0.55	1.6	0.25
U.A.E.	99	1,020	98.3	0.9	0.5	—	—
Qatar	47	310	97.9	—	—	0.7	0.9
Bahrain	143	260	56.7	37.2	4.9	0.8	0.4
Oman	41	100	91.1	1.9	0.9	1.7	—
TOTAL	1,483	5,760	86.7	10.7	1.8	0.65	0.15

Source: Akkad 1990.

MSF = multi-stage flash. RO = reverse osmosis. ED = electrodialysis. VC = vapour compression. MED = multi-effect distillation.

account the possible reduction in energy requirements and the lower operation and maintenance cost for RO.

2.9.2 *The world's largest seawater desalination with high-pressure pipeline system*

To meet the water demands of the increasing population and water-short regions in Saudi Arabia, the Saline Water Conversion Office (SWCO) under the Ministry of Agriculture and Water was made responsible for providing fresh water by desalination of seawater in 1965. The first seawater desalination plant was commissioned in 1970. With its increasing responsibilities to provide fresh water, the SWCO was changed in 1974 into an independent corporation, the Saline Water Conversion Corporation (SWCC), which then developed an elaborate plan to construct dual-purpose plants on both the east and west coasts of the kingdom.

The SWCC had constructed 24 plants by 1985, including 17 plants on the western coast along the Red Sea, from Haql on the Gulf of Aqaba in the north to the tiny Farasan island in the south, and 7 plants on the east coast along the Arabian Gulf from Al-Khafji to Al-Khobar (fig. 2.48). These plants were producing 1.82 million m³ (481 million gal.) of fresh water per day and 3,631 MW of electric power. By the

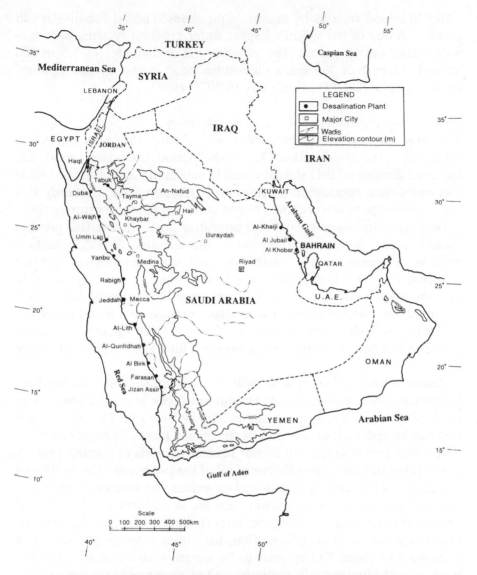

Fig. 2.48   **Desalination plants and water supply in Saudi Arabia**

end of the 1980s the total production of fresh water was estimated to have been increased to 2.17 million m³ (572 million gal.) of fresh water per day and 4,079 MW of electric power by the addition of six co-generation plants (SWCC 1988).

In addition to desalination and power plants, the SWCC provides

117

water to inland regions by means of pipelines. The Al-Jubail–Riyadh pipeline is one of the world's largest water pipeline systems with sea-water desalination plants. The pipeline has a diameter of 1.5 m (60 inches), a length of 466 km, a differential head of 690 m, and a pumping capacity of 830,000 m³ per day (SWCC 1988).

2.9.3 Cost constraints of seawater desalination

The MSF process has served very well during the past ten years, especially in the Middle East. During this period, operating experience has been developed that should result in substantial extensions to what was heretofore considered a reasonable operating life. Certainly this favourable experience will be a factor in the selection of future plants.

However, the lower capital and operating costs for the RO process should receive increasing attention in the selection of a desalination process in coming years. There are still opportunities for further lowering of costs through improved membrane technology, notably in increasing membrane life. Another new development with good potential for reducing costs for the RO process are membranes for operating at high pressures up to 1,500 psi (105 kg/cm²) and 50% conversion when operating on seawater with 45,000 mg of TDS per litre.

Another alternative process will be low-temperature multi-effect horizontal-tube evaporators. If aluminium tubes and tube sheets can be shown to have a reasonable life in Middle East seawater, the capital cost can be reduced, or a higher performance ratio can be achieved.

Another factor which will favour reverse osmosis in coming years is that it is the most energy-efficient of all of the processes. This will be of increasing importance if in fact fuel-oil prices rise further as expected and environmental considerations increase in importance. The cost of energy consumption is also the largest single item in the cost of desalted water. It is significant that, for either a single-purpose or a dual-purpose plant, RO appears to be the most cost-effective. On the basis of world fuel costs in 1989, the RO process would save over 10% compared with multi-effect distillation and 32% compared with MSF (Leitner 1989).

2.9.4 Hybrid RO/MSF seawater desalination to compromise quality-cost constraints

It seems that the race for the second generation of seawater desalters has been settled, with RO and low-temperature multi-effect horizontal-tube evaporators as front runners. Both systems are characterized by

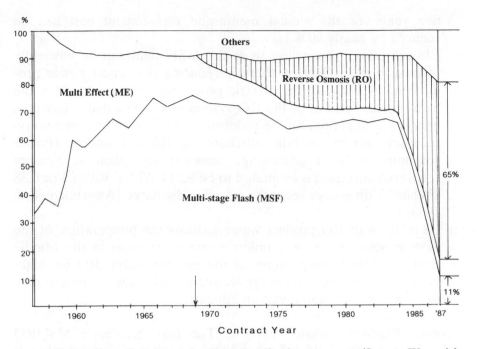

Fig. 2.49 **World market share of various desalination processes** (Source: Wangnick and IDA 1988)

their low energy requirements compared with the MSF system. As shown in fig. 2.49, which gives the worldwide market shares of various desalination processes, RO accounted for 65% of market share in 1987 (Wangnick and IDA 1988). Beside these two options, there are combination possibilities of different desalting plant types. In the hybrid MSF/RO desalination-power process, a seawater RO plant is combined with either a new or existing dual-purpose MSF plant with the following advantages:

» The capital cost of the combined RO/MSF plant can be reduced.
» A common seawater intake is used.
» Product waters from the RO and MSF plants are blended to obtain suitable product-water quality. Taking advantage of the fact that the MSF product (25 mg of TDS per litre) typically exceeds potable water specifications (WHO standard: 500–1,000 mg/l), the product-water specification in the RO system can thereby be reduced.
» A single-stage RO process can be used and the RO membrane life can be extended because of the reduced product-water specification. (The life of the RO membrane can be extended from three to

119

five years, or the annual membrane replacement cost can be reduced by nearly 40%.)

» Electric power production from the MSF plant can be efficiently utilized in the RO plant, thereby reducing net export power production. In addition, the electric power requirement to drive the high-pressure pumps of the RO system, which is a major factor of energy consumption, can be reduced by 30% by adding an energy-recovery unit to the brine discharge in the RO system. (Power consumption for a single-stage seawater RO plant at 30% of recovery/conversion is estimated to be 9.24 kWh/m^3 without or 6.38 kWh/m^3 with energy recovery on brine discharge [Awerbuch et al. 1989].)

» Blending with RO product water reduces the temperature of the MSF product water. A problem common in areas in the Middle East is the high temperature of the product water. RO for high-pressure brine when no energy recovery is used can be used to cool the MSF product water with an eductor.

JEDDAH RO/MSF HYBRID PROJECT. The first large-scale MSF/RO hybrid project, the Jeddah I rehabilitation project in Saudi Arabia, is now in operation by the Saline Water Conversion Corporation. This 15 million gal. (56,800 m^3) per day RO plant, the world's largest facility for seawater conversion, has demonstrated the attractiveness of the hybrid concept. The Jeddah I MSF desalination plant was completed in 1970, with an installed capacity of 5 million gal. (18,925 m^3) per day. It was one of the world's largest plants in the early 1970s and therefore has a significant place in history. The installed capacity of the Jeddah desalting complex was expanded by steps to a nominal capacity of 85 million gal. (321,725 m^3) per day, all by MSF.

In 1985 the operation and maintenance of the Jeddah I MSF plant had become increasingly costly. To keep pace with the increasing water demand, the 5 million gal. per day Jeddah I MSF plant was replaced by a 15 million gal. per day RO plant (phase I) in 1986–1989, which is incorporated in a hybrid RO/MSF desalination system. The RO unit has the following design criteria (Muhurji et al. 1989):

— feed-water quality: TDS = 43,300 mg/l, chloride as Cl$^-$ = 22,400 mg/l, pH = 8.2, water temperature 24.5–32.5°C;

— operating pressure at 60 kg/cm^2 (maximum design pressure: 70 kg/cm^2);

— a single-stage design, including 10 RO trains, with each train including 148 RO modules;

— hollow fine fibre (Toyobo Hollosep made of cellulose triacetate) RO module with 10 inch diameter;
— recovery ratio of 35% of product water;
— product-water salinity as specified at 625 mg of chloride per litre (=1,250 mg of TDS per litre).

Since MSF product water has a salinity as low as 25–50 mg of TDS per litre, the salinity of the permeate from the Jeddah I RO plant (phase I) was specified as 625 mg of chloride (1,250 mg of TDS) per litre, which is a major factor in minimizing the cost of the RO. In a cost analysis done by Bechtel (Muhurji et al. 1989), it was shown that the product water cost from the RO system in a hybrid MSF/RO plant can be reduced by 15% compared with a stand-alone RO plant.

2.10 Groundwater-hydro development in Chile and Libya

Groundwater-hydro has been studied in two development projects in the arid regions of north-west Chile and the Sahara desert in Libya. The Chilean plan will involve constructing a high-pressure pipeline to exploit the height difference between the wellfield in the Andes and the coastal terrain. The Libyan plan will involve installing a mini-hydro station at the end of the Great Man-Made River pipeline to exploit the height difference of 200 m.

2.10.1 Groundwater-hydro in multi-purpose Salar del Huasco scheme in Chile

The coastal plains in the northern part of Chile may be classified as arid to extremely arid (fig. 2.50). The extremely arid Iquique region is located in the northern corner of Chile, where rainfall is only 10 mm or less per year. No water resources are available in these arid coastal regions except for a very limited amount of groundwater, whose quality is likely to be saline or brackish. By contrast, huge renewable groundwater resources with excellent quality can be tapped in the Andes mountain ranges. The hydro-potential of the Andes mountain ranges in South America is one of the world's largest, and includes both surface water and groundwater.

The Salar del Huasco project is being planned to develop groundwater for water supply, irrigation, and hydroelectric power. The groundwater-hydro scheme would use the substantial head difference between the wellfield on the mountain range (3,750 m) and the irrigation area on the coastal terrain (1,400 m). The water will be supplied from a wellfield 76 km away by a pipeline that will cross the mountains

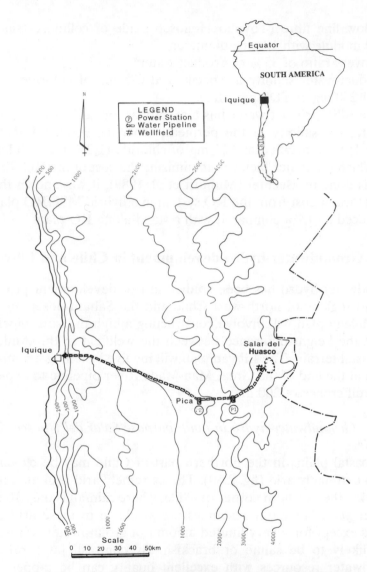

Fig. 2.50 **Salar del Huasco groundwater development scheme and water pipeline system in Chile**

using pumping stations. The project will assure adequate drinking water supplies to Iquique until the middle of the next century and will increase the local availability of irrigation water by 50%. This will suffice for the cultivation of 4,800 ha of land on the extremely arid terrain.

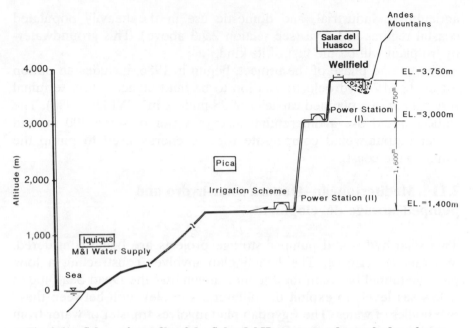

Fig. 2.51 **Schematic profile of the Salar del Huasco groundwater-hydro scheme**

The hydro units will have a combined capacity of 50 MW (WPDC 1988).

The scheme will comprise the extraction of 2.4 m³ of groundwater per second from 54 wells in the area of Lake Huasco, which is at an elevation of 3,785 m. The water will be piped through a central collector to Iquique and Pica, and the available head will be used to generate electricity. The first or upper station will be built between the wellfield and Pica, at an elevation of 3,000 m, and the second or the lower station will be built in Pica, at an elevation of 1,400 m (fig. 2.51). The theoretical hydro-power is estimated to be 50 MW in total, 16 MW at the first power station and 34 MW at the second. The installed capacities of the power stations are preliminarily estimated to be 42 MW in total, consisting of 13 MW at the first station and 29 MW at the second.

2.10.2 Groundwater-hydro in the Great Man-Made River project, Libya
A hydroelectric power station will be installed in part of the massive Great Man-Made River project, which will carry an eventual 6 million m³ of water per day from beneath the southern Sahara desert for

agricultural, industrial, and domestic use in the heavily populated coastal regions in Libya (see section 2.7.3 above). This groundwater-hydro plant will be the first of its kind.

The second phase of the project, begun in 1986, includes an option for an 18 MW hydroelectric station to be built adjacent to a terminal reservoir with a planned capacity of 28 million m^3 (WPDC 1986). The station would use a differential head of water of some 200 m, and power output would compensate for the energy used to pump the water to the coast.

2.11   Mediterranean–Qattara solar-hydro and pumped-storage development

Two solar-hydro and pumped-storage projects are being considered, in Israel and Egypt. The Israeli plan involves constructing a long pipeline/tunnel between the Mediterranean and the Dead Sea (400 m below sea level) to exploit the differences in elevation between these two bodies of water. The Egyptian plan involves transfer of water from the Mediterranean to the Qattara depression (a basin in the Western desert of about 26,000 km^2, the floor of which is 120 m below sea level). Both plans involve an initial development stage in which the basins are filled with water from the Mediterranean Sea up to a certain design level that will be maintained later by the transfer of water to replace the amount evaporated. A very similar type of solar-hydro scheme has also been studied for the Assal lake in Djibouti, which has the shortest conduit, with a length of about 15 km from the Red Sea to the Assal depression.

This particular type of hydroelectric project, generally known as solar-hydro, would be made possible by the combination of such factors as the existence of a vast depression at a distance not too far from the sea in a region with characteristically scarce rainfall and a resulting high degree of evaporation. The world's five deepest depressions are shown in table 2.11.

The Mediterranean–Qattara solar-hydro scheme was the first project of its kind for developing solar-hydro energy in a large desert depression in a hot-arid climate. The scheme would include pumped storage to cover peak power demand, which is becoming increasingly important owing to the forced reduction of hydroelectric power generation on the Nile in the 1980s. Pumped storage of seawater is further examined in this section to evaluate the development alternatives for pumped-storage schemes in Egypt.

Table 2.11 **World's deepest depressions**

	Location	Lowest elevation (m)	Area below sea level (km²)	Distance from sea or ocean (km)
Dead Sea	Israel, Jordan	−401	3,800	72
Lake Tiberias (Sea of Galilee)	Israel, Syria	−212	—	50
Assal	Djibouti	−174	80	15
Turfan	China	−154	5,000	1,500
Quattara	Egypt	−133	44,000	56

2.11.1 The scheme

The scheme would involve flooding a natural depression in the Western desert (the Qattara) through a canal or tunnel from the Mediterranean Sea, 56 km away (fig. 2.52). At its lowest point, the depression is 134 m below sea level. The plan envisages generating power utilizing the difference in elevation to the lake that will eventually be formed, whose surface will be 60 m below sea level, with an area of 19,500 km². The scheme could supply 670 MW of basic load without pumped storage (WPDC 1978).

2.11.2 Topography of the Qattara depression

The Qattara depression is located in the north-western part of Egypt and is the world's fifth deepest natural depression. The depression is bounded to the north and west by deep escarpments but becomes comparatively flat towards the south and the east (fig. 2.53). The lowest point is found at a level of 133 m below sea level. The depression has a length of about 300 km at sea level, a maximum width of 145 km, and an area of 19,500 km². The northern edge of the escarpment is bounded by a hilly ridge with an elevation of about 200 m above sea level, in which the shortest distance from the Mediterranean Sea is 56 km.

2.11.3 Previous studies

The utilization of the Qattara depression to develop hydroelectric power was first suggested by the Berlin geographer Professor Penk in 1912, and later by Dr. Ball in 1927. Dr. Ball studied in particular the possibility of utilizing it for hydroelectric purposes by the formation of

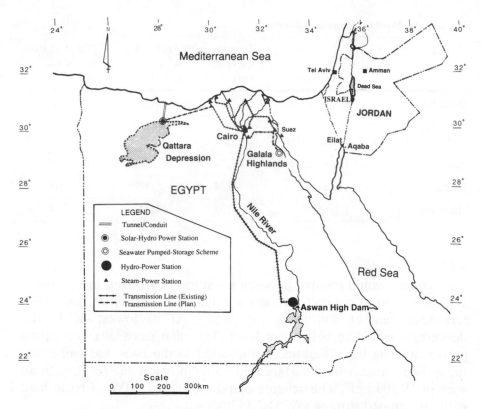

Fig. 2.52 **Qattara depression and electric power supply system**

lakes at final levels of 50 m, 60 m, and 70 m below sea level, to which the corresponding surface areas were 13,500, 12,100, and 8,600 km². Moreover, he indicated the most convenient water inflow routes (lines D, E, and F in fig. 2.53) with reference to the formation of the lakes. After examining the effect of climatic changes, evaporation, seepage, minor transmission losses, and the lowest cost per kW installed, he showed that the most convenient solutions were those relating to lakes at 50 and 60 m below sea level. From geological and topographical considerations, he finally recommended −50 m below sea level with the supply system along route D.

Dr. Ball, moreover, anticipated the possibility of using a power surplus during the period of off-peak demand to pump some part of the inflowing water into a high-level reservoir on top of the escarpment and to use the 200-m head to generate power to meet peak-load requirements (Martino 1973).

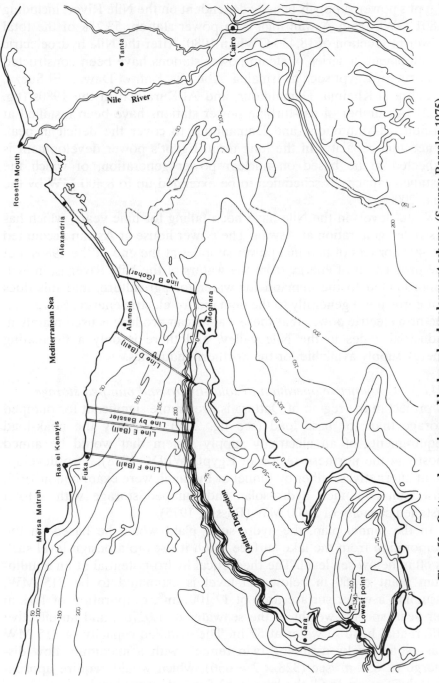

Fig. 2.53 **Qattara depression and hydro-solar development scheme (Source: Basseler 1975)**

2.11.4 Pumped-storage application

Egypt's power supply is heavily dependent on the Nile River, including 9,801 GWh from Aswan high dam power station, 53.2% of the total power production of 18,430 GWh in 1980. After the Nile hydroelectric development, a series of steam power stations have been constructed in northern Egypt such as Ismailia, Abu Qir, Kafr el-Dawar, El-Suezu, Shoubra el-Kheima, Damanhour, and Al-Kuraimat in the 1980s (fig. 2.52). A number of gas-turbine power stations have been installed at El-Suif, El-Mahmodia, and Damanhour to cover the deficit in peak generation capacity. In the long term, Egypt's power development is expected to be based on nuclear power generation, of which the installed capacity is scheduled to be extended up to 8,400 MW by the year 2000.

Water levels in the Nile have been falling for nine years, which has restricted generation at Aswan. The power house at Aswan accounted for 40% or less of national power supplies at the end of the 1980s, but the production of energy from the waters of the Nile River is, in fact, subordinated to the demand for water for agriculture, and this does not correspond generally to the demand for electric energy. Moreover, the firm electric power that these waters can produce is used mainly in industrial zones in the Nile valley, and there is only a fluctuating energy supply available for the northern industries.

2.11.5 Conjunctive operation of solar-hydro and pumped storage

A project in the region of Qattara is even more significant for pumped storage than for base load (see fig. 2.54) to satisfy the peak-load requirements of an electricity supply system that would be aimed mostly at the northern region of Egypt (WPDC 1978). Two development alternatives, either by tunnel or by canal, were examined in 1975, based on combined hydro-solar and pumped storage with a total installed capacity of 2,400 MW (Bassler 1975).

In the tunnel plan, the hydro-solar plant would be based on the evaporation from the lake surface when it rises to a design level such as 60 m below sea level. The theoretical hydro-potential at an equilibrium point of 60 m below sea level is estimated to be 315 MW, assuming a water surface area of 12,100 km², evaporation of 1.41 m per year, specific weight of the seawater of 1.02782, and an effective differential head of water at 57 m. The installed capacity of 315 MW was estimated by assuming twin tunnels with a maximum flow discharge of 656 m³/sec ($328 \times 2 = 656$), which would require approximately 35 years to fill the lake to 62.5 m below sea level.

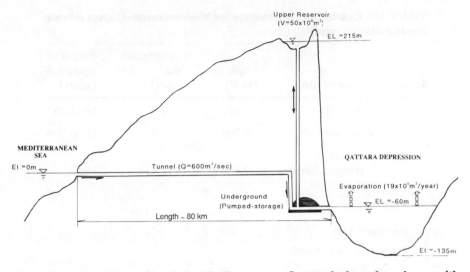

Fig. 2.54 **Schematic profile of the Mediterranean–Qattara hydro-solar scheme with pumped storage** (Source: Basseler 1975)

The pumped-storage portion was estimated to be 2,085 MW (2,400 − 315 = 2,085 MW). For this an additional discharge of 936 m³/sec would be required from the upper reservoir, assuming the specific weight of Mediterranean Sea water of 1.02782, pumping efficiency of 84.3%, and a differential head of water at 262 m. The upper basin would be situated in a natural depression at an elevation of 188.0 m above sea level with a maximum capacity of about 45 million m³. The design volume of the upper reservoir was estimated to be 15.16 million m³ per day, assuming 4.5 hours of peak operation per day.

In the canal plan, nuclear blasting was a given condition for excavating the open canal with a total length of 60 km. The construction programme for the nuclear-blasted canal scheme was estimated as outlined in table 2.12. The plan could have doubled the hydro-solar capacity by 15 years after the commencement of taking water from the Mediterranean Sea, but the nuclear method for open blasting, which was proposed in the 1970s, could have created serious environmental and socio-psychological problems and was put aside. Today excavation by a tunnel-boring machine would be practical and economical in the un-saturate rocks of the Neogene Tertiary.

2.11.6 *The Galala–Red Sea seawater pumped-storage scheme*
Planning for new thermal or nuclear power stations in Egypt has encouraged the Electric Authority to build a pumped-storage plant.

Table 2.12 **Construction programme for Mediterranean–Qattara scheme (nuclear-blasted canal)**

Stage	Type of plant	Capacity (MW)	Construction time (years)	Period of operation (years)
1	solar-hydro	670	7	1st–10th
2	solar-hydro	1,200	3	11th–15th
3	solar-hydro + pumped storage	2,400	4	16th–

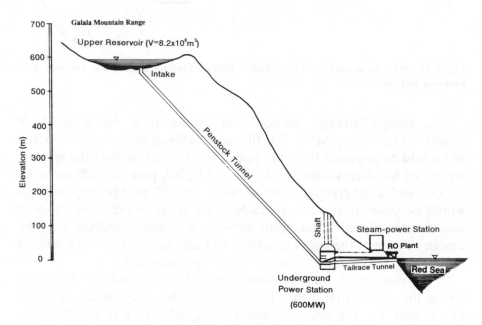

Fig. 2.55 **Schematic profile of the Galala–Red Sea pumped-storage scheme**

In 1989 a feasibility study was carried out for a 600 MW seawater pumped-storage scheme in the north Galala plateau, 55 km south of Suez (fig. 2.55). The scheme would utilize seawater pumped directly to a natural basin 587 m above sea level with a storage capacity of 8.2 million m³ (WPDC 1989a). In comparison with the Qattara scheme, the Galala–Red Sea scheme would have two advantages: (1) it would avoid the substantial capital cost of an intake tunnel or canal with a length of 60–80 km; (2) there are likely to be fewer environmental problems with the artificial lake.

The Galala project would be the world's first seawater pumped-storage scheme. Some technical problems, such as corrosion of the pipes and the turbine system, remain to be solved, but this unique application of non-conventional hydro-power would be marginally feasible in an arid region where the peak power deficit is substantial. The same type of seawater pumped-storage scheme is contemplated in Israel, with two development alternatives at Lake Tiberias and the Dead Sea (WPDC 1989b). For further details, including application studies of seawater pumped-storage schemes with hydro-powered RO desalination for hybrid co-generation, see sections 5.4 and 5.6.

2.12 Concluding remarks

2.12.1 Remarks on the review study

This study was initiated to review the problems and constraints of water-resources development and management in the arid zone, including non-conventional water-resources development alternatives as summarized below.

In the Middle East the potential for the development of renewable water resources is limited, owing to the scarce rainfall with very high potential evaporation.

MULTINATIONAL RIVER DEVELOPMENT. There are two major water-resources issues in the world's large river developments in the arid region: the quantity issue in inter-state water allocation, and the quality issue of salinity problems. Various and serious salinity problems have been major issues in the basin management of large rivers since the mid-twentieth century, including the Indus River in South-West Asia, the Tigris, Euphrates, and Jordan Rivers in the Middle East, the Nile River in North Africa, and the Colorado River in south-western Arizona in the United States of America.

RIPARIAN ISSUES. Many countries of the Middle East, except for those in the Arabian peninsula and Libya, depend on three major river basins: the Tigris-Euphrates, the Nile, and the Jordan and Litani. Given that these rivers do not respect national boundaries and that those states located upstream have obvious advantages both political and economic over those downstream, the potential for conflict over water is great.

Salinity control in the rivers is needed to protect the quality of the environment in the river system and to maximize the quantity of water available for downstream irrigation or other water supply. Reverse osmosis desalination of brackish water will be a key technique for sustainable basin management in the twenty-first century.

Owing to increasing demand and limited recharge potential for conventional renewable fresh groundwater resources, many states in the Middle East have already over-exploited the sustainable yield. Careful groundwater management will be essential to sustain further development.

NON-RENEWABLE GROUNDWATER RESOURCES DEVELOPMENT. A vast amount of the non-renewable or fossil groundwater is trapped in the Palaeozoic to Mesozoic-Neogene (Nubian) sandstones that underlie wide areas of the Arabian peninsula and the eastern Sahara desert in Saudi Arabia, Jordan, Egypt, and Libya. The dominance and importance of this resource will be paramount in water-resource planning and strategy in many countries, especially Egypt, Libya, Saudi Arabia, Kuwait, Qatar, and Bahrain.

Non-renewable or fossil groundwater resources should be saved as a strategic reserve except for emergency or short-term use.

DESALINATION OF SEAWATER. Desalination of seawater is likely to be required more and more to make up deficiencies in supplies of water from other sources.

The prevailing multi-stage flash desalination will be replaced by processes requiring lower capital and lower operating costs such as low-pressure types of reverse osmosis. The role of the ocean, which contains the largest water reserves on earth, will be important for sustaining water-resources development in the twenty-first century.

SOLAR-HYDRO DEVELOPMENT. The Mediterranean–Dead Sea canal scheme should now be reassessed in the joint development.

Groundwater-hydro and solar-hydro are likely to be a strategic priority to save fossil energy and the global environment with economic feasibility.

Strategic priority should be given to reverse-osmosis desalination, including research into hydro-powered co-generating applications, which will result in developing more low-energy-dependent membranes with significant cost reductions.

Water conservation and sustainable water-resources management will be key measures to sustain the economic development of the arid states, and may even include the cutting of part of the national water supply from non-renewable sources. The conservation approach has to be performed in parallel with developing non-conventional water resources, taking into account new developments in the technology of desalination, waste-water treatment, and water-saving techniques.

Water-resources planning studies in arid regions, especially in developing countries in the Middle East, must consider the following strategic development alternatives:

>> water conservation, including the diversion of existing water systems from one use to another;

>> maintaining fossil or non-renewable groundwater resources at strategic reserves, with the exception of emergency or short-time use for specified purposes;

>> non-conventional water-resources development, including desalination and reuse of treated sewage;

>> inter-state water transfer or importation.

Priority will have to be given to domestic water-resources development, management, and conservation, including non-conventional measures, rather than reliance on importation from outside countries. Inter-state riparian issues of water allocation have to be resolved in a context of basin master planning.

Water-resources planning, especially master planning for inter-state basin development, must include recognition of techno-political issues. It is suggested that techno-political feasibility should be evaluated and resolved in the context of a master plan. For further details on techno-politics see sections 5.5 and 5.6.

2.12.2 Marginal waters as potential non-conventional water resources

After reviewing the problems and constraints of water-resources development and management, the study focuses on marginal waters as non-conventional water resources in arid to semi-arid regions. Almost all the fresh and renewable natural water resources in the rivers, lakes, and aquifers in the arid zone, which are referred to as "conventional" water or "traditional" water, have already been exploited or will be fully developed by the end of the twentieth century. Furthermore, all major rivers in the arid zone have already been seriously contaminated by accumulated salt in the return flow from irrigated land, and severe water shortages are being felt in many urban centres as populations continue to grow. After completing the exploitation of renewable water resources, we may have only limited options to sustain water development, including:

>> making more efficient use of available water supplies,

Table 2.13 **Conventional and non-conventional water resources categorized by hydrological system**

System	Conventional	Non-conventional (marginal)
Atmosphere	Rainfall	Cloud seeding, or artificial rain
Surface water	Rivers Streams Lakes	*Treated sewage effluents* *Return flow with accumulated salts from* *irrigation drainage* Urban storm drainage Wadi run-off Playa lake water
Groundwater	Renewable groundwater	Non-renewable groundwater (fresh) Non-renewable groundwater (saline) *Desalinated brackish groundwater* Artificial recharge
Oceanic		*Desalinated seawater*

≫ diverting water from one use to another,
≫ developing marginal waters as non-conventional water resources,
≫ importing fresh water from neighbouring countries,
≫ importing food commodities as a proxy for water (e.g., 1 ton of wheat = 1,200 tons of water).

Marginal waters may occur in any category of hydrological system—atmospheric, surface water, groundwater, and ocean systems—as shown in table 2.13.

Potential applications in the atmospheric system include cloud seeding, or artificial rain, which is possible in some very limited areas in high mountain ranges such as the Anti-Lebanon where winter precipitation is 1,000 mm or more (Kally 1974).

Marginal waters in the surface-water system such as waste water and irrigation return flow are major sources of water reclamation. The probability that the results will be economically feasible is high, but this will depend on advanced waste-water-treatment technologies to be applied in the twenty-first century. The increasing demand for water supply, especially in urban centres, may create an increasing potential for water reclamation. Such water will be used mainly for secondary purposes such as garden/landscape irrigation and irrigation of specific crops (Wesner and Herndon 1990).

Marginal waters in the groundwater system include non-renewable or fossil groundwater, brackish groundwater, and artificial recharge from surface waters and treated sewage effluents. Artificially recharged groundwater is a marginal water in the arid zone, and may be involved in conjunctive surface-groundwater uses.

Brackish groundwaters with higher salinities such as 2,000–10,000 mg of TDS per litre have not been developed except for use in blending with fresh surface water or distilled water from desalination plants. In the arid zone, however, the reserve potential of brackish groundwaters in deep aquifers is great as compared with fresh groundwaters in shallow aquifer systems near the recharging area. RO desalination of brackish water has been only marginally feasible in the 1980s, but it is becoming more cost-effective and is regarded as an energy-conserving measure for developing water resources in the arid region. It will be a key technology for non-conventional water-resources development in the arid countries.

An extremely slight amount of seawater is being used for water supply through desalination plants. Seawater desalination has been practised mainly in oil-rich desert countries of the Arabian Gulf where conventional renewable water resources are scarce. In the 1970s, large-scale seawater desalination projects were considered that would be both technically and economically feasible as water-supply alternatives today (Buras and Darr 1979). Cost constraints remain, but there is no doubt that seawater will be the ultimate water resource in the arid zone, coupled with food imports as a proxy for water. Current innovative research in desalination technology, especially on reverse-osmosis membranes, is changing the cost environment by reducing both capital costs and operation and maintenance costs over the conventional MSF process which has been used so far almost exclusively in the Middle East states (see Appendix A).

Potential marginal waters as non-conventional water resources thus comprise primarily brackish waters, seawater, and reclaimed urban waste waters. These are the keys to developing water resources in the twenty-first century, taking into account that almost all the arid states in the Middle East are completing or depleting the development of their conventional water resources.

The cost and viability of technology are the key factors in the development of non-conventional water resources. Desalination of brackish water can provide a relatively reliable source of water for costs ranging from US$0.25 to US$1.00 per m^3 in the mid-1980s and is becoming even more cost effective by the development of low-pressure (low-energy) types of RO membranes. Seawater desalination and water transport by tanker may provide water for costs of US$1.25 to US$8.00

Table 2.14 **Hydro-potential and thermal-energy applications in water-resource systems**

System	Potential-energy applications	Thermal-energy applications
Surface water	Hydro-power	Stream heat pump
	Pumped storage	
	Reclaimed waste water	
Groundwater	*Groundwater-hydro*	Aquifer heat exchange
Seawater	*Solar-hydro*	*Solar pond*
	Pumped storage	Ocean thermal-energy conversion
	Tidal power	

per m^3 (DTCD 1985). The reuse of waste water gives a lower quality water at the cheapest price, while weather modification has the potential to provide a low-cost but relatively unreliable source of water and technology for it.

2.12.3   Applications in hydro-power and co-generation developments
The use of marginal waters should not be limited to exploiting water for municipal and industrial water supply and irrigation. After the Iraqi invasion of Kuwait in August 1990, worldwide attention was focused on the energy crisis and the need to minimize or reduce world energy consumption to sustain both human life and the global environment. The application of non-conventional water resources development with co-generation of thermal and hydro-power energy conversion may be used (1) to reduce capital investments, (2) to cut power-supply costs, and (3) to contribute to saving precious energy. Table 2.14 lists possible measures to develop hydro-potential and thermal energy in a water-resources system. Co-generation applications of seawater pumped-storage schemes with hydro-powered RO desalination are discussed in section 5.6.

2.12.4   Integration of marginal waters in national water master plans
This study has aimed to identify techno-political development alternatives for marginal waters as non-conventional water resources. These development alternatives are likely to be integrated in nationwide and/or multinational-level water master plans.

The study is focused on the development and management of saline water resources, including desalination by reverse osmosis with appli-

136

cations of co-generation alternatives, and suggests that marginal waters produced by RO desalination will play an increasingly important role in the twenty-first century's water-resources planning in the arid countries in the Middle East. It is not intended, however, to suggest that the RO process will necessarily be the only or best one in the future, taking into account potential progress in research on and the development of other new technologies.

3

Hydro-powered reverse-osmosis desalination in water-resources development in Kuwait

3.1 Background and objectives

3.1.1 Background

Kuwait is located at the north-western corner of the Arabian Gulf, between latitudes 28°30′ and 30°05′ north and longitudes 46°30′ and 48°30′ east. The country is bounded to the north and north-west by Iraq and to the south-west and south by Saudi Arabia, and has a land area of 17,818 km² and a coastline of 195 km (fig. 3.1).

The population was estimated at 1.79 million in 1987. Crude-oil production and petroleum-related investments provide the main governmental revenue. The gross national product (GNP) per capita was estimated to be US$19,610 in 1987. The occupation of Kuwait by Iraq in August 1990 and its subsequent liberation in March 1991 are too recent for further comment except that water development is the key to the future habitability of Kuwait as it was before.

During the period 1925–1950, Kuwait imported fresh water by dhow from the Shatt al-Arab in Iraq, some 100 km north-west from Kuwait, to supplement water obtained from wells. Further exploitation of water resources was initiated by the rapid development of the oil industry and commerce in the 1950s, when shortage problems became a constraint to economic development.

138

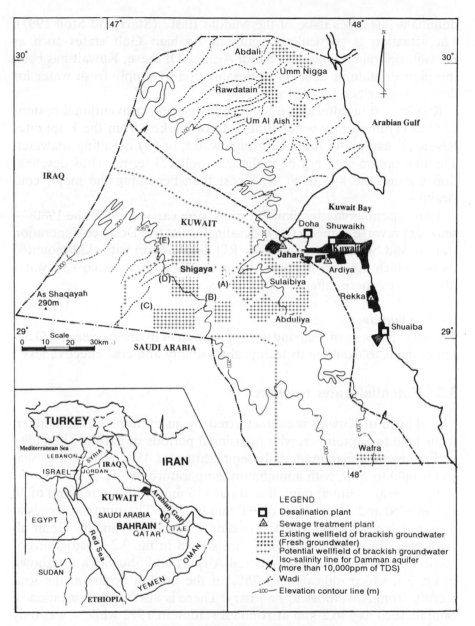

Fig. 3.1 **Kuwait and water resources**

Limitations of water are likely to impact increasingly on the economic development of other states in the Middle East and North Africa to the extent that "by the year 2000, water—not oil—will be the dominant resources issue of the Middle East" (Starr and Stoll 1987). The situation is particularly acute in Arabian Gulf states such as Kuwait, Bahrain, Qatar, and Saudi Arabia. Of these, Kuwait has been the pioneer state in developing desalination to supply fresh water for domestic use since the 1950s.

Kuwait had no alternative but to develop non-conventional options such as (1) importing water from Iraq or Turkey from the Euphrates River, (2) exploiting brackish groundwater, or (3) desalting seawater. The first option may not be realistic in political terms. Thus desalination became the key issue, with cost then becoming the major constraint.

Two experimental desalination trials were carried out in the 1980s—seawater reverse-osmosis (RO) desalination at the Doha co-generation station, and brackish-groundwater RO desalination with skid-mounted units—which give an opportunity to compare the unit cost of water produced by these different approaches.

3.1.2 Objectives

The main purpose of studying the application of hydro-powered RO desalination is to examine its technical feasibility and cost effectiveness.

3.2 Potential water resources

The climate of Kuwait is characterized by an extremely hot summer, from June to September, with occasional periods of extreme humidity and an average maximum daily temperature of 45°C. The winter season is mild to cool, with a minimum temperature of −1°C.

The average annual rainfall is about 115 mm, with a minimum of 30 mm in 1960 and a maximum of 360 mm in 1954. The rainfall records at four gauging stations—the International Airport, Ahmadi, Umm al-Aish, and Shuwaikh—since 1952 are shown in fig. 3.2. Histograms of monthly rainfall at the International Airport and Shuwaikh are shown in fig. 3.3, which indicate that 75% of the rainfall occurs in the four months from November to February. There is also spatial variation of rainfall, such as 136.2 mm at Ahmadi station in 1972 while it was only 18.1 mm at Alomaria.

The mean annual potential evaporation values as measured by class A-pan and Piche evaporimeters were 3,460 mm (1962–1977) and 5,460 mm (1957–1977) respectively. The theoretical annual average potential evaporation as estimated by the Penman method was approximately 2,630 mm (1957–1977). The monthly average potential evaporation and rainfall at Kuwait International Airport is shown in fig. 3.4.

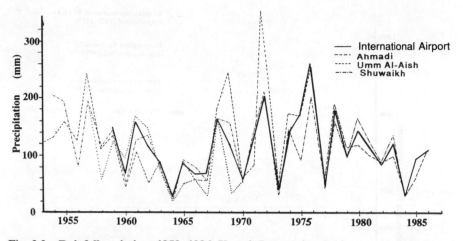

Fig. 3.2 **Rainfall variation, 1953–1986: Kuwait International Airport, Ahmadi, Umm al-Aish, Shuwaikh** (Source: Abusada 1988)

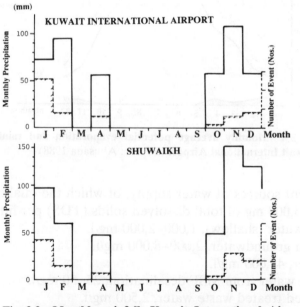

Fig. 3.3 **Monthly rainfall, Kuwait International Airport and Shuwaikh** (Source: Abusada 1988)

Kuwait is a hyper-arid state without rivers or fresh-water aquifers. Non-conventional water resources, including brackish groundwater, seawater desalination, and reclamation of treated waste water are the

141

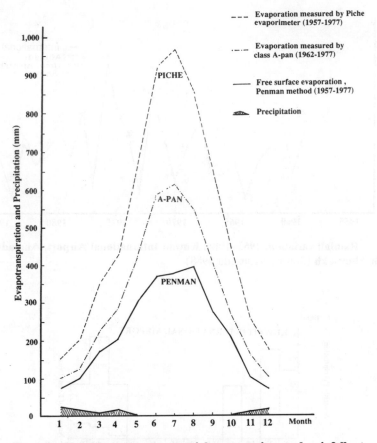

Fig. 3.4 **Monthly average potential evaporation and rainfall at Kuwait International Airport** (Source: Abusada 1988)

main current sources of water supply, of which the quality is as saline as 1,000–45,000 mg of total dissolved solids (TDS) per litre:
— groundwater (shallow), 1,000–2,000 mg/l,
— brackish groundwater, 2,000–8,000 mg/l,
— seawater, 45,000 mg/l,
— product water from MSF desalination, 25–50 mg/l,
— reclaimed treated waste water, 2,500 mg/l.
The WHO standard for the maximum permissible level for drinking water is 1,000 mg of TDS per litre.

3.2.1 Surface water
The prevailing hyper-arid climate of Kuwait is not favourable to the existence of any river systems in the country. There are no rivers or

lakes, but small-scale wadis are developed in the shallow depressions in the desert terrain. Surface run-off sometimes occurs in the large wadi depressions during the rainy season from November to April. There is no permanent stream-gauging station, but flash floods are reported to last for only a few hours to several days. Due to the extremely high evaporation losses and the high deficit in soil moisture, only a small percentage of the precipitation infiltrates into the ground-water. The run-off ratio must be extremely small.

The average annual rainfall within Kuwait is estimated to be 1,780 million m^3, assuming a mean annual rainfall of 100 mm. However, with such high evaporation losses, the net annual run-off is estimated to be merely 17.8 million m^3, assuming a run-off ratio of 1%.

3.2.2 Groundwater

Thick geological sequences are of sedimentary origin from Palaeocene to Recent, in two groups, known as Hasa and Kuwait. The Hasa group, which consists of limestone, dolomite, anhydrite, and clays, comprises three formation units, known as Umm el-Radhuma in the Palaeocene to Middle Eocene, Rus in the Lower Eocene, and Damman in the Middle Eocene. The Kuwait group, which consists of fluviatile sediments of sand and gravel, calcareous sand and sandstone with some clays, gypsums, limestones, and marls, comprises three formation units, known as Ghar in the Miocene, Fars in the Pliocene, and Dibdibba in the Pleistocene (fig. 3.5).

Two economic aquifers are found in the Damman formation in the Hasa group and the Dibdibba formation in the Kuwait group.

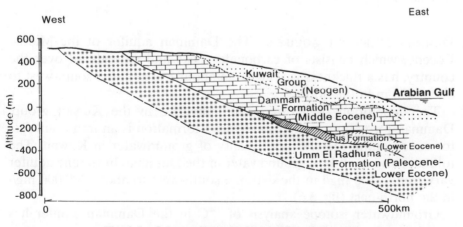

Fig. 3.5 **Schematic geological profile of Kuwait**

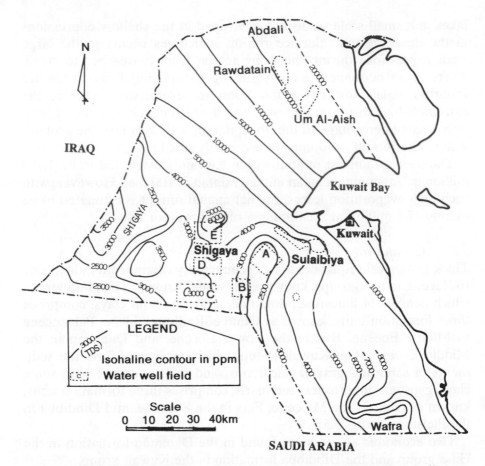

SAUDI ARABIA

Fig. 3.6 **Salinity (TDS) contour map of the Damman aquifer in Kuwait** (Source: Abusada 1988)

DAMMAN LIMESTONE AQUIFER. The Damman aquifer of the Middle Eocene, which consists of carbonate rocks and extends all over the country, has a thickness varying from about 150 m in the south-west to about 275 m in the north.

The dissolution of gypsum and anhydrite in the Kuwait group, Damman formation, and Rus anhydrite formation is an important factor conditioning the chemical quality of groundwater in Kuwait. The total dissolved solids of groundwater in the Damman limestone aquifer vary from 2,500 mg/l in the extreme south-west to about 200,000 mg/l in the north-east (fig. 3.6).

Groundwater isotope analysis of ^{14}C in the Damman aquifer has been performed by taking water samples from 13 wells in south-western Kuwait. From the absence or zero concentration of ^{14}C, the age of the groundwater in the Damman aquifer is estimated to be more than 400,000 years, while the ^{14}C concentration in the Kuwait group groundwater indicates an age of 14,000–22,000 years (Abusada 1988).

Owing to the nature of limestone geology, the permeability of the Damman limestone aquifer varies considerably. The aquifer para-meters vary from 27 to 7,100 m^2/day transmissivity and 3.4–8.9 × 10^{-4} storage coefficient, based on results obtained from 38 testing sites in south-western and southern Kuwait (Abusada 1988).

No natural groundwater recharge from rainwater is likely in the confined Damman limestone aquifer, although there is some lateral inflow or recharge through the Saudi border, which is preliminarily estimated to be 8.3–24.9 million m^3 per year (Abusada 1988).

DIBDIBBA AQUIFER. The Dibdibba aquifer, which is composed of unconsolidated sands and gravels, is generally a water-table aquifer with fresh to brackish groundwater.

Most of the groundwater recharge of the Kuwait group is dependent on upward leakage from the underlying confined Damman limestone aquifer. The quality of the groundwater is generally similar to that of the Damman aquifer. The total dissolved solids of the groundwater in the Kuwait group increase generally from about 3,000 mg/l in the south-west to about 130,000 mg/l in the north-east over a distance of about 150 km. Some lenses of fresh water with TDS ranging between 800 and 1,200 mg/l are perched on the brackish-groundwater body in the Rawdatain and Um al-Aish wellfields in northern Kuwait, which are recharged by infiltration through the wadi beds during occasional flash floods in the wadi depressions (fig. 3.1).

The piezometric level in the Kuwait group varies from about 90 m in the south-west to zero along the coast. The groundwater flows generally north-eastwards.

3.2.3 Seawater
Seawater is an unlimited water source for Kuwait, which has a long coastline along the Arabian Gulf, which covers an area of 3,683 million km^2 and holds 10.07 × 10^{12} m^3 of water (Korzun et al. 1976)

The high mineral content of water from the Arabian Gulf requires special attention for the control of salt deposition in plants located there. The total dissolved solids of the feed water from Kuwait bay at Doha average 44,885 mg/l (Al-Zubaidj 1989), which is as much as 1.3 times that of other standard seawaters, such as 33,600 mg/l in the Pacific Ocean and 36,000 mg/l in the Atlantic (Howe 1962). Seawater has been the major source of the fresh-water supply in Kuwait since the 1960s and is likely to continue to be the key source for developing water resources in Kuwait in the twenty-first century.

3.2.4 Treated sewage effluents

Marginal waters in the artificial category are composed primarily of municipal waste water and urban storm drainage water. The potential reclaimed sewage effluents in Kuwait city were estimated to be 190 million m^3 per year in 1988, assuming a water supply of 293 million m^3 per year with a 65% rate of return flow. The actual amount of reuse of sewage effluents in 1988 was 97 million m^3 per year, which was one third of the volume of water supplied. The potential for water reuse will increase, corresponding to the increasing water use in the future.

3.3   Water-resources development projects

The water needs of Kuwait expanded after crude-oil marketing was initiated in 1946, requiring the import of water by lighter and barge from the Shatt al-Arab in Iraq, some 100 km to the north-west. Intensive test well drillings in 1945 discovered an extensive brackish-water aquifer in the Abduliya area. The first desalination plant was commissioned in 1950 at Fahahil in Kuwait city. A parallel development followed to meet the growth of the city, including the Sulaibiya brackish-water wellfield. The combined development of co-generation and this brackish-water wellfield was commissioned in 1953. Kuwait is now dependent on distilled water to blend with brackish groundwater as the main source of its water supply. Another source of water is treated sewage effluents, which are being used for landscape irrigation and agriculture.

The present sources of water supply for municipal and industrial use in Kuwait, with their salinity (milligrams of TDS per litre) and annual volumes, are as follows:
— groundwater, shallow (1,000–2,000 mg/l), 2.5 million m^3,
— brackish groundwater (2,000–8,000 mg/l), 109 million m^3,
— seawater desalination by MSF (25–50 mg/l), 184 million m^3,
— reclaimed waste water (2,500 mg/l), 97 million m^3.

Small-scale crop irrigation is exploiting 57–67 million m^3 of brackish

groundwater per year. Water-resources development projects undertaken in Kuwait since the 1950s are described as below.

3.3.1 Surface water and artificial recharge

Kuwait's hydrology, topography, geology, and surface water resources
do not favour the country, and no promising storage-dam scheme may
be possible. The possibility of effective use of temporary surface run-
off in the wadis was examined in a research project on groundwater
recharge at Rawdatain in 1962, in which recharge pits with a total volume of 25,000 m^3 were dug in the wadi depression to evaluate the
infiltration potential of the run-off into the upper Kuwait group aquifer
where the water table is shallow. The prospects of increasing the
potential of fresh groundwater in the shallow Kuwait group are good,
but artificial recharge will not be a key application, owing to the
limited amount of surface run-off.

3.3.2 Groundwater exploitation

Groundwater has been exploited in two major aquifers, in the Kuwait
group of the Neogene-Quaternary and in the Hasa group of the Eocene.

The selection of wellfields in Kuwait has been governed by many
factors. In areas such as the Jahara, Abdali, and Wafra farms, groundwater exploitation has been concentrated on the shallow-water-table
aquifer with a salinity of 2,000–8,000 mg of TDS per litre for local
irrigation. At the initial stage of development, large-diameter hand-
dug wells were constructed in the shallow aquifer at a depth of
between 10 and 15 m. Later, tube wells 50–60 m deep were drilled in
the saturated section of the Kuwait group at the end of 1960s. Relatively deep groundwater wells penetrating into the upper part of the
confined Damman aquifer were drilled by the Kuwait Oil Company in
the early 1940s to provide brackish water for the oil industry and gardening at Abdali and other areas. The Sulaibiya wellfield was developed in the early 1950s to supply water for gardening and mixing with
distilled water. The exploitation of fresh groundwater resources in
Rawdatain and Umm el-Aish was later initiated for Kuwait city. In
view of the limited sustainable yield of the aquifer system and possible
leakage contamination from the underlying saline water body, the
abstraction has been controlled since the mid-1970s. The Damman
aquifers in remote areas were also explored by steps in the mid-1960s
to coordinate with the substantial increase in water demand in Kuwait
city. The Shigaya wellfield south-west of Kuwait city was commissioned for use in the early 1970s.

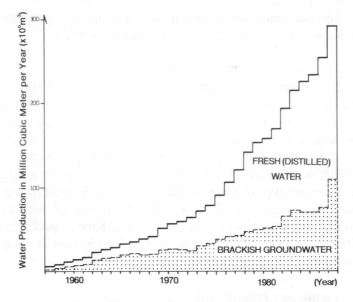

Fig. 3.7 **Production of brackish groundwater and distilled water in Kuwait**

Annual abstraction of groundwater for water supply is estimated at 109 million m³ of brackish water and 2.5 million m³ of rather fresh water (fig. 3.7). Crop irrigation is being carried out by pumping 53–67 million m³ of brackish groundwater per year from the wellfields in Wafra and Abdali–Um Nigga. The existing yield, estimated potential yield, and water salinity of each wellfield are shown in table 3.1.

3.3.3   Seawater desalination
Kuwait is one of the world's leaders in the production of fresh water from the sea. Co-generation stations, using the multi-stage flash process to distil seawater, were developed in the early 1950s and have been in use since then (table 3.2). The annual production of fresh (distilled) water is estimated to be now 184 million m³, as shown in fig. 3.7.

SHUWAIKH CO-GENERATION STATION.   Shuwaikh was the first co-generation station in Kuwait to be built since 1953. Between 1965 and 1982 distillation units were installed in response to a rapid increase in the demand for fresh water. In 1987 the installed capacities of the power generation units and distillation plants were 324 MW and 32

148

Table 3.1 **Wellfields in Kuwait, 1985**

Field	Aquifer	No. of wells	Yield (million m³/year) Existing	Potential	Salinity (TDS, mg/l)	Purpose
Rawdatain and Um al-Aish	Dibdibba F	52	2.5	6.6	700–1,200	water supply
Shigaya A, B, C	Kuwait G	60	53	66	3,000–4,000	water supply
Shigaya D, E	Damman F	54	—	42	3,000–4,500	water supply
Sulaibiya	Damman F	133	25–33	33	4,500–5,500	water supply
Abduliya	Damman F	14	8	—	4,500	water supply
Wafra	Kuwait G	(110)	33–42	50	4,000–6,000	irrigation
Abdali-Um Nigga	Dibdibba F	(110)	20–25	33–42	3,000–7,000	irrigation

Source: Kuwait Institute for Scientific Research, in 1990.

Table 3.2 **Installed capacity of co-generation stations in Kuwait**

	Fresh water production Million m³/year	Mig/day	Power generation (MW)	Date
Shuwaikh	53	32	324	1960–70
Shuaiba North	23	14	400	1965–71
Shuaiba South	50	30	804	1971–75
Doha East	71	43	1,158	1978–79
Doha West	159	96	2,400	1985
Az-Zour South stage I	10	6	—	
stage II	(119)	(72)	(2,511)	(1991)
Total	366	221	5,769	

Source: Kuwait Institute for Scientific Research, in 1990.

mig (145,500 m³) per day respectively. Distillation plants were installed as a part of the following co-generation stations (Al-Farhoud 1988).

SHUAIBA CO-GENERATION STATION. The Shuaiba station is composed of two stations, Shuaiba North and Shuaiba South. The installed capacity of the power generation units is 1,204 MW in total, being 400 MW at Shuaiba North and 804 MW at Shuaiba South. Distillation plants with a total installed capacity of 44 mig per day were installed between 1965 and 1975, including 14 mig (63,650 m^3) at Shuaiba North (1965–1971) and 30 mig (136,400 m^3) at Shuaiba South (1971–1975).

DOHA CO-GENERATION STATION. The Doha station is also composed of two stations, Doha West and Doha East. The installed capacity of the power generation units is 3,558 MW in total, 1,158 MW at Doha East and 2,400 MW at Doha West. Distillation plants with a total installed capacity of 139 mig per day were installed between 1978 and 1985, including 43 mig (195,500 m^3) at Doha East (1978–1979) and 96 mig (436,500 m^3) at Doha West (1983–1985).

AL-ZOUR CO-GENERATION UNIT. The Al-Zour station, scheduled to be completed by 1991, was designed to have an installed capacity of 2,511 MW of power generation and 72 mig (327,300 m^3) of distillation per day.

The problem with seawater distillation is the high cost of the MSF evaporation process. The cost of the thermal process is largely dependent on the rate of energy (fuel) consumption for operating the system, which can account for as much as about 50% of the unit water cost and is sensitive to the unstable world market price of crude oil.

3.3.4 Reuse of treated sewage effluents

The amount of reuse of the sewage effluents in Kuwait in 1988 was 97 million m^3, which was one third of the volume of water supply.

Three municipal waste-water treatment plants, at Ardiya, Rekka, and Jahara, were designed to treat municipal waste-water through tertiary treatment for reuse in landscape irrigation. The installed capacity of these plants is 290,000 m^3 per day in total, comprising 150,000 m^3 at Ardiya, 65,000 m^3 at Rekka, and 80,000 m^3 at Jahara. The output is 265,000 m^3 per day, including 175,000 m^3 at Ardiya, 30,000 m^3 at Rekka, and 60,000 m^3 at Jahara. After tertiary treatment by sand filtration, the quality of the treated water is controlled to be 10–20 mg of BOD, 3–40 mg of NH$_3$-N, and 2,500 mg of TDS per litre

Table 3.3 **Sewage treatment plants for reuse in Kuwait**

Plant	Installed capacity (m³/day)	Present output (m³/day)
Ardiya	150,000	175,000
Rekka	60,000	30,000
Jahara	80,000	60,000
TOTAL	290,000	265,000

Water quality (mg/l)		
	Actual	Standard
BOD	10–20	
NH₃-N	3–40	1–10
TDS	2,500	1,500–4,500

Source: Kuwait Institute for Scientific Research, in 1990.

(table 3.3). Some of the reclaimed sewage water is being used for landscape irrigation and some for agriculture.

3.4 Experimental seawater reverse-osmosis desalination

3.4.1 Background

As has been indicated, Kuwait has been producing fresh water by distilling seawater since the 1950s. The multi-stage flash desalting process, which has been used exclusively in the Arabian peninsula, has proved to be very simple and reliable, but it requires extensive materials and energy. The MSF system reached its maturity with very few improvements. It seems, however, that the race for the second generation of seawater desalters will be won by reverse osmosis and low-temperature multi-effect horizontal-tube evaporators (Darwish and Jawad 1989a). Both systems are characterized by their low energy requirements, as compared with MSF. Energy consumption is the largest single cost item in desalination. Intensive efforts were made in the 1980s to evaluate the feasibility of RO desalination of seawater, including the installation of a pilot RO plant in Doha, where a cost analysis was made to compare the costs of the experimental RO and the existing MSF systems.

151

3.4.2 The Doha experimental RO plant

This pilot plant, with an installed capacity of 3,000 m^3 per day, was installed in 1984 to evaluate membrane and operating systems. It has three lines, equipped with different types of modules, namely spiral-wound, hollow fine fibre, and plate-frame (Darwish and Jawad 1989b):

— line 1: first stage, spiral-wound (UOP-PA 1501); second stage, spiral-wound (UOP-PA 8600);
— line 2: first stage, hollow fine fibre (Dupont B10); second stage, hollow fine fibre (Dupont B9);
— line 3: first stage, plate and frame (Enro + Scheicher & Schuell Film Tec.); second stage, spiral-wound (Hydronautics 8040B).

The feed seawater to the RO plant usually contains high concentrations of inorganic salts and foreign materials that can foul membranes and decrease their productivity. The main foulants associated with feed seawater are due to biological slime formation, suspended solids, colloids, metal oxide, and scale formation. Pre-treatment is essential to control the life of the membranes. Different methods of conventional pre-treatment were examined in each line.

Since the beginning of the plant's operation, pre-treatment has been running satisfactorily, with an availability of more than 96%. Most of the time, it has been successfully controlled to give a silt density index of less than 4, but in some cases it has failed to produce an acceptable quality, owing to clogging of the dual-media filters, absence of or overdosing with FeClSO4, breakdown of the destabilizer mixer, and climatic conditions such as temperature, dust storms, and wind.

3.4.3 Cost evaluation

The cost effectiveness of the membrane (RO) process can be assessed by comparison with the cost of the predominant thermal (MSF) process. These costs have two major components: (1) direct capital cost, and (2) operation and maintenance costs. The cost of equipment forms a major part of the capital cost, while the cost of the energy and chemicals consumed forms a major part of the operating and maintenance cost.

An evaluation was undertaken to compare the cost per unit of water produced by large-scale MSF and RO plants of typical design, each with an installed capacity of 27,300 m^3 (6 mig) per day. The feed water is assumed to be of the quality of seawater in the Arabian Gulf, with concentrations per litre of 45,000 mg of TDS, 800 mg of Ca^{++}, 1,700 mg of Mg^{++}, 12,500 mg of Na$^+$, 500 mg of K$^+$, 3,600 mg of SO$_4^{--}$, 24 mg of CO$_3^{--}$, 24,000 mg of Cl$^-$, 180 mg of HCO$_3^-$, 12 mg of Sr^{++}, and

0.04 mg of Ba^{++}. The evaluation further assumes the unit electric energy cost to be US\$0.07/kWh, the rate of replacement of the membranes 20% per year, twenty years' plant life, a 90% load factor, and an interest rate of 10% a year. The results of the comparison were as follows (Darwish and Jawad 1989b):

FACILITIES.   The seawater intake size and flow rate of the MSF unit are twice those of the RO unit.

The volume of the MSF unit is about three times that required for the RO permeators. The land area required for the MSF unit is at least four times that required for the RO permeators.

Extensive and heavy materials are used in the MSF unit, which are more than ten times those required for the RO unit. The heavy weight of the MSF unit requires heavy foundations and extensive civil engineering work.

ENERGY CONSUMPTION.   Thermal energy is consumed only by the MSF unit, and amounts to 89 MW. This thermal energy can be very expensive if it is obtained directly from boilers (not extracted from steam turbines).

The energy consumption for pumping seawater to the pre-treatment system and the high-pressure feed pump in the RO plant was estimated to be 0.25 and 7.98 kWh/m^3 respectively, or a total of 8.23 kWh/m^3, which is about 25% more than that required for the MSF unit. However, the pumping energy for RO can be decreased about 30%, from 8.23 to 5.9 kWh/m^3, by installing an energy-recovery unit such as a reversed centrifugal pump or Pelton wheel.

The average energy consumption per cubic metre of the product water for the MSF unit was 15.27 kWh/m^3, which was about three times as high as the rate of 5.9 kWh/m^3 for the RO plant.

UNIT COST OF PRODUCT WATER.   From the above analysis, the on-site unit water costs of seawater desalination were estimated to be US\$2.7/m^3 by MSF and US\$1.7/m^3 by RO. These are about twice as high as the costs of US\$1.00/m^3 for municipal water supply and of US\$0.95/m^3 for waste-water treatment in Japan (MFJ 1991), which are often used as a world standard for comparison.

CONJUNCTIVE USE PLAN FOR MSF AND RO.   Introducing RO seawater desalting plants in Kuwait does not mean phasing out older desalting units. A combination of new RO and existing MSF units could be cost-effective in a water-supply plan, as illustrated in fig. 3.10 in section 3.6 below.

3.5 Experimental brackish-groundwater reverse-osmosis desalination

3.5.1 Background

The groundwater in Kuwait is mostly brackish, with total dissolved solids of the order of 2,000–8,000 mg/l. Brackish groundwater with salinity two to eight times as high as the WHO standard maximum allowable level for drinking water (TDS = 1,000 mg/l) is being blended with permeate from MSF distillation plants or used to irrigate garden crops. No direct use of brackish groundwater for drinking purposes is possible without desalination. Reverse osmosis is the best means of demineralizing brackish waters and has been in use in the United States since the 1970s. Brackish-groundwater desalination is usually three to five times less expensive than seawater desalination (Buros 1989) and has the following advantages:

— low initial capital cost,
— compact design,
— short construction time and easy mobilization,
— lower energy requirement,
— cost flexibility in small- to large-scale units.

Thirteen skid-mounted mobile brackish-water RO units designed to supply fresh water for emergency purposes, equipped with standby power-generating units and with an installed capacity of 0.25 mig (1,137 m^3) per day each, have been installed since 1987 in various locations in Kuwait—the Labour Institute for Juveniles, the Shuwaikh storage area, two army camps, and nine hospitals. Kuwait is the first country to use such mobile RO units for the desalination of brackish groundwater. The technical and cost feasibilities are reviewed here before examining the concept of a hydro-powered RO desalination system in section 3.6.

3.5.2 The experimental RO unit

The first of the thirteen skid-mounted RO units began a one-year test operation in 1988 and ran continuously for 8,260 hours according to specifications. During the test operation, no membrane unit was added or replaced, but frequent changes of cartridge filter elements were needed to avoid bio-fouling. The test operation was successfully completed without encountering any significant problems (Malik et al. 1989).

THE RO SYSTEM UNIT. The RO unit is housed in two standard containers. The first, the operation container, includes the membranes, high-pressure pumps, cartridge filter, flushing/cleaning tank, transfer pump, dosing stations, control panel, electrical switch board, etc. The second contains two dual-media filters, the feed pump, a backwash air blower, and associated pipes and valves.

Brackish water is supplied to the feed-water tank (227 m^3) through the existing brackish-water pipeline network.

The pre-treatment system consists of dual-media filters (hydro-anthracite/fine sands) and cartridge filters (5-μm size). Sulphuric acid (5 mg/l) and antiscalant flocon (6 mg/l) are added before the cartridge filters and sodium bisulphate (2 mg/l) at the suction of the feed pump.

After the feed water passes through the cartridge filter, the pressure is increased up to the operating level of 15–25 kg/cm^2 by centrifugal pump.

The RO unit consists of eight pressure vessels. The membrane is a low-pressure type, spiral-wound BW-8040 composite module, 8 inches in diameter.

The permeate from the modules flows to the flushing/cleaning tank. A neutral pH value is achieved in the final product water by dosing with caustic soda (5–10 mg/l). Sodium hypochlorite (1 mg/l as Cl$_2$) is injected to sterilize the product water.

BIO-FOULING PROBLEMS. The brackish feed water contains bacteria with count-concentrations of the order of 60–400 CFU/ml, which was the main cause of blockage in the cartridge filter elements. Cleaning or replacement of the elements was needed every 300–400 hours, which is five times as frequent as the standard rate of 1,500–2,000 hours. To combat this problem the feed-water tanks and sand filters were disinfected with 5 mg of chlorine per litre, which improved the rate of filter replacement up to 700–800 hours. Shock-chlorinating the cartridge filter periodically with 5 mg of chlorine per litre further significantly improved the replacement time to about 1,800 operating hours.

MEMBRANE CLEANING. Cleaning the membrane every 1,000 hours with a solution of NaOH (0.1%) and EDTA (0.1%) and replacing the cartridge filter every 1,800 hours was found to be more economical and

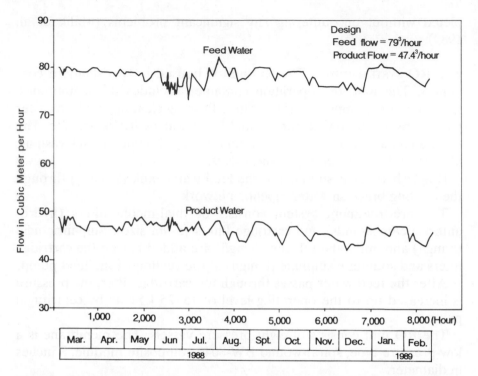

Fig. 3.8 **One-year test operation of brackish-groundwater RO desalination in Kuwait** (Source: Malik 1989)

safer than any other method, such as increasing the chlorine dose rate (from 0.2 to 2 mg/l) in the feed water.

3.5.3 Technical performance
One year of test operation (8,260 hours) of the brackish-water reverse-osmosis desalination was successfully completed in 1989. The skid-mounted RO unit can operate continuously with an availability of 94.3%. The average discharge of product water was 46.83 m³/hour, which was 98.9% of the designed value of 47.4 m³/hour (fig. 3.8).

QUALITY OF FEED WATER AND PRODUCT WATER. The salinity of the brackish feed water varied from 3,134 to 3,874 mg of TDS per litre, with an average of 3,407 mg/l. The salinity of the product water averaged 73.5 mg/l, with a minimum of 62 mg/l and maximum of 122 mg/l. The feed-water temperature was between 26°C and 37°C. The pH of the feed water was 7.87 on average, with a minimum of 7.65 and a maximum of 8.0.

156

OPERATING PRESSURE AND POWER CONSUMPTION. The operating pressure varied from a minimum of 15 kg/cm² to a maximum of 21 kg/cm². The average power consumption during the 8,260 hours of operation—including all auxiliary functions such as air conditioners, lights, mixers, etc.—was 2 kWh per m³ of product water.

RECOVERY AND SALT REJECTION. The recovery of fresh water was 59.86% on average, ranging between 56% and 64%. The average salt rejection was 98.4%, with a minimum of 98%.

3.5.4 Cost performance

This case study on a very small-scale brackish-water RO desalination unit was aimed at evaluating the cost-effectiveness of supplying fresh water to remote or isolated towns and for emergency needs by using a skid-mounted unit. The cost estimates for the initial capital cost and operation and maintenance costs assumed the following:
— 15 years of plant life,
— 3-year membrane replacement frequency,
— interest rate at 8%,
— electricity charges of KD 0.020 (US$0.07) per kWh,
— source cost of brackish groundwater not included.

The initial capital cost comprised: mechanical equipment, 49.8%; membranes, 19.5%; electric generators, 17.5%; instrumentation equipment, 5.0%; training, 4.5%; and civil, 3.5%. The operation and maintenance (O&M) cost, comprising labour, chemicals, spare parts, energy/electricity, and membrane replacements, was estimated to be KD 0.160 (US$0.48) per m³. O&M is the most important cost item in a small-scale plant and is five times as high as the capital cost. The energy costs and labour costs are the dominant elements in O&M, accounting for 31.7% and 27.0% respectively. Other costs account for less than half of O&M, including 14.6% for membrane replacement, 14.4% for chemicals, and 12.3% for spare parts. The unit cost of the product water from this particular small-scale skid-mounted mobile system was estimated to be as high as KD 0.726 (US$2.18) per m³ (Malik et al. 1989).

3.6 Hydro-powered brackish-groundwater reverse-osmosis desalination: A new proposal

In this study I propose the use of hydro-powered reverse-osmosis desalination to minimize the cost of energy consumption, which is the largest single cost element in desalination engineering. Hydro-powered desalination makes effective use of the hydro-potential energy in a water pipeline system carrying brackish groundwater from a wellfield to the terminal reservoir where the differential head is 200 m or more. This section examines this new concept for the existing Shigaya groundwater development project in Kuwait to evaluate its cost feasibility.

3.6.1 Brackish groundwater wellfield

The proposed wellfield is located in the potential wellfields of West Shigaya and a part of North Shigaya, about 100 km west of Kuwait city (fig. 3.9). The ground elevation is 200–300 m above sea level. The Damman limestone at this point has a thickness of about 150 m. The piezometric levels, however, are rather low, being in the range of 50–100 m above sea level. The groundwater is brackish, with a salinity of 2,500–7,000 mg of TDS per litre. The potential yield has been estimated to be 68,000 m^3 per day in each potential wellfield (Abusada 1988). For this study, the potential yield is assumed to be 45 million m^3 per year (123,400 m^3 per day), with the wellfield within an area with an elevation of more than 200 m. It is estimated that 46 production wells would be required, assuming a unit rate of 2,700 m^3 per day per well.

3.6.2 Pressure pipeline system and pre-treatment plant

The proposed hydro-powered scheme would use the piezometric head difference between the collecting reservoir (elevation, 230 m) and the Jahara RO plant (elevation, 20 m). The pre-treatment plant would be sited immediately east of the collecting reservoir, where the feed water gravitates to the Jahara plant. A ductile iron pressure pipe 750 mm in diameter and 60 km long, with a pressure limitation of 25 bar maximum, would carry the feed water to the Jahara plant. The design discharge and velocity in the pressure pipe are 1.42 m^3/sec and 3.2 m/sec, respectively.

3.6.3 Estimate of hydro-potential energy in the trunk main

The head difference between the collecting reservoir (230 m) and the RO plant (20 m) is 210 m. The energy loss would consist mainly of friction loss in the pressure pipe, together with other losses, and is estimated to be 10 m of water head, which is only 5% of the total head of 210 m. From the effective head of water at 200 m, or 20 kg/cm^2, the theoretical hydro-potential of the scheme is estimated to be 2,780 kW.

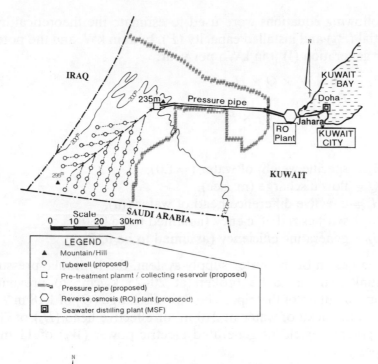

LEGEND

▲ Mountain/Hill
○ Tubewell (proposed)
▢ Pre-treatment planmt / collecting reservoir (proposed)
⇒ Pressure pipe (proposed)
⬡ Reverse osmosis (RO) plant (proposed)
▣ Seawater distilling plant (MSF)

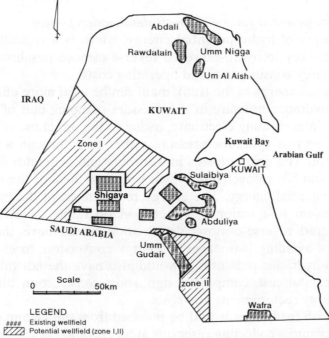

LEGEND

Existing wellfield
▨ Potential wellfield (zone I,II)

Fig. 3.9 Proposed layout of hydro-powered RO desalination system in Kuwait

159

The following equations were used to estimate the theoretical hydro-potential (P_{th}) and installed capacity (P), both in kW, and the potential power generation (W_p) in kWh per year:

$$P_{th} = 9.8 \times W_s \times Q \times H_e,$$
$$P = P_{th} \times E_f,$$
$$W_p = 365 \times 24 \times G_f \times P,$$

where

W_s = specific weight of water ($=1.0$),
Q = flow discharge (m³/sec),
H_e = effective difference head of water (m),
E_f = synthesized efficiency (assumed to be 0.80),
G_f = generating efficiency (assumed to be 0.68).

In the design of the water supply system, the hydraulic pressure in the trunk main is to be broken at 20–25 kg/cm² to prevent the mechanical failure of the pipe. The flow discharge (Q) of 1.18 m³/sec at a differential head of water of 210 m, or effective head (H_e) of 200 m, has a potential yield of generated electric power (W_p) of 11 million kWh per year.

3.6.4   *Hydro-powered reverse-osmosis desalination system*

The application of hydro-potential energy, which is a typically clean energy, is the key to hydro-powered reverse-osmosis desalination, to minimize energy consumption and operating costs.

The potential energy in the trunk main can be used more effectively to provide hydraulic pressure in the pressure-pumping unit of an RO system than in generating electricity, owing to the direct use of hydro-potential energy as hydraulic pressure rather than through a turbine and generator. The energy losses in a turbine and generator are generally 16% and 5% respectively, which is in total 20% of the theoretical hydro-potential energy. The energy requirement of the pressure-pumping system is a major cost factor in operating an RO plant. Hydro-powered reverse-osmosis desalination would have the great advantage of avoiding two stages of energy conversion, to electricity and then to hydraulic pressure. It would also have the advantages of low initial capital cost, compact design, short construction time, and minimal energy requirements and costs.

The brackish feed water would be pumped from the Damman limestone aquifer into a collecting reservoir at an elevation of 235 m above sea level (fig. 3.10). The feed water is estimated to have an average

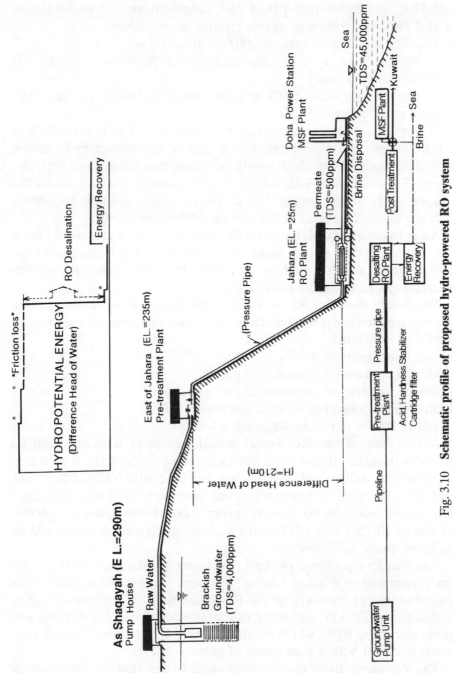

Fig. 3.10 **Schematic profile of proposed hydro-powered RO system**

161

salinity of 4,000 mg of TDS per litre, a temperature of between 26°C and 37°C, and an average pH of 7.87, ranging from 7.65 to 8.0 (Malik et al. 1989). The following design criteria were assumed:

— installed capacity of system, 100,000 m³ per day;
— design feed water (85% operating factor), 86,400 m³ per day (31 million m³ per year);
— design product water (60% of feed water), 51,840 m³ per day (18.9 million m³ per year).

The reverse-osmosis unit would be in two parts. The first would be a pre-treatment unit sited immediately east of the collecting reservoir, with dual-media filters (hydro-anthracite and fine sands) and cartridge filters (5-μm size) and with sulphuric acid (5 mg/l) and antiscalant flocon (6 mg/l) added before the cartridge filters. Sodium bisulphate (2 mg/l) would be added at the suction of the feed pump.

After passing through the cartridge filter, the feed water would enter a pressure pipeline (trunk main) to sustain a hydraulic pressure head of 20 kg/cm², which would be used directly to overcome the osmotic pressure to permeate the membrane.

The 8-inch diameter RO module would have a low-pressure, spiral-wound composite-type membrane. The specifications of the module would be as follows:

— salt rejection rate, 87.5%,
— design operating pressure, 20 kg/cm²,
— design quantity of permeate, 30 m³ per day,
— maximum operating water temperature, 40°C,
— pH of feed water to be adjusted, 6.0–6.5.

A unit line of the RO vessel would consist of a circuit with six modules in series. Recovery is estimated to be 70% of the feed water, yielding 31.5 million m³ of permeate per year with TDS at 500 mg/l, and 8.0 million m³ of brine reject per year with TDS at 17,700 mg/l. The membrane will be cleaned every 1,000 hours using a solution of NaOH (0.1%) and EDTA (0.1%), and the cartridge filters will be replaced every 1,800 hours.

The effective pressure of the brine reject is estimated to be 17 kg/cm², assuming a friction loss of 3 kg/cm² in the RO circuit. The potential energy recovery of the RO brine reject is preliminarily estimated to be 333 kW, assuming the total efficiency of the turbine and generator to be 80%, which would generate 1.98 million kWh of electricity per year with a load factor of 65%.

The permeate from the modules would then flow to the flushing/

cleaning tank. A neutral pH value would be achieved in the final product water by dosing with caustic soda (5–10 mg/l). Sodium hypochlorite (1 mg/l as Cl_2) would be injected to sterilize the product water.

3.6.5 Cost effectiveness

The investment cost of the proposed hydro-powered desalting plant is preliminarily estimated to be US$94,065,000 in total, with an annualized capital cost of US$5,656,000, comprising US$74,488,000 of capital cost and US$19,577,000 of design and construction supervision. The capital cost would include the following major cost elements:
— pre-treatment, US$13,898,860,
— desalting plant, US$22,144,570,
— RO membrane, equipment, US$26,679,960,
— control and operating system, US$1,871,900,
— appurtenant works, US$8,495,200,
— power-line and substation, US$1,142,680,
— energy recovery/turbine, US$254,940.
Financial expenditure is estimated to be US$24,428,700, based on 1990 prices with 8% interest during three years' construction.

The annual cost of operation and maintenance is estimated to be US$5,653,600, made up of the following main items:
— labour, US$1,169,200,
— material and supplies, US$584,920,
— chemicals, US$2,339,690,
— membrane replacement, US$1,559,790.

The costs of source water and benefits from energy recovery are not included in this cost estimate. The above cost estimates are based on the following assumptions:
— plant life, 20 years,
— membrane life (replacement), 3 years,
— unit price of RO module, US$1,300.

The unit water cost of the hydro-powered reverse-osmosis desalination for 31.5 million m^3 of product water per year is estimated to be US$0.40/$m^3$, which is lower than the cost of such other methods as seawater desalination by MSF (US$2.70/m3), seawater desalination by RO (US$1.70/m3), and brackish-groundwater desalination by RO without the use of hydro-power (US$0.60/$m^3$), as shown in fig. 3.11. Such an application of hydro-potential energy recovery in a pipeline system is likely to have a strategic value in saving fossil-fuel energy and the global environment in addition to minimizing costs in desalination

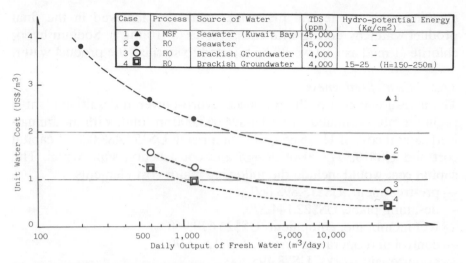

Case	Process	Source of Water	TDS (ppm)	Hydro-potential Energy (Kg/cm2)
1 ▲	MSF	Seawater (Kuwait Bay)	45,000	–
2 ●	RO	Seawater	45,000	–
3 ○	RO	Brackish Groundwater	4,000	–
4 ▣	RO	Brackish Groundwater	4,000	15-25 (H=150-250m)

Fig. 3.11 **Unit water cost of desalination in Kuwait** (Sources: Darwish 1989; Murakami 1991; Murakami and Musiake 1991)

engineering in many parts of the world where there are groundwater resources at an appropriate elevation.

3.7 Development alternatives and a conjunctive-use plan

3.7.1 Development alternatives
The predominant multi-stage flash (MSF) desalination facilities in Kuwait, which consume extensive materials and more energy than RO, will be replaced in stages after the completion their plant life of about 15–20 years. RO seawater desalting plants will replace the old MSF desalter units. The unit cost of RO brackish-groundwater desalination is also much lower than that of seawater desalination, implying lower energy consumption and less capital investment. Hydro-powered RO desalination is the method with the lowest cost, minimizing both energy consumption and capital cost. The development alternatives include the following:

» MSF distilling of seawater (existing plant; highest cost);
» RO desalination of seawater (experimental stage now being completed);
» RO desalination of brackish groundwater (existing skid-mounted RO units);
» Hydro-powered RO desalination of brackish groundwater (as proposed here; the lowest-cost method).

164

3.7.2   Conjunctive-use plan

A number of old MSF plants in Kuwait are going to be phased out by the year 2000. Seawater RO will replace the old MSF in stages, but almost pure water from the existing MSF system will also be blended with RO product water with a salinity of about 500 mg of TDS per litre to obtain water of a quality suitable for drinking.

The salinity ranges of the product water from the various processes are as follows:
— MSF-distilled seawater, 25–50 mg/l,
— RO-desalinated seawater, 300–1,500 mg/l,
— RO-desalinated brackish water, 100–500 mg/l.
These may be compared with the WHO drinking-water standards of 250–500 mg of TDS per litre for Europe, the United States, and Japan and 500–1,000 mg/l for the Middle East.

In a hybrid RO/MSF seawater desalination system, a seawater reverse-osmosis plant is combined with either a new or an existing MSF co-generation plant, with the following advantages:
» Both the capital and operating cost for the RO system are reduced.
» A single-stage RO process can be used, and the life of the RO membrane can be extended by reducing the water-quality specification for the permeate.
» The temperature of the MSF product water is reduced by blending the hot product water from MSF distillation with the RO permeate.

The combination of the new RO system with the existing MSF will be the key approach to developing the Kuwait water supply system in the 1990s.

Combining the proposed hydro-powered RO desalination system with the present MSF system would make more effective use of brackish-groundwater desalination at the lowest cost, taking into account the limited potential of brackish-groundwater resources and the unlimited potential source of seawater. The salinity of the permeate from brackish-groundwater RO desalination can be controlled in the range 100–500 mg of TDS per litre, while the brine reject water has a salinity as high as 10,000 mg/l or more. The salinity of the product water from MSF distillation is as low as 25–50 mg/l. Brackish-groundwater RO desalination will contribute (1) a direct supply of good quality drinking water to meet WHO standards and (2) an indirect supply by blending brine reject water from RO with almost pure water from the existing MSF system. The conjunctive-use plan suggests the following priority uses of the water and energy elements:

165

≫ RO product water (permeate)—31.5 million m³ per year with 500 mg of TDS per litre—for direct use for drinking-water supply;

≫ RO brine reject water—8 million m³ per year with 17,700 mg of TDS per litre—for indirect use to blend with MSF product water;

≫ MSF product water—632,000 m³ per day maximum with 25–50 mg of TDS per litre— to be blended with RO brine reject water;

≫ MSF brine reject water—>45,000 mg of TDS per litre—to be safely disposed of offshore in Kuwait Bay;

≫ energy recovered from the RO process—1.98 million kWh of electricity per year—to be used to supply electricity for treatment and/or pumping.

A tentative conjunctive-use plan is illustrated as a flow diagram in fig. 3.10.

3.7.3 Remarks on future development planning

The desalination of saline water by a membrane separation with low-energy requirements will play an increasingly important role in the water-resources planning of arid states in the twenty-first century. Reverse osmosis is the least costly process today, but it may not be the optimum solution, which may be neither reverse osmosis nor thermal desalination. Membrane desalination, however, will be a key application for water-resources planning in the twenty-first century. A new desalination system using reverse osmosis either with or without the use of hydro-power will be incorporated in the existing MSF system in Kuwait by stages to make a reality of energy-saving desalination technology.

4

Hydro-powered reverse-osmosis desalination in water-resources planning in Jordan

4.1 Background and objectives

4.1.1 Background

Jordan is located to the north-west of the Arabian peninsula and extends from 29° to 33° north latitude and from 35° to 39° east longitude, with an area of 89,555 km² (fig. 4.1).

More than 80% of the country is covered by almost unpopulated desert. The population was estimated to be about 2.8 million in 1985, about 90% of whom live in the north-west quadrant of the country. Greater Amman, which is a metropolitan district within a 30 km radius from the centre of Amman city, occupies 3% of the area of the country, but its population is as much as 1.62 million (573 people per km²), or about 60% of the whole population of Jordan. The national population growth rate was about 3.7% per year in the 1970s (Huang and Banerjee 1984), mainly due to migration from the West Bank and the Gaza Strip.

The population growth rate is expected to decline slowly to about 3.2% by the year 2010. Municipal and industrial water use is expected to increase from 24% of total water use in 1985 to 30% in 2005 and 45% in 2015, assuming a modest consumption rate of 83 litres per

167

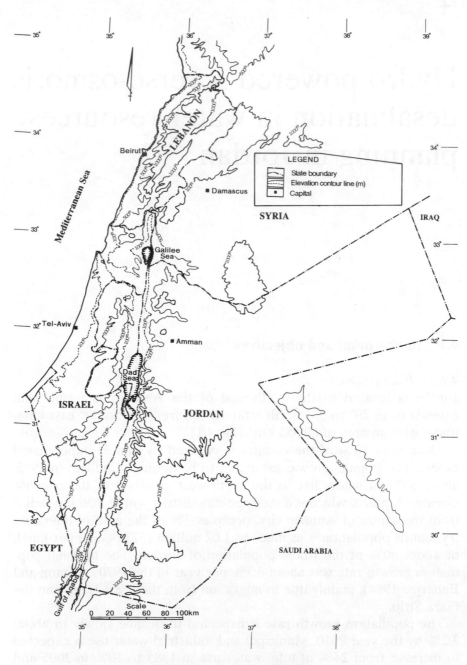

Fig. 4.1 **Jordan and Israel**

capita per day for domestic use. The national water demand was simply projected to increase to 1,209 million m³ per year by the year 2000, assuming a growth rate of 2.5%–3.5% in population, 5% in industrial uses, and 4% in agriculture uses (MPJ 1990). Effective rainfall as the potential renewable water resource was estimated to be 1,123 million m³ per year, with 245 million m³ becoming groundwater and 878 million m³ running off as surface flow (World Bank 1989).

Limitations of water, one of the important resources of Jordan, are likely to have a major impact on the economic development of the country. By the year 2000 most of the conventional water resources in the country will have been fully exploited by conventional measures such as constructing dams and drilling wells. The development of marginal non-conventional water resources will therefore become a key measure in the twenty-first century for sustaining economic development.

Non-conventional water in Jordan consists primarily of brackish water, seawater, and reclaimed urban waste water. In the 1970s it was considered that large-scale seawater desalination projects would become both technically feasible and economically viable as water supply alternatives in the early 1990s (Buras and Darr 1979). Innovative research in 1980s on membrane technologies for desalination has been changing the world market by reducing the share of conventional MSF distillation, which has so far been the only method used in Middle East countries (see Appendix A). The development of saline water resources by desalting with reverse osmosis and other membrane processes will play an increasingly important role in the context of the national water master plan.

4.1.2 Objectives

The main purpose of studying the application of hydro-powered RO desalination in a case study on the Aqaba-Disi groundwater development and water supply project is to evaluate the technical feasibility and cost-effectiveness of the proposed co-generation system.

The proposed co-generation system aims not only to conserve the fossil groundwater resources in the Disi aquifer but also to retrieve the hydro-potential energy in a pipeline system for both the generation of electricity and desalting brackish groundwater from the Kurnub aquifer.

Potential non-conventional water-resource applications such as the proposed hydro-powered RO desalination are examined in the context of the national water master plan for sustainable development in Jordan in the twenty-first century.

4.2 The water resources of Jordan

Hydro-meteorologically, Jordan is semi-arid to arid, with relatively abundant water resources as compared with other states in the Middle East such as Kuwait. About 80% of its territory is steppe and desert where water is only minimally available. Jordan, however, has various sources of water, such as rivers and streams, springs, wadi flash floods, renewable and non-renewable groundwater, and reclamation of treated sewage effluents.

4.2.1 Water-resources potential

Water resources in Jordan depend mainly on precipitation within the country, except for the Yarmouk River, whose flow is mainly fed by rainfall on Syrian territory. Average rainfall ranges from 600 mm per year in the northern uplands to less than 500 mm per year in the southern and eastern desert areas. The rainfall occurs between October and May, and is at its height between December and March, when over 80% of the annual rainfall occurs.

The average annual volume of rainfall within Jordan has been estimated to be 8.5×10^9 m^3. However, with high evaporation losses, the average net annual yield is only about 1.12×10^9 m^3 (13%), with 875 million m^3 (10%) in the form of surface water and 242 million m^3 (3%) in groundwater (Huang and Banerjee 1984). About two-thirds of Jordan's potential usable water resources is surface water. About 400 million m^3 per year of the surface flow, which is 46% of the total run-off, forms the discharge in the Yarmouk River. Sustained-yield and/or renewable groundwater resources are preliminarily estimated at 3% of the annual rainfall; their recharge is mostly dependent on rainfall on the western highlands. In addition, it is estimated that over 11×10^9 m^3 of stored fresh groundwater exists within the state, but this is mostly non-renewable groundwater which may offer opportunities for short-term and emergency uses.

4.2.2 Surface water resources

Surface water resources, which constitute two-thirds of Jordan's potential usable water resources, are at present used exclusively for agriculture, except for spring water, which is sometimes collected for municipal use. Most of the municipal water supply systems and industries in Jordan at present depend on groundwater and springs. Although surface water resources exist on the northern border such as in the Yarmouk River, in the Jordan valley, and in some of the wadis flowing into the Jordan River, exploitation of surface water for municipal and industrial water supply has not so far occurred to any great extent because of sporadic flow patterns, priority use for irrigation, relatively low elevation, and the long distances to population centres.

River flows are generally of a flash-flood nature, with large seasonal and annual variation. Annual base flows, moreover, whose volume is estimated at 540 million m³, vary by at least 15%–20%, depending on rainfall patterns with a return period of five years (Huang and Banerjee 1984). The base flow of 150 million m³ per year in the Yarmouk River has been developed by the East Ghor Main Canal (EGMC) irrigation project since 1965. Corresponding to the rapid increase in water demand in the metropolitan area, 45 million m³ of canal water has been diverted from the EGMC to Amman for municipal and industrial use by constructing a treatment plant and pipeline with a total difference (pumping) head of 1,300 m.

Since the beginning of the 1960s, a number of storage dams have been constructed that together hold an estimated 452 million m³ of water. The Al-Wuheda dam, which is being built on the Yarmouk River near the Syrian border to store 225 million m³, will supply irrigation water for downstream in the Jordan valley and will generate electric power. Syria will use part of the water and 75% of the total hydroelectric power (World Bank 1988).

4.2.3 *Groundwater resources*

Major potential aquifers are found in the pervious sequences in the basalt system of the Pleistocene, the Rijam (B4) formation of the Lower Tertiary, the Amman–Wadi Sir (B2/A7) formation of the Upper to Middle Cretaceous, the lower Ajlun (A1–6) formation of the Middle Cretaceous, the Kurnub-Zarqa formations of the Lower Cretaceous, and the Disi formations of the Palaeozoic age.

The shallow aquifer systems of basalt-Rijam (B4) form a locally important aquifer in the central part of the Jafr and Al-Azraq–Wadi as-Sirhan basins. Groundwater irrigation has been practised in and around the town of Jafr since the 1970s, but the underlying aquifer B4 has been contaminated by stages by irrigation return flows, increasing salinity (TDS) from 500 mg/l to 4,000 mg/l during the ten years of operation. The sustained yield is estimated to be less than 2 million m³ per year, because of the limited groundwater recharge through the wadi beds during the occasional flash floods. The basalt-Rijam system in the Azraq basin has been intensively exploited for the purpose of Amman municipal water supply. Annual abstraction from the Azraq wellfield reached 15.6 million m^3 in 1985, which exceeded the safe yield, lowering the piezometric head and increasing water salinity. Groundwater in the Sirhan basin, of which the recharge mechanism is the same as that of the Jafr basin, is untapped.

The most important aquifer system is the Amman–Wadi Sir (B2/A7), which consists of limestone, silicified limestone, chert, sand limestone, and sandstone of Upper to Middle Cretaceous age. This system extends throughout the entire country with thicknesses of about 100–350 m. The depth of the groundwater table below ground level generally ranges from 50 to 250 m in the uplands. Good groundwater recharge occurs from the western highlands, where the annual rainfall ranges from 200 to 600 mm. To the east, the aquifer is confined by thick marl such as the Muwwaqar (B3) formation, and water salinity is high. This economic aquifer system, B2/A7, has been excessively exploited in the northern part of the country, lowering the piezometric levels and causing deterioration in water quality. In the southern part of the country such as the Mujib basin, the Upper Hasa basin, and the Jafr basin, the B2/A7 aquifer is the most important economic aquifer, of which the quality is as good as less than 500 mg of TDS per litre. The groundwater is being pumped for M&I water supply from the wellfields of Qastal, Siwaqa, Qatrana, Sultani, Karak, Shoubak, and Hasa.

An intermediate aquifer system is the lower Ajlun (A1–6), which consists of alternating limestone, marl, shale, chert, and sandstone of Middle Cretaceous age. This system is underlain by the Amman–Wadi Sir (B2/A7) formation, which is mostly confined by its relatively impervious layer of marl and shale in the A5/6A or upper unit of A1–6. The lower Ajlun formation extends throughout the country with variable thickness and litho-facies. Southwards, aquifers in the lower Ajlun formation become more sandy, and salinity becomes as little as 350 mg of TDS per litre. The aquifer system is mostly untapped, however, because of its complicated hydrogeology and deep formation.

Deep sandstone aquifers are the Kurnub/Zarqa of Lower Cretaceous age and the Disi of Palaeozoic age, which are unconformably separated by a less permeable layer of sandstone, siltstone, and shale. The Kurnub formation intercalates frequent argillaceous layers in the south, while the Disi is composed of massive and rather homogeneous arenaceous layers. Groundwater in these aquifers is mostly non-renewable because of limited groundwater recharge through small outcrop areas. The quality of the groundwater in the Kurnub-Zarqa system varies from fresh to brackish. Excellent quality with low salinity, however, is found in the Disi aquifer in the southern part of the country, which has been exploited for the water supply of Aqaba and local experimental irrigation. The development potential of Disi groundwater has been estimated to be about 100–200 million m^3 per year for a period of over 50–100 years. The aquifer complex, however, forms a huge groundwater reservoir extending under the whole of the country. This groundwater storage offers opportunity for short-term and emergency uses.

Groundwater is presently used for municipal, industrial, and agricultural purposes. In the northern uplands, which include the heavily populated Greater Amman and Irbid areas, groundwater in the Amman–Wadi Sir aquifer has been over-exploited in the 1980s. Significant irrigation water use is also found in the Zarqa River basin, where about 70% of the water is from groundwater. Abstraction in the northern uplands is estimated at about 120 million m^3 per year against an estimated sustainable yield of 90 million m^3 per year.

It is said that 96% of the kingdom's population is now supplied with drinking water from springs and groundwater wells. A series of water supply schemes have been carried out, including the following groundwater projects—the Wadi Arab scheme west of Irbid (20 million m^3 per year), the Azraq project (15 million m^3), the Amman-Zarqa project, (14 million m^3), the Qatrana-Siwaqa-Qastal project (9 million m^3), the Sultani project near Karak (3.5 million m^3), the Shoubak project (1.5 million m^3), and the Disi project (17 million m^3)—and the Deir Alla–EGMC pipeline project (45 million m^3) (World Bank 1988). The Mukheiba wellfield (26 million m^3 per year), which was developed for irrigation water supply downstream of the Yarmouk/Ghor, will be diverted to upland water supply by taking advantage of the difference in the water head of about 200 m between the artesian wellfield and the Ghor.

4.2.4 Treated sewage effluents

Significant work on sewerage has taken place during the last decade, and about 40% of the urban population (25% of the country's population) is now being served. In many urban areas, however, household cesspits and septic tanks are still commonly used, with liquid effluents discharging into the soil via open-joint pipes or openings in pit wells. This return flow mixes with groundwater recharge from rainfall, which is reused for water supplies, and incremental increases in mineral content and high nitrate concentrations have been monitored in the groundwater under some densely populated areas.

Groundwater in the Wadi Arab wellfield, which draws from the Amman–Wadi Sir aquifer (B2/A7), was contaminated by direct infiltration from sewage effluents in 1988 through an outcrop of B2/A7 in the upstream area. Drainage of sewage effluents from Irbid city was diverted to the north to protect the quality of groundwater in and around the outcrop area of the B2/A7. Direct recharge of sewage effluents into the limestone aquifers is not planned.

The Zarqa River, which runs through the heavily populated cities of Amman, Zarqa, and Ruseifa, collects the return flows of sewage effluents. The sewage effluents mix with surface water in the river system and are stored in the reservoir of King Talal dam, which is used exclusively for irrigation water supply in the Jordan valley downstream and not for municipal water supply.

4.3 Water-resources development and management

The United Nation's partition proposal of 1947, which divided Palestine into Jewish and Arab states, ignored water problems. The 1948 Arab-Israeli war aggravated the difficulties of cooperative water development and management. The failure of negotiations to develop a multilateral approach to water-resources development and management reinforced unilateral action. Though the Unified Plan (see Appendix C) was not ratified, both Jordan and Israel undertook to operate within their allocations. Their two major projects undertaken were the Israeli National Water Carrier and Jordan's East Ghor Main Canal.

The design of the East Ghor Main Canal (EGMC) was begun in 1957; its construction began in 1959, and the first phase up to Wadi Zarqa was commissioned in 1966. The King Talal dam, situated on the Zarqa River, with a storage capacity of 56 million m^3, and an 18-km extension of the EGMC were completed in 1977 at a cost of US$52 million (fig. 4.2).

Smaller dams were built on the rift-side wadis from the late 1960s, including the Kafrain dam (3.8 million m^3) and the Wadi Ziqlab dam (4.3 million m^3). The rift-side dam scheme on the Wadi Shueib was intended to store winter flows for downstream irrigation; however, it could not effectively store the design volume, owing to substantial leakage through a gravel formation and limestone geology in and

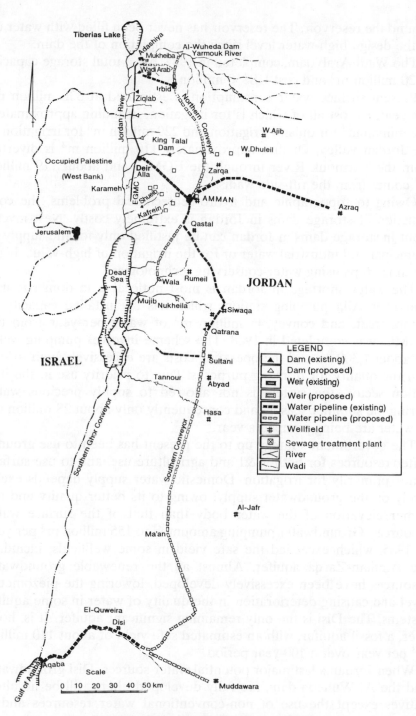

Fig. 4.2   Water resources system of Jordan

175

around the reservoir. The reservoir has never been filled with water up to the design high-water level since the completion of the dam.

The Wadi Arab dam, completed in 1987, has a total storage capacity of 20 million m^3 and cost US$50 million.

Present surface water consumption is estimated at 336 million m^3 per year, almost all of which is for irrigation, including approximately 102 million m^3 for upland irrigation and 229 million m^3 for irrigation in the Jordan valley. Of this, approximately 110 million m^3 is diverted from the Yarmouk River through the EGMC, and about 119 million m^3 comes from the rift-side wadis.

Owing to topographic and hydro-geotechnical problems, the construction of storage dams in Jordan is extremely costly. New investment in storage dams in Jordan can be justified only for the supply of municipal and industrial water or for the irrigation of high-value, high-yielding crops using water-conserving technologies.

The water shortage in Jordan is most noticeable in domestic use. The Deir Alla pumping station, which has an installed capacity to pump, treat, and convey 45 million m^3 of water per year from the EGMC, was completed in 1988. The scheme involves pumping water up about 1,300 m, and the operating costs are excessively high to sustain the quality for drinking purposes. Due to priority use in the irrigation sector, the system is not allowed to supply precious water during the summer season, and consequently only about 28 million m^3 of water are being pumped a year.

The government strategy up to the present has been to use groundwater resources for both M&I and agriculture use, and to use surface water primarily for irrigation. Domestic water supply depends exclusively on the groundwater supply, owing to its better quality and the higher elevation of the water body than that of the surface water resources. Groundwater pumping amounted to 155 million m^3 per year in 1985, which exceeded the safe yield in some wellfields, including the Amman-Zarqa aquifer. Almost all the renewable groundwater resources have been excessively developed, lowering the piezometric level and causing deterioration in the quality of water in some aquifer systems. The Disi is the only remaining significant aquifer. It is, however, a fossil aquifer, with an estimated safe yield of about 110 million m^3 per year over a 100-year period.

When Jordan's last major potential water sources, Disi groundwater and the Al-Wuheda dam, are fully developed, there will be no alternatives except the use of non-conventional water resources and/or importation of water from other countries.

4.3.1 Surface water resources

Surface water resources are dominated by the Yarmouk and Zarqa Rivers, which provide the majority of the irrigation water for the Jordan valley. Irrigation in the Jordan valley in the past has been made possible only by large-scale public investments in water diversion such as the East Ghor Main Canal and water storage dams, including the King Talal and the Wadi Arab, to utilize the potential of surface water resources. The King Talal dam on the Zarqa River was completed in 1979 to collect not only natural flows in the river system but also sewage effluents, both treated and untreated, from the population centres of Amman and Zarqa. Sewage effluents constitute an increasing proportion of the water stored behind the dam, and the amount of treated sewage in northern Jordan is expected to increase from 29 million m^3 in 1985 to 116 million m^3 in 2005 and 165 million m^3 in 2015 (World Bank 1988). Although the water quality of the reservoir is still good and suitable for the cultivation of most crops through drip irrigation except for leafy vegetables, use of King Talal water for M&I, even after treatment, has to be avoided on account of the health risks.

Small dam schemes have been implemented to provide embankment dams with heights of 30–38 m on small streams in the rift-side wadis, including the Ziqlab (4.3 million m^3 of storage), the Shueib (2.3 million m^3), and the Kafrain (3.8 million m^3) since 1968. As mentioned earlier, the dam on the Wadi Shueib was intended to store winter flows for downstream irrigation, but it could not effectively store the design volume owing to substantial leakage through the gravel foundation and limestone geology in and around the reservoir.

The Wadi Arab dam was originally planned to store 30 million m^3 of spring flow per year. However, the flowing spring suddenly stopped because of groundwater development in the adjacent wellfield in the wadi in 1985. The dam design had to be amended to store increased winter flow from the EGMC by pumping up 100 m for M&I water supply during the summer season. This was made possible by raising the dam height and changing the supply objectives, including the M&I use. The combined capacity of the King Talal and Wadi Arab dams was increased to 130 million m^3 when the dam heights were raised at the end of the 1980s.

WATER-RESOURCES DEVELOPMENT IN THE YARMOUK BASIN The Yarmouk River, which has a mean discharge of 400 million m^3 per year, provides almost half of Jordan's surface-water resources. The water in this river, after allowing some 17 million m^3 per year for downstream

177

users in neighbouring countries, is diverted through the EGMC, an irrigation canal that runs along the Jordan River to serve agricultural water needs in the Jordan valley. The shortage of groundwater resources to meet growing municipal and industrial water demands in north Jordan has required the conveyance of 45 million m³ of water per year from the EGMC to Amman by pumping an extremely high head of 1,300 m from the Deir Alla treatment and pumping station (200 m below sea level) to the terminal reservoir (1,100 m above sea level). The schematics of water-transport systems in north Jordan are shown in fig. 4.3.

THE AL-WUHEDA (MAQARIN) STORAGE DAM SCHEME.   The Al-Wuheda dam, first conceived as early as 1956, is soon to be constructed in the northern area of Maqarin, about 20 km north of Irbid, to store the waters of the Yarmouk River.

The estimated stream-flow at the Maqarin gauging station is 273 million m³ per year on average, which includes the flood waters that are discharged downstream without any use. On the basis of the riparian agreement between Syria and Jordan in 1988, preliminary work for an 800-m-long diversion tunnel was completed at the end of 1989. The reservoir is to have a gross capacity of 225 million m³, with an effective storage volume of 195 million m³ annually. The water would irrigate an additional 3,500 ha in the Jordan valley and supply 50 million m³ of water a year to the Greater Amman area and the eastern heights. A power station near the dam would generate an average of 18,800 kWh of electricity a year. Syria will use part of the water and 75% of the total hydroelectric power generated. The project was stopped, however, by opposition from Israel, which wanted more water in the Yarmouk River downstream.

4.3.2   Groundwater resources

Groundwater has been exploited extensively in northern Jordan because the population was originally concentrated in this region. Groundwater has been used exclusively for M&I water supply, owing to its better quality and higher elevation than any of the surface water resources.

The Amman and Zarqa wellfields, which were developed to supply water for the municipalities of Amman and Zarqa, had the capacity to provide 16–17 million m³ per year in the 1950s to supply 50% of the demand. Azraq oasis, 100 km east of Amman, was developed to supply M&I water for Amman municipality. To meet the increasing demand for M&I use in the 1980s, both the Amman-Zarqa and Azraq well-fields were over-developed, lowering their piezometric heads, which caused deterioration in their quality.

Two important artesian wellfields, the Mukheiba and the Wadi Arab wells, were exploited in the mid-1980s in north-west Jordan. The Mukheiba wells, near the Adasiya intake site of the EGMC, are currently used for irrigation in the Jordan valley through an 11.5-km canal with a capacity of 3 m³/sec. The sustained yield of the wellfield is estimated to be 20–25 million m³ per year, and its quality is suitable for drinking purposes. The Mukheiba wells represent the best available source for incremental supply of M&I water to the Jordan uplands. The Wadi Arab wellfield, located just upstream of the Wadi Arab dam and reservoir, has been developed to tap the aquifers in the Amman formation (B2) with an estimated safe yield of 10 million m³ per year. The highly confined groundwater in the Amman formation is believed to supply a group of springs in the wadi beds which were the source of base flow of the Wadi Arab; abstraction of the artesian water from the formation has substantially reduced the base flow of the Wadi Arab and the Wadi Arab reservoir. The Wadi Arab dam is now largely dependent on pumping from the EGMC for recharge and storage.

Two other wellfields, the Wadi Ajib (15 million m³ of safe yield per year) and the Wadi Dhuleil (20 million m³ of safe yield per year), situated to the north and north-east of Amman, have been exploited for the purpose of local upland irrigation and M&I use (World Bank 1988). The Wadi Ajib wellfield is being over-developed to abstract 14 million m³ per year for M&I water supply and 14 million m³ for irrigation, while the Wadi Dhuleil wellfield is developed exclusively for irrigation purposes. The quality of the aquifer below the irrigated land has suffered progressive deterioration from over-pumping and contamination by irrigation return flows.

The Disi aquifer (350 km south of Amman) is the most precious and extensive aquifer in Jordan. It is being exploited both for M&I use for Aqaba and for arid-land irrigation. Greatly enlarged areas of land have recently been developed for agriculture or are being planned for, which implies much higher extraction rates. As the aquifer is extremely expensive to develop for irrigation because of its depth, irrigated agriculture is unlikely to be economical. Furthermore, Disi as a typical fossil groundwater, source, which with the Al-Wuheda dam, represents Jordan's last substantial unexploited fresh water resource, should be regarded as a strategic water reserve.

179

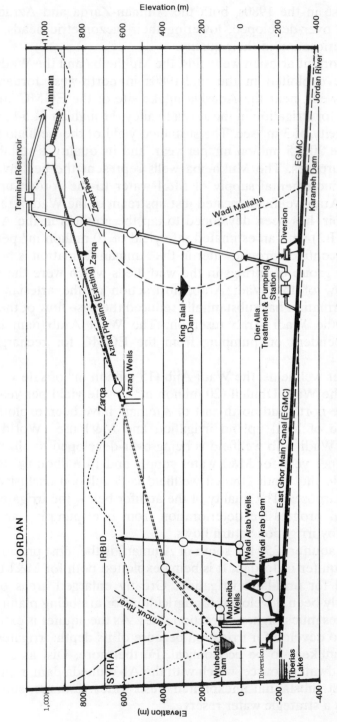

Fig. 4.3A Water transport systems in Jordan—northern portion

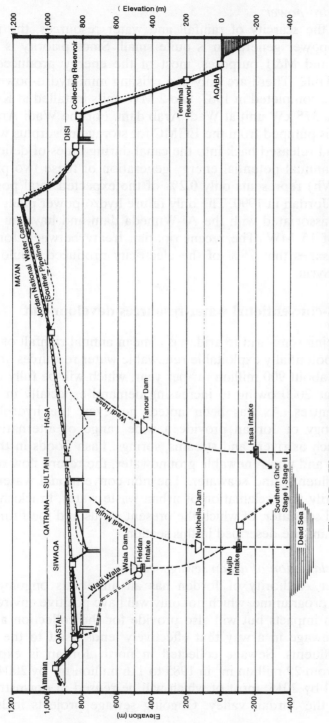

Fig. 4.3B Water transport systems in Jordan—southern portion

4.3.3 Hydro-power

Owing to the scarcity of rainfall and water resources, the potential for hydro-power generation is quite small. Since priority is given to irrigation and M&I purposes, most of the energy produced cannot be dependable. There are only two existing mini-hydro-power plants, which were completed in 1987: two 2 MW units installed at King Talal dam, and a 375 kW unit at Wadi Arab dam. For the Wadi Arab plant, the water is pumped from the EGMC for storage of surplus water (1.2 m^3/sec) and released back into the canal during times of deficit (1 m^3/sec). The annual potential energy generation of these two plants (12 million kWh) represents only 0.2% of the expected total power generation in Jordan in 1990. The only future hydro-power plant foreseen would be associated with the Al-Wuheda dam and have an installed capacity of 15 MW. The recent riparian treaty between Jordan and Syria envisages that 75% of the electricity produced would be consumed in Syria.

4.4 Non-conventional water-resources development

Jordan, being semi-arid to arid, has a mean annual rainfall of only 114 mm. The potentially exploitable renewable water resources are further limited to about 900 million m^3 per year, which will be fully exploited by the year 2000 owing to increasing demand especially in the population centres. As has been noted, however, the hydrology and hydrogeology of Jordan provide a wide range of alternative water sources such as rivers and streams, springs, flash floods in the wadis, renewable and non-renewable groundwater, the return flow of treated sewage effluents, and seawater. The non-conventional water sources are primarily the reclamation of urban waste water, brackish groundwater, and seawater, of which the present status and the future development plans are described in this section.

4.4.1 Reclamation of urban sewage waters

The Water Authority of Jordan has an ambitious ongoing sewage treatment programme, which not only will have positive environmental and health impacts but will also provide for the collection and treatment of sewage in a way that effectively lends itself to the reuse of treated effluents. Sewage collected in north Jordan is expected to increase from 29 million m^3 in 1985 to 116 million m^3 by 2004 and 165 million m^3 by 2015, most of which will be reused in downstream irrigation in the Jordan valley. Ongoing sewage projects include construction of new sewage treatment plants in Baqa and Wadi Sir and extension of the existing plants in Salt and Jerash. These plants have priority because their effluents are discharged upstream of the Zarqa basin and will be reused in downstream irrigation through regulation by the King Talal reservoir.

4.4.2 Brackish groundwater

Brackish groundwater is generally stored in deep aquifers except in the south-west, where the Disi formation or Precambrian complex out-crops. The quality of the brackish groundwater ranges from 1,000–2,000 mg of TDS per litre to 5,000–10,000 mg/l, which is good for neither domestic use nor irrigation. Brackish groundwater with salinity of less than 2,000–3,000 mg/l can be used directly for some crop irrigation, depending on pervious or sandy soil conditions. Another potential use for brackish groundwater is for specific purposes in the mining industry such as for washing water. In general, brackish groundwater can be safely used after desalination or mixing with very fresh water.

Brackish groundwater has been found in some places in the Jordan valley, and has been accidentally detected in some deep sandstone aquifers such as the Kurnub formation on the uplands during either exploratory or exploitation drillings, but no systematic study or inves-tigation of brackish-water potential has been undertaken. However, a large storage potential for brackish groundwater is conceivable in the rather shallow aquifers of the eastern desert of Jordan, including the areas of Azraq, Sirhan, and Hamad. In these areas, the target aquifers will be the Amman–Wadi Sir (B2/A7) formation, which is underlain by the shallow aquifer unit of Rijam (B4). These brackish aquifers may exist at depths of 200–300 m and 500–700 m with TDS of 2,000–5,000 mg/l. From the scanty piezometric data, the depth to the water table from ground level is expected to be only 100–200 m in wadi depres-sions including the Azraq and Sirhan. This brackish groundwater potential is situated only 100–150 km east of Amman, which suggests a potential source of water supply for the Amman municipalities if cost-effective desalination is performed. The most important cost factor in such desalination is the energy cost, which can be controlled by intro-ducing off-peak power operation, taking into account the dominant steam-power generation with high peak demand in Jordan. Recent innovative research in the high-molecular membrane industry could provide the necessary energy saving through the use of low-pressure reverse-osmosis modules for brackish water demineralization.

A large amount of exploitable brackish groundwater is conceivably stored in the deep sandstone aquifers in southern Jordan, such as the Kurnub and Khreim formations. A case study on their nature and potential use for desalination and water supply is provided in the following section.

4.4.3 Seawater

Desalination of seawater for M&I water supply is the principal source of water in the oil-producing Gulf countries. Conventional distillation by the dominant multi-stage flash (MSF) method will be too expensive in Jordan, except for specific projects. Furthermore small-scale MSF desalination, for example to satisfy local water demand for the Aqaba municipal water supply, has a scale demerit to achieve the cost feasibility. Adding seawater desalination by reverse osmosis, however, may improve costs even for small- and medium-scale desalination plants. Thus the Aqaba steam-power station might be viable as a co-generation station either with MSF or RO. Hybrid desalination with MSF-RO and power will be a key element for regional water-resources planning in Aqaba district. Techno-political alternatives, including seawater pumped-storage hydro-powered RO desalination for co-generation, are described in section 5.6 in a case study on the inter-state Aqaba regional economic development plan for peace.

4.5 Case study on hydro-powered brackish-groundwater desalination by reverse osmosis: A proposal for co-generation in the Disi–Aqaba water supply scheme

Aqaba, with a population of 42,400, is the largest city in the Ma'an governorate and the fourth largest city in Jordan (DSJ 1988).

The port of Aqaba is Jordan's only access to the sea and therefore of strategic importance to commerce and industry. The highest growth of water demand is projected in the Ma'an governorate, from 11 million m^3 per year in 1990 to 29 million m^3 in 2005, with the greatest increase being in water demand for industrial use (World Bank 1988). Aqaba regional development will be even more constrained by water shortage for municipal and industrial use because of complete dependence on non-renewable or fossil groundwater in the deep sandstone Disi aquifer, about 50 km north-east from the city of Aqaba.

This section examines the application of mini-hydro-power from groundwater for brackish-groundwater reverse-osmosis desalination, proposing that mini-hydro-power plants and a RO desalting plant

184

should be added to the existing Disi–Aqaba water pipeline system. This new proposal for co-generation would include the following objectives to sustain regional economic development:

» recovery of the potential energy in the existing groundwater pipe-line (trunk main) system, which is being wasted;
» conservation of the non-renewable fresh groundwater in the Disi aquifer, replacing it by developing the brackish groundwater in the Kurnub sandstones;
» desalting the brackish groundwater by hydro-powered reverse osmosis, using some of the recovered hydro-potential energy in the existing pipeline;
» testing the technical feasibility and cost-effectiveness of the pro-posed co-generating application with mini-hydro-power and RO desalination;
» conservation of energy and water resources by introducing hybrid hydro-powered RO desalination with an energy-recovery system.

4.5.1 Background of the Aqaba water supply

Aqaba is situated at the head of the Gulf of Aqaba on the Red Sea, at the southern end of Wadi Araba (fig. 4.2). Only 40 years ago Aqaba was a sleepy little fishing village whose small population lived in mud-brick houses nestling among palm groves which are still a delightful feature of the town.

However, as well as being Jordan's only outlet to the sea, Aqaba occupies a strategic position, providing an important link between the Middle East and East Africa. The port of Aqaba was a strategic point in the war between Iraq and Iran in the 1980s, and again in the Gulf war of 1990–91. It now handles all the sea imports and exports of Jordan as well as much of those for Iraq, Syria, and Lebanon. The volume of traffic through the port has increased spectacularly since just before the Gulf war, and Aqaba is still an important commercial centre. This expansion has been accompanied by rapid growth in industrial development along Jordan's limited coastline.

As a small fishing town, its water needs were readily met from shallow wells dug near the sea which produced sufficient quantities of good fresh water permeating to the sea through the alluvial fan of Wadi Araba. But shortly after World War II, as the demand for water increased, boreholes were drilled further inland. Well No. 1 was constructed in 1958, 2 km north of the sea. In 1964 well No. 2 was drilled further inland and water pumped to a 2,250 m³ reservoir, augmenting the supply.

Over-pumping of these wells resulted in the intrusion of seawater. To satisfy the increasing demand, additional holes were drilled in the deep alluvial deposits of Wadi Yutm. Until the middle 1970s these wells provided the entire water supply for Aqaba, but, with the limited yield of the alluvial aquifer, there have been increasing shortages, especially during the hot summer months, and rationing has been necessary for a number of years.

4.5.2   The Disi aquifer

Since the heart of the project is the water source, and the success of the scheme depends entirely on a correct assessment of the yield of the aquifer, intensive hydro-geological studies have been carried out since 1976 (NRAJ 1977, 1978).

Groundwater flow through the Disi area originates in the Um Sahm mountains, discharging in a north-easterly direction around each end of the geological feature called the Kharawi dyke, which forms a natural underground barrier. The new wellfield at Qa Disi will intercept a large proportion of the flow at present passing round the north-western limit of the dyke and will slowly develop in the groundwater a large depression, centred at Disi. The extent and rate of development of this depression has been simulated by digital computer models (NRAJ 1982). From the model simulation studies that have been carried out it was concluded that the aquifer will support a maximum abstraction from the Qa Disi area of between 17 and 19 million m^3 per year for at least fifty years. The maximum capacity of the scheme has therefore been fixed at 17.5 million m^3 per year.

4.5.3   Disi–Aqaba water supply scheme

The Aqaba water supply scheme comprises four main elements: (1) the wellfield and headworks complex, (2) the trunk main from Disi to Aqaba, (3) the trunk distribution main from Aqaba to a fertilizer factory near the Saudi border, and (4) a distribution network within the town (fig. 4.4). The scheme was completed and has been in operation since the end of 1981.

HEADWORKS.   For the first-stage development to exploit 10 million m^3 per year, seven boreholes 400 m deep were drilled to penetrate the Disi sandstone aquifers. The finished diameter of the upper half of the boreholes is 219 mm and of the lower half 171 mm. Each borehole is equipped with twin submersible pumps delivering water through collecting mains into a reservoir from where the water gravitates to

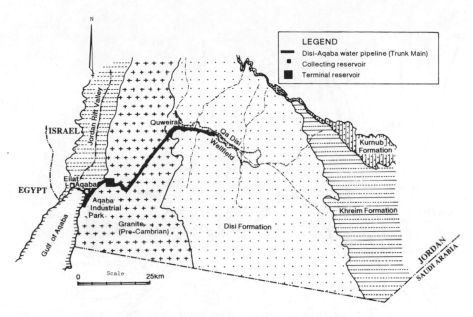

Fig. 4.4   **Disi–Aqaba water supply system**

Aqaba. Power for the pumps is provided by a power station equipped with four diesel generating sets of 550 kW each.

TRUNK MAINS.   A ductile iron trunk main 800–450 mm in diameter and 92 km long carries the water to Aqaba and southwards to the fertilizer factory near the Saudi border. Pressure is broken at three locations along the pipeline, as shown in the profile of the trunk main (fig. 4.5), to limit pressure to a maximum of 25 bar, which is the ceiling bearing capacity of the ductile iron steel pipe used in this project.

A large reservoir of 9,000 m^3 capacity, sited immediately north of Aqaba, provides a buffer to absorb fluctuation in demand downstream and reservoir storage in the event of a pipeline failure. A 4,500 m^3 reservoir is constructed at the fertilizer factory to provide service storage for the factory and for other industrial developments expected in the same area.

PROJECT COST.   The total cost of the Disi–Aqaba water supply project was estimated at JD 11 million (US$44 million at 1978 prices of the Jordan Water Supply Corporation), including the following main cost elements:

187

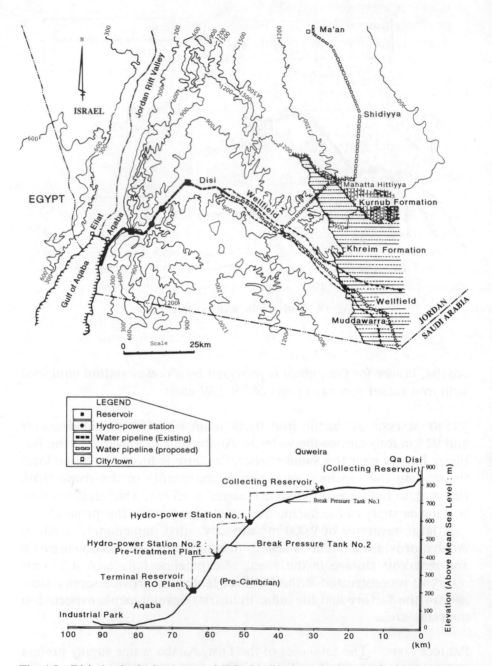

Fig. 4.5 Disi–Aqaba hydro-powered RO desalination scheme and brackish groundwater

— borehole construction, US$5,464,000,
— borehole pumps, US$1,110,000,
— generating (diesel) equipment, US$2,648,000,
— pipeline/trunk main, US$21,172,000,
— distribution, US$13,104,000,
— valves and specials, US$444,000.

The total cost of the project is estimated to be US$74.8 million, assuming price escalation at 170% from 1978 to 1990 (IMF international financial statistics, 1990/1978).

4.5.4 Introduction of mini-hydro development

The theoretical hydro-potential of the Qa Disi wellfield, which is situated at an elevation of 840 m above sea level, is preliminarily estimated to be 5.2 MW by assuming a flow discharge of 0.663 m^3/sec with an effective differential head of water of 800 m (95% of the total head). This hydro-potential energy is being wasted by breaking the water pressure at three locations along the pipeline as described above.

This study aims to evaluate the effectiveness of using the hydro-potential in the trunk main between Disi and Aqaba by installing a series of mini-hydro stations in the existing trunk main at each point with a difference head of water of about 200 m. The head difference between the collecting reservoir (840 m) and the terminal reservoir (220 m) is 620 m. The hydro-potential of the existing trunk main between the collecting reservoir and the terminal reservoir is estimated to be 3.2 MW, using the equations given in section 3.6.3 to evaluate the hydro-potential and power.

The flow discharge is assumed to be 17.5 million m^3 per year (0.555 m^3/sec), which is equivalent to a design capacity of 0.663 m^3/sec with a unit operating time of 21 hours per day. The effective differential head of water is estimated to be 589 m, assuming a 5% friction head loss.

From the optimal layout of the pressure pipeline system (fig. 4.5), two hydro-power stations would be installed, at ground elevations of 630 m and 410 m respectively.

By assuming a synthesized efficiency of 0.80 and a generating efficiency of 0.873, the installed capacity and annual power output are estimated to be 2 MW and 15,900 MWh per year respectively. The details are shown in table 4.1.

4.5.5 Conservation of fossil groundwater in Disi

Disi is currently exploited for M&I water supply for Aqaba (8.5 million m^3 per year) and for irrigated agriculture. The recorded extraction for

Table 4.1 **Installed capacity and annual power output of Disi–Aqaba groundwater-hydro scheme**

Station	Elevation (m)	Effective head (m)	Installed capacity (kW)	Potential power generation (MWh/year)	
				Hydro-power[a]	RO recovery[b]
1	630	200	1,039	7,946	—
2	410	200	1,039	7,946	—
3	220	180	—	—	810
TOTAL			2,078	15,900	810

NOTE: Friction head loss assumed to be 5% of the total head. Synthesized efficiency assumed to be 0.80. Load factor of mini hydro-power generation, 83.7% (0.555/0.663). Elevation of collecting reservoir, 840 m above sea level. Elevation of terminal reservoir, 220 m above sea level.

a. Groundwater hydro-power potential.
b. Energy recovery from hydro-powered RO desalination.

1986 is 14.5 million m³, but 3,000 ha have now been developed for agriculture, implying an extraction of over 30 million m³ per year, and licences have been granted to drill wells for the irrigation of over 20,000 ha, implying an annual extraction of over 200 million m³. It should be noted that the aquifer is extremely expensive to develop for irrigation for growing wheat: the water table lies 250–300 m below the surface and wells have to be drilled to a depth of 500–1,000 m. Furthermore, Disi represents, with Al-Wuheda dam, Jordan's last substantial unexploited water resource and deserves to be regarded as a strategic water reserve. A World Bank study (1988) recommended that the aquifer be monitored at present abstraction levels to confirm the most reasonable long-term yield for M&I supply in south Jordan.

4.5.6 Brackish groundwater resources

The Kurnub group of Lower Cretaceous age underlies almost all of Jordan. It is composed of sandstones with poorly to very well cemented facies interbedding silts, clays, shales, and occasionally dolomitic layers. It is thought to be a deep aquifer unit with a large storage potential and a maximum thickness of about 1,000 m or more. The water table, however, is about 200–300 m or more below the ground level, and permeability and salinity vary in place and depth. The quality of the groundwater varies from 300 to 2,800 mg of TDS per litre, but it is considered to be mostly brackish except for minor recharging areas in the north-western highlands.

190

In southern Jordan, the Disi aquifer is unconformably overlain by the Khreim formation, which is about 100–300 m thick and stores brackish groundwater in its upper to middle sections. Brackish groundwater is also found in the Kurnub formation along the southern edges of the Jafr basin about 25 km north from the Disi (fig. 4.5). The depth of the pumping water level will range from 100 to 250 m in the Khreim formation between Disi and Muddawwara, while it is as deep as 230–325 m in the Kurnub formation along the southern fringe of the Jafr basin. These brackish waters with salinity between 1,000 and 5,000 mg of TDS per litre in southern Jordan would mostly be fossil with limited amounts of natural recharge from rain. The storage potential, however, has been estimated to be as large as 16,600 million m³ (NRAJ 1986). Brackish-groundwater development with desalination may thus be able to replace existing fossil-groundwater abstraction from the Disi aquifer.

4.5.7 *Hydro-powered brackish-groundwater desalination by RO*

Co-generation, that is annexing of a brackish-groundwater RO desalination unit to a groundwater-hydro system would develop the hydro-potential energy in the differential head of water between the Disi wellfield at 840 m and the Aqaba terminal reservoir at 220 m. Two-thirds of the differential head of water would be used to generate hydro-powered electricity and one-third to produce the hydraulic pressure for permeating the RO (fig. 4.5). The proposed co-generating system for the Disi–Aqaba water supply scheme would include the following objectives and measures:

» developing clean hydro-potential energy in the existing water trunk main between Disi and Aqaba, amounting to 620 m of differential head of water, thus indirectly conserving fossil (oil) energy in generating electricity;

» co-production of hydro-powered electricity and fresh water for Aqaba M&I water supply;

» development of brackish groundwater resources in the Khreim and/or Kurnub formations, conserving fossil groundwater in the Disi aquifer, which has been being abstracted for M&I water supply for Aqaba since 1970;

» direct use of hydro-potential energy for generating pressure for reverse osmosis, utilizing part of the hydro-potential energy at 150–250 m of differential head of water in the trunk main, whose pressure at 15–25 kg/cm² is the optimum requirement for operating reverse osmosis;

» pioneer research on brackish-groundwater RO desalination in Jor-

191

dan, evaluating the cost-effectiveness of minimizing operation and maintenance costs, which are a major cost factor in desalination engineering.

Brackish groundwater would be pumped at a rate of 0.663 m³/sec from the Khreim and/or Kurnub formations underlying the area of Disi-Muddawwara-Shidiya, and be conveyed to a collecting reservoir at an elevation of 840 m. For the purpose of this case study, the design value of the salinity of the feed water is assume to be 4,000 mg of TDS per litre.

The brackish water would flow down from the collecting reservoir at 840 m elevation to the desalination plant and terminal reservoir at 220 m through the existing pipeline system, passing two mini-hydro-power stations by steps at 630 m and 410 m respectively. The installed capacity of the two stations is estimated to be 2,078 kW and the annual power output 15,900 MWh.

The hydro-powered RO system would have three parts: a pre-treatment unit, a pressure pipeline unit, and the RO unit itself. The pre-treatment unit would be sited just beside the outlet of the second mini-hydro-power station at 410 m elevation and would include dual-media filters (hydro-anthracite and fine sands) and cartridge filters (5-μm size). After passing through the cartridge filter, the flow would pass through a pressure pipeline (the trunk main) between 410 m and 220 m to obtain a hydraulic pressure of 18 kg/cm², which would be used directly to overcome the osmotic pressure and permeate the RO membrane. The main heart of the RO unit is a low-pressure-type membrane, spiral-wound in a composite-type 8-inch-diameter module, with the following specifications:

— salt rejection rate, 87.5%,
— design operating pressure, 18 kg/cm²,
— design quantity of permeate, 30 m³ per day,
— maximum operating water temperature, 40°C,
— pH of feed water, 6.0–6.5 (controlled at the pre-treatment unit).

A unit line of the RO vessel would consist of a series circuit of six modules. Recovery is estimated to be 70% of the feed water, including 40,100 m³ per day of permeate with a salinity of 500 mg TDS per litre and 10,200 m³ of brine reject with 17,700 mg/l. The effective pressure of the brine reject is estimated to be 15 kg/cm², assuming a friction loss of 3 kg/cm² in the RO circuit. The potential energy recovery from the RO brine reject is preliminarily estimated to be 136 kW, assuming the total efficiency of the turbine generator to be 80%, which would generate 810,000 kWh of electricity per year with a load factor of 68%.

Another alternative would be to develop 0.72 m³/sec of brackish groundwater to produce 43,400 m³ of permeate per day, which is equivalent to the current water supply volume of 15.8 million m³ per year.

UNIT WATER COST.   The total investment cost for the proposed hydro-powered RO desalination, based on 1990 prices with 8% interest during three years' construction, is preliminarily estimated to be US$56,088,000, with an annual capital cost of US$2,677,000, comprising the following major elements:
— pre-treatment, US$6,468,000,
— desalting plant, US$10,306,000,
— RO membrane/equipment, US$12,417,000,
— control and operating system, US$871,000,
— appurtenant works, US$3,954,000,
— powerline and substation, US$1,143,000,
— energy recovery/turbine, US$255,000
— *subtotal* (US$35,414,000);
— design and construction management, US$9,111,000;
— financial expenditure, US$11,563,000.
   The annual cost of the operation and maintenance is estimated to be US$2,631,000, including the following main cost elements:
— labour, US$544,000,
— material supply, US$272,000,
— chemicals, US$1,089,000,
— membrane replacement, US$726,000.
   The above cost estimates are based on 1990 prices and the following assumptions:
— plant life, 20 years,
— membrane life (replacement), 3 years,
— cost benefit from energy recovery not included,
— costs for source water (groundwater) and pipeline/distribution not included.
   The unit water cost for 14.6 million m³ of design annual product water is estimated to be US$0.41/m³.

COST FOR GROUNDWATER HYDRO-POWER.   The capital cost of the proposed two mini-hydro-power stations, each equipped with a 1 MW Pelton turbine, is preliminarily estimated to be US$2 million, accounting for only 5.7% of the capital cost of the RO unit. The generated power of 16 million kWh per year will be used in part to supply electricity for pumping the groundwater wells and in part to recover the investment cost of the plants. The costs of existing hydraulic structures such as pipelines and reservoirs are referred in section 4.5.3 above.

OTHER DEVELOPMENT ALTERNATIVES.   After yielding its hydro-potential energy in the recovery unit, the pressure-free brine water at 17,700 mg of TDS per litre would be discharged directly into the Gulf of Aqaba, where it would combine harmlessly with seawater at 45,000 mg/l; or it could be used for blending with distilled water if a thermal or solar seawater desalination system were constructed. The desalination of seawater at Aqaba will be an important means of supplying fresh water from non-conventional sources, which may include the following four options:
— distillation by conventional MSF,
— RO desalination,
— solar-distillation,
— hybrid MSF and RO desalination.
   Non-conventional water-resources development alternatives including hydro-powered brackish-groundwater desalination and seawater desalination at Aqaba can therefore be integrated into the framework of a regional water master plan that would make the region self-supporting.
   A pumped-storage application with seawater RO desalination for co-generation in the context of an inter-state Aqaba regional economic development plan is discussed in section 5.6.

4.6   Non-conventional water-resources development in the national water master plan of Jordan

The potential contribution of non-conventional water-resources development, including the proposed co-generation with hydro-powered RO desalination, in a national water master plan for Jordan for the twenty-first century is studied here, taking into account that 95% or more of the national renewable water resources are going to be fully exploited to meet the increasing demand, especially in the population centres, by the year 2000. Non-conventional water-resources development will be increasingly important in such planning.

4.6.1   Development alternatives and priority
A general characteristic of non-conventional water resources is that they are generally more complex to develop and operate than con-

ventional sources, and they are almost always more expensive. In most cases, non-conventional measures involve considerably more risk than conventional solutions, and no single non-conventional solution is suitable for all water-short areas. At the same time, by providing water to an arid area, non-conventional water resources may offer an opportunity for development previously considered impossible.

In any situation where a conventional source of water can be developed, it will almost always be preferred to a non-conventional source. However, if conventional groundwater or surface water supplies are inadequate, consideration should be given to some of the non-conventional water-resource techniques. Accordingly, non-conventional water resources are considered here in the context of a national water master plan for Jordan.

CONVENTIONAL ALTERNATIVES. Conventional alternatives comprise fresh surface water and fresh renewable and non-renewable ground-water.

The main potential for further *surface water* utilization in Jordan is through the construction of new water-storage facilities on the Yarmouk River and rift-side wadis, including:
>> the Al Wuheda dam on the Yarmouk,
>> development of the northern Ghor side wadis (Karameh, Kifranja, Al-Yabis, and raising the Kafrein dam),
>> development of the southern Ghor side wadis (Wala recharge dam, Nkheila dam, Tannour dam).
The most important of these will be the Al-Wuheda dam, with a gross capacity of 230 million m^3. The total gross water storage potential of the proposed projects has been estimated to be 300–350 million m^3.

The potential for further development of *renewable groundwater* resources is small. Current intensive abstraction amounts to 333 million m^3 per year, which accounts for more than 90% of the estimated long-term safe yield of 356 million m^3. More attention needs to be given not to development but to management of the aquifer system, taking into account the need for sustainable development to avoid over-extraction and deteriorating quality.

The main potential for *non-renewable groundwater* lies in the fossil aquifer of Disi, Jordan's last major exploitable source of good-quality water after the Al-Wuheda dam. The Disi groundwater scheme will require expensive conveyance over a distance of about 350 km to the population centres of the north-west highlands (Amman). The mining yield potential, which has been evaluated by a series of computer model simulation studies, has been estimated to be 110 million m³ per year for over 100 years. This non-renewable alternative should be regarded as a strategic reserve, guided by careful monitoring of the aquifer and stepwise development over a decade.

The Disi aquifer is part of an extensive inter-state deep sandstone aquifer system in the Arabian peninsula underlying south-eastern Jordan and north-western Saudi Arabia. In the early 1980s Jordan feared that the hydraulic influence of Saudi Arabia's intensive abstraction might cross the state boundary. However, the rapid increase in Saudi abstraction from the Tabuk wellfield between 1982 and 1985 dropped the pumping levels by more 120 m of water head, and in its Fifth Development Plan (1990–1995) the government of Saudi Arabia decided to cut part of the national water supply by decreasing the abstraction of non-renewable groundwater for the supply of irrigation. From the experience in Saudi Arabia, the economic limit of abstraction from the Disi aquifer will probably be reached much sooner than expected.

NON-CONVENTIONAL ALTERNATIVES.   Alternatives for the development of non-conventional water resources available to Jordan include the following:

» desalination of brackish groundwater and seawater, including co-generation, groundwater-hydro, and hydro-powered RO desalination,
» the reclamation and reuse of municipal sewage effluents,
» weather modification,
» inter-state water transportation, including the Euphrates–North Jordan transmission scheme and the Peace Pipeline project.

Brackish groundwater reserves are found in most deep aquifer systems, including the Middle to Lower Cretaceous sequences such as the Ajlun and Kurnub formations. In the extensive eastern desert, groundwater generally has a brackish nature, and is even found in shallow aquifer systems, including the Amman–Wadi Sir formation. The salinity of such brackish groundwater is in the range of 2,000–5,000 mg of TDS per litre, which fits within the effective range of reverse-osmosis desalination.

In 1982 Jordan's first RO desalination plant, with an installed capacity of 80,000 US gallons (300 m³) per day, was commissioned at the Zarqa oil refinery, where the supply source of the groundwater had been contaminated with increasing salinity, from a TDS content of 336 mg/l in the 1960s to 1,700 mg/l in 1980 (Alawin 1983).

The most promising brackish groundwater resources are to be found in the Amman–Wadi Sir (B2/A7) formation in and around the Azraq springs, about 100 km east of Amman/Zarqa. The priority use for brackish-groundwater RO desalination of the Azraq wellfield will be for M&I water supply, since the piezometric head of the B4 aquifer system is being lowered by over-pumping and is suffering from increasing salinity. The Azraq wellfield has the following characteristics:
— piezometric elevation, 500–600 m (Amman is at 800–1,000 m),
— depth to groundwater table, 50–200 m,
— 100 km distant from the population centre of Amman,
— suitable salinity range between 1,000 and 5,000 mg of TDS per litre.

Brackish groundwater in deep aquifer systems such as the Kurnub formation has a depth to the water table of more than 200–250 m. The storage potential for brackish groundwater in deep aquifer systems is more than that for fresh water reserves in shallow aquifer systems. The hydrological characteristics of brackish groundwater systems, however, range between renewable and non-renewable. Careful assessment and management of the brackish groundwater resources would be required to sustain development by the application of desalination.

Seawater desalination is possible only in the Gulf of Aqaba. Small-scale seawater RO desalination has been carried out for boiler water supply at the Aqaba steam-power plant since the mid-1980s. It is quite clear that the cost of desalting seawater is usually three to five times as high as desalting brackish water (see Appendix A). Water for Aqaba is presently being supplied by developing fossil groundwater from the Disi aquifer, and it is recommended in this study that this source should be replaced by the desalination of brackish groundwater in the adjacent Kurnub aquifer by a hybrid hydro-powered RO system, which can be expected to reduce both the cost and the energy requirement and will help to sustain valuable groundwater resources as a long-term policy. A proposal for seawater desalination, to be coordinated with the National Water Carrier of Jordan, which would convey water from the sea to the population centre of Amman, would require lifting water about 1,000 m or more. At present, seawater desalination has no feasibility except to supply water for M&I use in the Aqaba coastal region. There is still the opportunity to desalinate seawater and lift the product water up to a 1,000 m elevation in the future by developing new renewable-energy alternatives, including solar-energy conversion and ocean-thermal-energy conversion in the hot and arid climatic region of the Gulf of Aqaba.

It is proposed that priority should be given to the development of

197

brackish-groundwater desalination for municipal water supply and that feasibility studies might be undertaken of the following two possibilities:

» the desalination of brackish groundwater at Azraq to supply water for Amman,

» hybrid hydro-powered RO desalination of brackish groundwater from the Kurnub aquifer to supply water for Aqaba.

The *reclamation and reuse of municipal sewage effluents* as an additional water resource continues to increase potential water resources, corresponding to the increases in water demand and supply in Greater Amman, which consumes about 60% of the total water supply in Jordan. Almost all the sewage effluents in the Amman-Zarqa region are discharged into the Zarqa River system, whether treated or not. The Kherbet Samra sewage plant, which collects the effluents from metropolitan Amman and Zarqa, treated 33.2 million m^3 in 1989 and discharged it into the Zarqa River to enhance the base flow of the river system. The King Talal dam on the lower reaches of the Zarqa River subsequently harvests all the sewage effluents that flow into the river system. The Zarqa is mainly polluted by the untreated sewage effluents in its upper reaches, while there is some natural purification in both the flowing and impounding processes. The sewage effluents harvested in the King Talal reservoir are reused exclusively for irrigation water supply in the Ghor (Jordan valley). The exceptional topography of the north-west plateau and the escarpment of the Jordan valley permits reuse for irrigation in the valley of the bulk of the return flow of water used in the uplands.

Weather modification, which includes artificially induced precipitation, or cloud seeding, could probably provide an inexpensive source of water under certain meteorological conditions. However, specific verification is necessary in each mountainous region of Jordan. Experiments on the upper Jordan River in Israel provided encouraging results under the particular orogenic and climatological conditions on the southern slopes of the Anti-Lebanon range (Mount Hermon), where the ground elevation exceeds 1,500–2,000 m, with an annual rainfall of more than 500–1,000 mm (Kally 1974). In Jordan, the potential area for cloud seeding is limited to Ajlun mountain. Cloud seeding may not be very promising, however, since the orogenic and climatic conditions of the Ajlun mountain zone are less attractive than those of the upper Jordan River in Israel. Cloud seeding on the south-eastern slopes of Mount Hermon in Syria, where the headwaters of the Yarmouk River originate, may have the same effect as experienced in

Israel. In any case, international cooperation is needed to develop a weather-modification program.

Inter-state water transportation alternatives may include the Euphrates transmission scheme to Jordan and the Peace Pipeline scheme. The transport of water by tanker and barge is a more remote alternative for Jordan, since the main demand area is in northern Jordan, where the ground elevation exceeds 800–1,000 m.

A feasibility study of the Euphrates–North Jordan transmission scheme was made in 1983. This would transport water from the Euphrates River in Iraq to north Jordan (Amman) by water pipeline. Al Qaim, situated on the Euphrates where it enters Iraq, at an elevation of 163–165 m, offers the highest abstraction level, thereby minimizing the overall static lift between the river and the delivery point in north Jordan. The scheme was scheduled to abstract up to 160 million m^3 of water annually (5 m^3/sec) from the Euphrates River. The pipeline system was designed for a 5 m^3/sec rated capacity, 605 km in length, 1.5–2.0 m diameter, 830 m static lift, and 1,380 m of total pumping head (NPCJ 1983). Such an inter-state water transport scheme might be technically and economically feasible if the water were to be used for domestic purposes.

Turkey's ambitious Peace Pipeline proposal, which aims to transfer water from the Ceyhan and Seyhan Rivers in Turkey to eight states in the Arabian peninsula, includes an assumed potential water delivery of 600,000 m^3 per day (219 million m^3 per year) to Jordan.

Both the Euphrates–North Jordan and the Peace Pipeline schemes have been put aside, however, owing to political constraints, including interstate riparian-rights questions on the Euphrates River, where the use of water as a political weapon has been increasing. These interstate water-transportation projects have now been emphatically rejected by all Arab states, who have said that if necessary they will depend on non-conventional waters in their territories, including seawater desalination. Development priority is therefore likely to be given to marginal waters as non-conventional water resources, taking into account not only technical, financial, and economic but also political feasibility.

4.6.2 Desalination development strategy in the national water master plan

Desalination to develop previously unusable brackish groundwater and seawater as sources of potable water, including energy-saving applications of co-generation and hydro-powered RO processes, should be included in the context of a master plan for the development of the water resources of Jordan. In such a plan, the use of this relatively expensive water-treatment process should be entered into with caution, after the possibility of utilizing more conventional and possibly less expensive sources of water has been carefully weighed. The master plan should include measures for the conservation and optimum development and management of all these natural resources. Steps should be taken to ensure the rational use of water and minimize wastage. Water quality should be maintained at acceptable levels, and an appropriate pricing policy should be established, including the diversion of water from irrigation to municipal and industrial use. The use of fossil groundwater in Disi for growing wheat is one particularly questionable application.

Elements that should be included in a water master plan for the next twenty to thirty years may be delineated by decades into short-, medium-, and long-term development stages as follows, with special focus on the inclusion of non-conventional water resources:

≫ short-term development strategy (1990–2000)
— water conservation and management, including rehabilitation and enhancement of existing hydraulic structures,
— the Al-Wuheda dam,
— the North Jordan National Water Carrier,
— storage dams on the side wadis,
— retention dams on the wadis, including the Wala groundwater recharge dam,
— renewable groundwater development in southern Jordan,
— *waste-water treatment and reuse*, Zarqa River–King Talal dam system;

≫ medium-term development strategy (2000–2010)
— diversion of water from irrigation to M&I use, including the application of more efficient irrigation techniques,
— *desalination of brackish groundwater*, including co-generation and hydro-powered RO applications,
— *desalination of seawater*,
— Mediterranean–Dead Sea conduit scheme, including *solar-hydro and hydro-powered RO desalination* by joint development between Israel, Palestine, and Jordan;

≫ Long-term development strategy (2010–2020)
— *inter-state water transportation*, including transportation by pipeline, tankers, and barges,
— *weather modification*, including an artificial-rain project on the

upper Jordan and Yarmouk Rivers to be undertaken jointly by Israel, Syria, and Jordan.

The most important, and the highest-priority schemes will be the Al-Wuheda dam and other storage dams on the side-wadis of the East Bank. These storage, flood-retention, or groundwater-recharge dam schemes would reduce the inflow from the river system into the Dead Sea and be linked with the Mediterranean–Dead Sea conduit scheme in the context of an inter-state basin-development master plan which would be beneficial to Jordan, Palestine, and Israel. Further discussion of the water politics of inter-state basin development of the Jordan River system is included in chapter 5.

5

Solar-hydro power and pumped-storage co-generation in hydro-powered reverse-osmosis desalination in inter-state development of the Jordan River basin

5.1 Background and objectives

5.1.1 Background

By the year 2000, water—not oil—will be the predominant resource issue of the Middle East. The situation will be particularly acute in non-oil-producing countries such as Israel and Jordan, where the renewable water resources such as fresh surface waters and groundwater will have already been exploited or will soon be fully developed.

Concerns over the global environment and the Gulf (oil) crisis associated with Iraq's invasion of Kuwait in August 1990 have improved our understanding of the importance of clean energy such as non-polluting hydroelectric power.

A solar-hydro scheme using the evaporation power of the Dead Sea and known as the Mediterranean–Dead Sea (MDS) canal scheme was proposed by Israel in 1980. The scheme, which would have multiple socio-economic and political ramifications, was intended to convey water from the Mediterranean to the Dead Sea via canals and tunnels, utilizing the height difference of around 400 m to generate 600 MW of electricity. In addition, proposals were made to use the water for cooling nuclear power stations rated at 1,800 MW, and to investigate the feasibility of generating 1,500 MW from Dead Sea as a solar pond. Up till now there has been no presentation of the concept of sharing resources with riparian states and no effort at joint development. The MDS project was soon put aside, owing to strong opposition from Arab states and others and to confusion following the drop in world oil-market prices in 1984.

Major constraints to realizing the 1980 MDS project were:

>> Jordanian fears of environmental and economic effects—which may no longer be valid;

>> the failure to consider the concept of shared resources, including riparian rights to the Dead Sea, and the absence of any effort at joint development between the states—all of which could now be removed by linkage of the MDS and Al-Wuheda dam projects;

>> territorial questions on the West Bank—which, with cooperation with the Palestinians, could now be dealt with separately from cooperation in water development.

There have been several changes in the political situation since the Iraqi invasion of Kuwait in 1990–1991 that may facilitate a comprehensive resolution of Israeli-Arab problems. This may make integrated development not only technically and economically feasible but politically desirable and urgent.

5.1.2 Objectives

The objectives of this chapter may be stated as follows:

>> to delineate the strategic dimensions of water problems in one of the world's driest regions—Israel, Palestine, and Jordan—where the peace of the world has been at risk for more than forty-five years;

>> to evaluate the techno-political feasibility and cost-effectiveness of the proposed co-generation system for the MDS scheme, using hydro-power with seawater RO desalination to produce fresh drinking water for the inter-state region of the Dead Sea;

>> to elaborate techno-political alternatives in the inter-state basin-development master planning of the Jordan River system, by combining non-conventional alternatives with advanced water technologies;

>> to re-assess the much-discussed Mediterranean–Dead Sea conduit scheme, which has again been revived with the end of the Gulf war in 1992 and the international political drive for peace in the Middle East in 1993–1994 and an end to the Arab-Israeli conflict.

5.2 Water resources of Israel

In an average year rainfall over Israel is estimated to be 5×10^9 m^3; about 3.5×10^9 m^3 of this is lost through irretrievable absorption-evaporation, leaving only 1.5×10^9 m^3 per year to reach the country's water reservoirs on the surface and underground (Gisser and Pohoryles 1977).

The characteristics of Israel's water resources may be summarized as follows:

» Rain falls only in winter, with wide fluctuation, ranging from around 25% of the long-term average in dry years to 160% in particularly rainy years.

» Most water sources are situated in the northern and central regions of the country.

» Most water sources are located at low elevations, from which water must be pumped with high operation and maintenance costs.

Owing to the substantial fluctuations in annual rainfall, groundwater aquifers are conceived as more reliable potential reservoirs than surface storage. About one-third of Israel's water use is dependent on surface water resources, mainly the Jordan River. Groundwater is therefore a major source of supply, amounting to two-thirds of national consumption. The aquifers concerned are dependent on limestone formations 300–400 m thick and deep sandstone formations 600–800 m thick. The deepest groundwater wells penetrate to a depth of 1,000 m or more.

Marginal or non-conventional waters—brackish groundwater, seawater, and treated sewage effluents—are looked to mainly for additional water supplies for the next decade.

5.2.1 Potential water resources

Potential renewable water resources depend exclusively on precipitation, which, in addition to fluctuating considerably from year to year, has significant spatial variations. Over half of Israel receives annual rainfall of less than 180 mm, while it is 1,000 mm or more in the high mountains of northern Israel. Although renewable water resources accumulate in the north, the demand is concentrated in the central and southern regions. The rainy season begins in October or November and ends in April or May; for the rest of the year there is very little rain, three or four months being completely rainless. Replenishment of groundwater occurs exclusively in winter, while irrigation with its highest water demand occurs in the summer.

Of the average 1.5×10^9 m^3 of rainfall reaching the country's surface and underground water reservoirs per year, the Sea of Galilee in the north stores effectively receives 0.5×10^9 m^3, while aquifers in the coastal plain store 1×10^9 m^3.

5.2.2 Surface water resources

Surface drainage is mainly provided by a few streams flowing east and west. Throughout the southern half of the state, streams are ephemeral.

About one-third of Israel's potential usable fresh water is surface water, which depends largely on the Jordan River. The river is entirely land-locked, terminating in the Dead Sea. Its hydrology and water resources have been discussed in section 2.5.

Galilee as a whole is the wettest region of the state, receiving in places over 1,000 mm of rainfall per year, and both springs and streams are more numerous than in other areas.

The northern Harod (Bet She'an) River, a tributary of the lower Jordan, is replenished by abundant springs or groundwater flow but has high salinity and is useless for irrigation purposes. Its brackish water is the major source of contamination of the lower Jordan. However, RO desalination promises to salvage 20 million m^3 of water per year or more.

The Yarqon River is a short stream on the coastal plain fed by large springs at Rosh Ha'ayin, 15 km east of Tel Aviv. The Yarqon River basin lies on economic aquifers with high development potential.

The mountainous and hilly zones in Samaria and Judaea receive more than 500 mm of average annual rainfall, but surface water is not plentiful. The permeable strata dipping westward are valuable for groundwater recharge to the underlying potential aquifers.

5.2.3 Groundwater resources

The main aquifers to supply water for irrigation and municipal and industrial use are found in permeable strata of Cenomanian-Turonian carbonate rocks and Plio-Pleistocene sandstones.

Some of the main sources of groundwater are the thick carbonate rock aquifers of the Cenomanian-Turonian formations, which consist mainly of dolomite and limestone intercalating some clay and chalk layers. The total thickness amounts to 600-700 m in the central and northern parts of Israel. The aquifer supplies several hundred million cubic meters of water annually, which is a significant portion of Israel's water supply (Schneider 1967).

The coastal plain is rich in water resources from wells and springs. Up to 700 mm of precipitation may be received per year over the hills, and permeable strata dipping westward yield valuable groundwater for the coastal plains. This gave the early Jewish settlers a wide choice of sites for their villages, while today it is one reason why Israel wishes to retain control of the West Bank as a major source of groundwater recharge. The aquifer lies at depths of 18–120 m in the Middle Plio-Pleistocene formation. Groundwater abstraction from the coastal aquifer amounts to around 30% of the total water supply volume in Israel (Beaumont et al. 1988).

5.2.4 Non-conventional water resources

The marginal waters of Israel are composed primarily of brackish water, seawater, and urban waste water. The potential contribution of marginal waters to meet the anticipated water demand include the following alternatives:

>> reclaimed sewage effluents of the Dan region (Greater Tel Aviv),
>> water harvesting for the Sea of Galilee by artificial rainfall,
>> brackish waters to the north of the Sea of Galilee and in the south in the area adjoining the port town of Eilat on the Red Sea,
>> seawater desalination,
>> peak-demand power generation by seawater pumped storage by the Dead Sea,
>> RO desalination of water with co-generation of power for peak-demand needs, by the Mediterranean–Dead Sea conduit scheme,

The salinity of the brackish groundwaters in the north near Lake Tiberias and in the south in the area adjoining the port of Eilat on the Red Sea is in the range of 1,000–10,000 mg of total dissolved solid (TDS) per litre, which is suitable for desalination by RO at a reasonable cost. The M&I water supply for Eilat is heavily dependent on the RO desalination of this brackish groundwater. Renewable supplies from the underlying aquifers have been estimated at about 200 million m^3 per year (Buras and Darr 1979). Seawater desalination by distillation such as by the multi-stage flash (MSF) process used in the Gulf states is still too expensive for non-oil-producing countries such as Israel and Jordan.

The second source of marginal water is urban waste water, for which the demand has been increasing since the late 1970s and early 1980s. On the basis of returnable useful flows of 65% of domestic and 30% of industrial water consumption, the urban waste-water potential for 1985 was estimated at 370 million m^3 (Buras and Darr 1979).

Evaluation of the marginal waters in a national water master plan will be needed, taking into account recent innovative research on saline water conversion, including the desalination of brackish water and seawater by the RO process.

5.2.5 *Water consumption in Israel*

Almost all renewable water resources such as surface water in the upper part of the Jordan River and groundwater in the limestone and deep sandstones aquifers, of which the potential supply is preliminarily estimated at $1.5–1.6 \times 10^9$ m^3 per year, were already being exploited by the end of the 1970s. Indeed, the demand had already exceeded the potential of renewable resources by the late 1960s. Annual water consumption in Israel was 1,565 million m^3 in 1973, including 1,180 million m^3 (75.4%) for agriculture, 288 million m^3 (18.4%) for domestic use, and 97 million m^3 (6.2%) for industry. It was then predicted that by 1992 water-resource development to provide a further 8.1 million m^3 for agriculture, 20.5 million m^3 for domestic use, and 28.5 million m^3 for industry would be needed (Buras and Darr 1978).

Israel's per capita consumption (537 m^3 per year; 86 m^3 per year for domestic purposes only) is not out of line with other industrial nations, although it is as much as double that of its neighbours (Naff and Matson 1984). The agricultural sector is responsible for more than three-quarters of Israel's total water use.

5.3 Water-resources development and management in Israel

The primary users of the waters of the Jordan River are Israel and Jordan. Between them, the Jordan River system has been extensively exploited; it satisfies about half of their combined water demand. The other riparian states are Lebanon and Syria; their use of the Jordan River at present is minor as compared to the others, and satisfies about 5% of their total demand for water.

The most comprehensive water-resources development and management in the Middle East to date is undoubtedly found in Israel. Following the establishment of the state in 1948, the government decided to undertake a comprehensive programme of water-resource development based on the ideas outlined by Lowdermilk (1944; cf. Appendix C). Two factors had considerable importance in the initial stages of development: the first was the lack of capital in the new state, and the second was the urgent necessity to provide water supplies for the many immigrants pouring into the country.

207

Up to about 1965 and completion of the National Water Carrier, there was enough water awaiting development to satisfy all needs. All that was required was new schemes to tap the resources and make efficient use of them. From the late 1960s onwards it became extremely difficult to make any extra water supplies available, and so emphasis had to be shifted to making more efficient use of the available supplies.

In the late 1970s and early 1980s Israel had to face a growing demand for water from the urban and industrial sectors of its economy. It will now have to face the issue of diverting water from the agricultural sector, which still accounts for more than three-quarters of the country's total water use, to the municipal and industrial sectors of the economy.

5.3.1   Initial stage of water-resource development
Initially, attention was concentrated on low-cost projects, such as the drilling of wells, which produced quick results. These pumped wells permitted the irrigation of new lands on the coastal plain and in the northern Negev.

Efforts were made by Jewish rural settlers to improve the flow of the upper Jordan River in the Huleh valley during 1950–60. The Huleh valley, situated in the northernmost corner of Israel, was a marshy area where nobody could live before the 1950s. The marshy area was flooded by the winter flow of the upper Jordan River, and the stored water evaporated without productive use in the semi-tropical climate. Land-reclamation work was carried out by the immigrants to construct a series of canal and drainage systems to control both flood water and the groundwater levels in the depressions, to enable them to convert the valley from a useless marsh into fertile irrigation land.

Development of the upper river basin in conjunction with irrigation and drainage of the Huleh valley, however, both increased the saline-nutrient flows into Lake Tiberias (the Sea of Galilee) and has resulted in a heightened concern over eutrophication. The chloride ion concentration in the lake rose from below 300 to nearly 400 mg/l between the years 1949/50 and 1963/64, as shown in fig. 5.1. The increased utilization of water resources may not have been the only cause of this sharp increase in salinity, but it is conceivable that it played a major role in it.

5.3.2   Medium-term water-resource development
Medium-term development projects were chosen that permitted the maximum investment per unit of water supplied, were not technically

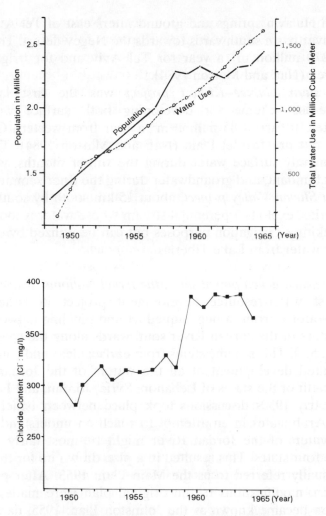

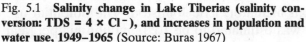

Fig. 5.1 **Salinity change in Lake Tiberias (salinity conversion: TDS = 4 × Cl⁻), and increases in population and water use, 1949–1965** (Source: Buras 1967)

complex, and allowed the investment to be divided into a number of stages. At the same time, the idea evolved that every project within the country, no matter what its size, should be able to be integrated into a nationwide hierarchical water-supply system. A number of long-term projects that had a regional rather than local significance were also implemented.

The Yarqon-Negev project, which was one of the early schemes of the National Water Carrier and was completed in 1955, carries water

209

from Rosh Ha'ayin springs and groundwaters east of Tel Aviv in the Yarqon River basin southwards towards the Negev desert. The system provides 270 million m³ a year for Tel Aviv and for irrigating the Lachish area (Naff and Matson 1984).

The Western Galilee–Kishon project was the first large-scale conjunctive-use scheme for developing both surface water and groundwater. It carries 85 million m³ a year from western Galilee to the fertile but dry Jezreel Plain (Naff and Matson 1984). The water source is mainly surface water during the winter months, when it is relatively abundant, and groundwater during the drier summer period.

The Beit She'an Valley project, about 15 km south by south-west of Lake Tiberias, exploits a perennial stream whose water is too salty for either drinking or irrigation purposes but can be utilized by diluting it with purer water from Lake Tiberias.

5.3.3 Integrated development stage: the Israel National Water System

The largest water-resource development project in Israel is the National Water Carrier, a huge aqueduct and pipeline network carrying the waters of the Jordan River southwards along the coastal plain region (fig. 5.2). This scheme stems from earlier ideas and concepts for the integrated development of all the waters of the Jordan for the mutual benefit of the states of Lebanon, Syria, Jordan, and Israel.

In the early 1950s discussions took place between Israel and the adjoining Arab states in an attempt to reach an understanding as to how the waters of the Jordan River might be most fairly allocated among the four states. This resulted in a plan drawn up for the United Nations usually referred to as the Main Plan: 1953. After prolonged negotiations, modifications to the original plan were made, and the new version became known as the Johnston Plan: 1955, named after the American mediator, Eric Johnston. The potential use of the Jordan's water was estimated to be 1,287 million m³ per year in total, of which 31% was allocated for Israel, 56% for Jordan, 10% for Syria, and 3% for Lebanon. It is widely assumed that the technical experts of the various countries involved agreed on the details of this plan, though soon afterwards the governments rejected it for political reasons. (See Appendix C for further discussion of these plans.)

With the failure of these negotiations, both Israel and Jordan decided to proceed with water projects situated entirely within their own boundaries. As a result, Israel began work on the National Water Carrier in 1958. The main storage reservoir, and also the starting point of the scheme, is Lake Tiberias. From there water is pumped through

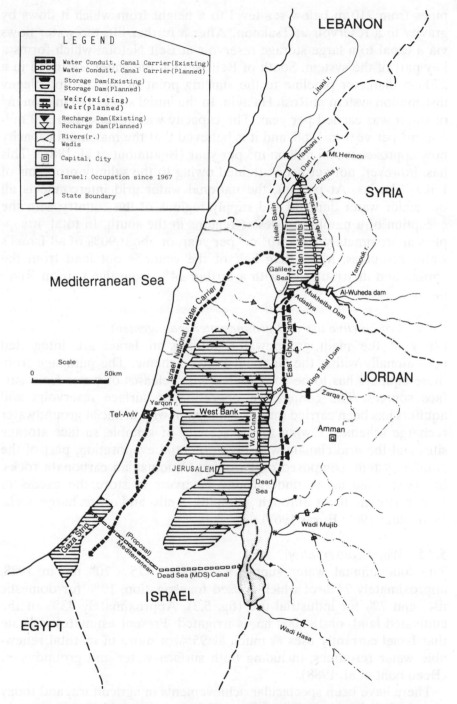

LEGEND

	Water Conduit, Canal Carrier(Existing)
	Water Conduit, Canal Carrier(Planned)
	Storage Dam(Existing)
	Storage Dam(Planned)
	Weir(existing)
	Weir(planned)
	Recharge Dam(Existing)
	Recharge Dam(Planned)
	Rivers(r.)
	Wadis
	Capital, City
	Israel: Occupation since 1967
	State Boundary

LEBANON

SYRIA

Litani r.

Hasbani r.

Dan r.

▲ Mt.Hermon

Banias r.

Huleh Basin

Golan Heights

Arab Diversion

Mediterranean Sea

Galilee Sea

Yarmouk r.

Al-Wuheda dam

Mukheiba Dam

Adasiya

East Ghor Canal

King Talal Dam

JORDAN

Zarqa r.

Israel National Water Carrier

Scale

0   50km

Yarqon r.

Tel-Aviv

West Bank

W.G.Canal

Amman

JERUSALEM

Dead Sea

Wadi Mujib

Gaza Strip

(Proposal)
Mediterranean-
Dead Sea (MDS) Canal

ISRAEL

EGYPT

Wadi Hasa

Fig. 5.2   **Water-resources development plan for the Jordan River system**

pipes from 210 m below sea level to a height from which it flows by gravity to a reservoir at Tsalmon. After a further lift, the water flows via a canal to a large storage reservoir at Beit Netofa, which forms a key part of the system. South of Beit Netofa, the water is carried in a 270-cm diameter pipeline to the starting point of the Yarqon-Negev distribution system at Rosh Ha'ayin. In the initial stages 180 million m^3 of water was carried per year. The capacity was increased to 360 million m^3 per year in 1968, and it is believed that the maximum capacity now approaches 500 million m^3 per year (Beaumont et al. 1988). This has, however, not yet been attained owing to the salinity problems of Lake Tiberias. At present, the national water grid interconnects all the major water demand and supply regions of the country with the exception of a number of desert regions in the south. In total, it supplies approximately 1.4×10^9 m^3 per year, or about 90% of all Israel's water resources. More than half of the water is obtained from the Jordan and its tributaries, with a further 14% from the Yarqon River basin.

5.3.4 Conjunctive use and groundwater management

Many of the main groundwater aquifers in Israel are integrated operationally within the National Water Scheme. The pumpage from these aquifers has to be coordinated with releases of water from surface sources. The conjunctive operation of surface reservoirs and aquifers has been carried out in conjunction with artificial groundwater recharge schemes. Owing to the scarcity of suitable surface storage sites and the arid climate with high potential evaporation, part of the aquifer system, composed of Turonian-Cenomanian carbonate rocks, has been used as an underground reservoir to store the excess of winter stream flows through pumping wells and/or recharge wells (Schneider 1967; Buras 1967).

5.3.5 Water conservation

The total annual water supply was about 1.75×10^9 m^3 in 1988, approximately 74% of which is used for irrigation, 19% for domestic use, and 7% for industrial use (fig. 5.3). Approximately 43% of the cultivated land, or 185,000 ha, is irrigated. Present estimates indicate that Israel currently uses as much as 95% or more of its total renewable water resources, including both surface water and groundwater (Beaumont et al. 1988).

There have been spectacular achievements in agriculture, and today almost all irrigation in Israel is carried out by sprinkler, drip, or sub-

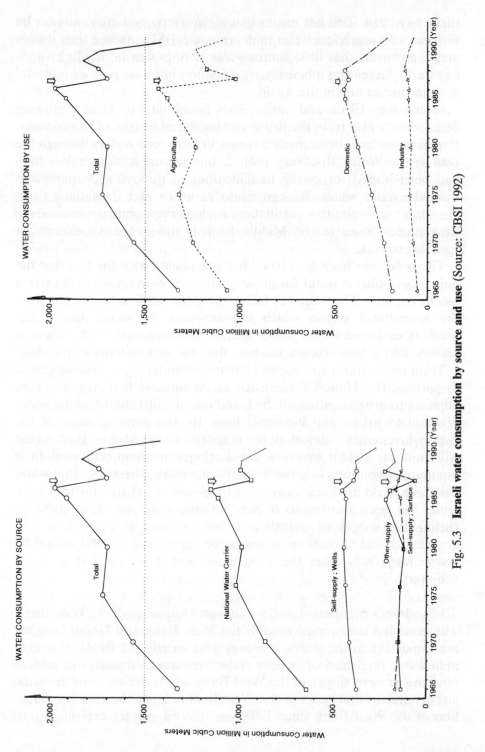

Fig. 5.3 Israeli water consumption by source and use (Source: CBSI 1992)

213

surface systems. This has meant that a given irrigated area can now be watered with much less water than previously. At the same time it does mean, however, that little future water savings can be made by agriculture by increasing efficiency, as irrigation in Israel is as economical in water use as any in the world.

In the late 1970s and early 1980s Israel had to face a growing demand for water from the urban and industrial sectors of its economy. Experiments have been made to reuse urban waste waters through the Dan Waste-Water Recovery project, but success has been less than had been hoped for owing to difficulties in removing contaminants from the waste water. Research into various water desalination systems has concluded that distillation, such as the dominant multi-stage flash process used in the Middle East, is too expensive except for specific projects.

The result has been that Israel has been faced with the fact that the only way to obtain water for growing cities is to divert water from one use to another. This requires facing the issue of diverting water from the agricultural sector, which still accounts for more than three-quarters of Israel's total water use, to the municipal and industrial sectors, taking into account the net effect on the economy of the state.

What seems likely to happen increasingly in Israel, as has happened in parts of the United States such as Arizona, is that irrigated land adjacent to urban centres will be taken out of cultivation and the water diverted to urban and industrial uses. By the early decades of the twenty-first century almost all the countries of the Middle East region will be facing similar severe water shortages in urban centres as their populations continue to grow. It seems inevitable, therefore, that water will have to be diverted away from irrigation to urban/industrial uses. Israel has been starting to reduce national water use since 1987 by cutting the supply of irrigation water, as seen in fig. 5.3. It was announced that allocations of water for agriculture in 1991 would be reduced by 30% from the 1990 level, and it seems that this was achieved.

5.3.6 Israel's occupation policy and water resources of the West Bank

The occupied lands, most notably the West Bank and Golan Heights, are important to the water economy and security of Israel. It is estimated that one-third of Israel's water resources originates in rainfall over the western slopes of the West Bank and is drawn from the same aquifer system that supplies the West Bank. Hence the Israeli occupation of the West Bank since 1967 has allowed greater exploitation of this aquifer by preventing new water-resource development by the Arab population. The effect has been to maximize groundwater recharge so that the aquifer under Israel can be more extensively developed. At the same time, Israeli settlements in the West Bank are also tapping the aquifer.

It should also be noted that another one-third of Israel's water comes from the Jordan River. The 1967 conquests are important in this light also because the Golan Heights afford control over the upper Jordan, enabling Israel to block any Arab attempt to divert its head-waters (fig. 5.2). Almost half of Israel's total water supply therefore consists of water that has been diverted or pre-empted from Arab sources located outside its pre-1967 boundaries (Naff and Matson 1984).

5.4   Joint Israel/Palestine/Jordan Mediterranean–Dead Sea conduit development with co-generation

A new co-generation method for Israel and Jordan is proposed here, which would produce both electricity and fresh water from the sea by means of a co-generation system combining solar-hydro power generation and hydro-powered RO desalination, based on exploitation of the 400 m elevation difference between the Mediterranean and the Dead Sea.

The co-generation system would produce 500 MW of electricity and 100 million m³ of fresh water per year from the Mediterranean Sea. The benefits would be shared by the riparians, including Gaza. It is assumed that the product of 100 million m³ of fresh water per year would be used exclusively to supply the central Ghor (the Jordan valley, in and around the Dead Sea), where the ground elevation is as low as 210–400 m below sea level.

The application of solar-hydro generation with RO desalination, which is a new type of co-generation system proposed here, is likely to be a key technological development in this region for the strategic objective of saving fossil energy and the global environment.

5.4.1   Background
This particular type of hydroelectric power development, also known as hydro-solar power, is made possible by the existence of a vast depression at a distance not too far from the sea, and the region's characteristically arid climate (with the resulting high degree of evaporation). Two such hydro-solar projects have been studied in depth:

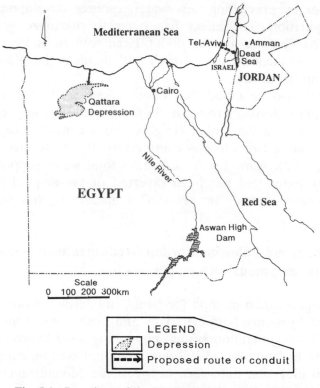

Fig. 5.4 **Locations of the Mediterranean–Qattara and Mediterranean–Dead Sea hydro-solar schemes**

the Mediterranean–Qattara canal scheme in Egypt (discussed in section 2.11 above) and the Mediterranean–Dead Sea canal scheme in Israel (fig. 5.4). Both plans would involve an initial development stage during which the basins would be filled with water from the Mediterranean Sea up to a certain design level, which would be maintained thereafter by transfer of water to replace the amount evaporated.

THE ISRAELI PLAN. Israel announced a feasibility study on a seawater hydroelectric power generation project in 1980, but this had been preceded by pre-feasibility studies over many years before that. The Mediterranean–Dead Sea Canal hydro-power project was designed to exploit the 400 m elevation difference between the Mediterranean Sea (0 m) and the Dead Sea (− 402 m) by linking the two seas.

Various routes for the conduit to connect the seas were studied (fig. 5.5). The shortest, the central route, would be 72 km long, including a 15-km section of open canal and a 57-km tunnel 5 m in diameter. The

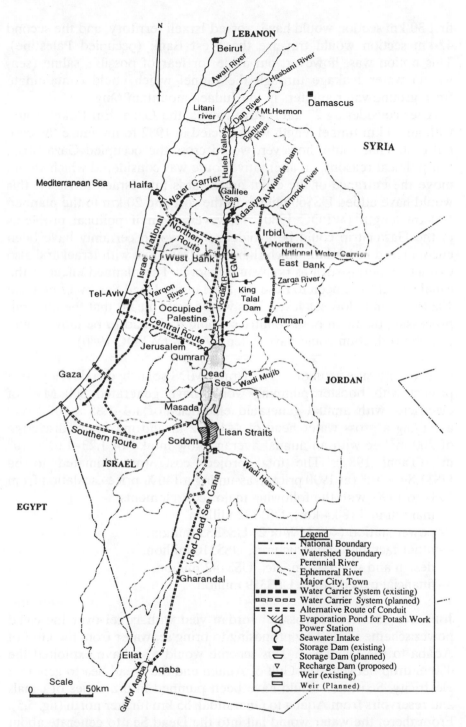

Fig. 5.5 **Israel-Jordan Mediterranean–Dead Sea hydro-solar scheme project**

217

first 30-km section would have crossed Israeli territory, and the second 42-km section would traverse the West Bank (occupied Palestine). This option was, however, put aside for fear of possible saline (sea-water) water leakage through the tunnel which could contaminate fresh groundwater aquifers in the Judaea mountain range.

After considering 27 alternative routes, the Gaza–Ein Bokek route with an 80-km tunnel length was selected in 1982 to minimize the capital cost. That route, however, would cross the occupied Gaza Strip. For political reasons, an alternative route was considered which would move the entrance of the canal northwards into Israeli territory; this would have added US$60 million to the cost and 20 km to the planned 100-km length (WPDC 1980). However, even if political problems in the Gaza Strip could be avoided, they would certainly have been encountered in Jordan, which shares the Dead Sea with Israel and also extracts minerals such as potassium from it. The planned effect of the canal would have been to raise the level of the Dead Sea by 17 m, from 402 to 385 m below sea level. This would have meant that the mineral-processing plants in both countries would have had to be moved, and potash production could have fallen by 15% (WPDC 1980).

COST OF THE MDS PROJECT.   The Israeli MDS solar-hydro development project with booster pumping would have generated 800 MW of electricity with annual generated electricity of $1.4–1.85 \times 10^9$ kWh, assuming a gross water head of 444–472 m and maximum discharge of 200 m^3/sec with an annual average flow intake of $1.23–1.67 \times 10^9$ m^3 (Tahal 1982). The total project cost was estimated to be US1.89×10^9 (at 1990 prices), assuming a 140% price escalation from 1982 to 1990, with the following major cost elements:
— main tunnel (80.4 km), US$732 million,
— power station (400 MW × 2) US$385 million,
— other facilities and structures, US$310 million,
— design and supervision, etc., US$142 million,
— financial expenditure, US$319 million.

JORDAN'S COUNTER-PROPOSAL.   Jordan vied with Israel over the canal power scheme in 1981 by proposing to bring seawater from the Gulf of Aqaba to the Dead Sea. This scheme would also have exploited the 400 m drop between the Gulf of Aqaba and the Dead Sea to generate electricity. Seawater would have been pumped into a series of canals and reservoirs from Aqaba to Gharandal, 85 km further north (fig. 5.5). From there, the water would fall into the Dead Sea to generate about 330 MW for eight hours a day at peak demand (WPDC 1983).

218

ENVIRONMENTAL PROBLEMS AND POLITICAL CONFLICT. The flow of water from the Jordanian carrier would have forced Israel to cut back its own influx of water into the Dead Sea, or the level would have risen so high as to flood the potash works (of both Israel and Jordan) and the surrounding hotels on the Israeli side. The Mediterranean–Dead Sea hydro-power project was then put aside. Israeli interest then turned to seawater pumped-storage from the Dead Sea (WPDC 1989; Naff and Matson 1984).

It should be noted that a United Nations mission found that the maximum level to have been reached by the Dead Sea would have been −390.5 m, which would not have flooded any religious or archaeological remains, nor would it have triggered earthquakes, as this level was comparable with previous equilibrium levels, and would not increase reflectivity. These studies therefore demonstrated that the project would not have had any adverse environmental effects (WPDC 1983). The possible increased evaporation through the introduction of Mediterranean water as discussed below could indeed have had additional beneficial effects.

DEAD SEA PUMPED-STORAGE SCHEME BY ISRAEL. Israel's Energy Ministry has recently shown renewed interest in a pumped-storage scheme on the Dead Sea, first proposed in the early 1980s but shelved in favor of a similar project proposed for the Sea of Galilee. Power could be produced even more cheaply and efficiently from pumped-storage on the Sea of Galilee in northern Israel, but the project could damage plant and animal life. The interest has therefore shifted back to the Dead Sea because of its almost total absence of flora and fauna. The Dead Sea pumped-storage scheme could produce 400–800 MW, equivalent to 7%–14% of the Israeli national grid's generation capacity of 5,835 MW in 1991. The total production of electricity amounted to 20.8×10^9 kWh in 1991.

CO-GENERATION WITH JOINT DEVELOPMENT: THE OPPORTUNITY FOR THE FUTURE. While Israel's MDS canal scheme was conceived to provide hydroelectric power, it did not offer any solution to the urgent need for fresh water supply (Glueckstern 1982). The use of hydroelectric power to make desalination cost-effective was a consideration of the scheme in the early 1980s, but it was not considered sustainable to use valuable clean energy from hydroelectricity for conventional desalination because the substantial energy losses that would be incurred through conversion and transmission. Discussion of the MDS canal scheme in the early 1980s overlooked the concept of shared resources and the

219

benefit of joint development. Indeed up until 1991 there was no attempt to conceive a comprehensive development plan for the Jordan River system including linkage of the MDS canal and the Al-Wuheda dam on the Yarmouk (Murakami 1991).

The new co-generation approach to the MDS canal scheme proposed here takes into account (1) recent innovative developments in membrane technology for RO desalination which aim to save energy and to make RO desalination more cost-effective and (2) recent changes in the Middle East political situation following the Gulf war that may make comprehensive basin development not only technically and financially feasible but politically desirable and urgent.

5.4.2   Hydrology of the Dead Sea and evaporation from it
The climate of the watershed ranges from "hot arid" in the bottom of the Jordan valley to "Mediterranean semi-arid" in the surrounding highlands. The Dead Sea is a brine water body with the extremely high salinity of 250,000 mg of TDS per litre. It is a closed lake with no outlet except by evaporation, which at present amounts to 1,500–1,600 mm per year (Calder and Neal 1984).

Evaporation from the surface of the saline lake is the key factor in estimating the capacity for generating electricity by solar-hydro development. For the same meteorological inputs and aerodynamic resistance, a decrease in salt concentration will increase evaporation rates and reduce lake temperature, whereas an increase in concentration will have the reverse effect. Increased use of water from the Jordan River, especially for irrigation, has increased salt concentrations, whereas the proposed introduction of Mediterranean Sea water into the Dead Sea via a canal for hydroelectric purposes would reverse this trend (Weiner and Ben-Zvi 1982).

A model analysis to predict the annual evaporation rate and surface temperature as a function of aerodynamic resistance and thermodynamic activities of water (Calder and Neal 1984) assumed that on an annual long-term basis the heat flux into the lake was negligible and that the available energy could be equated to the net radiation calculated from the following parameters for the Dead Sea: air temperature $(T) = 23.6°C$, vapour pressure of air $(e) = 15.9$ mbars, saturation vapour pressure of water at temperature T $(e_s(T)) = 29.05$ mbars, and total available energy $(H) =$ net radiation flux density $(R_n) = 146$ $W - m^2$. The activity of the water in solution $(a_w;$ the a_w of pure water $= 1.00)$ was assumed to have changed from 0.75 before 1958 to 0.71 in the 1980s. If the proposed canal development were completed, the formation of an unmixed Mediterranean water surface layer ($a_w = 0.98$) overlying the denser Dead Sea water would (possibly on a localized scale in the vicinity of the canal outlet) decrease the surface water salt concentration and raise the a_w values. The model prediction suggests a large increase in the (local) mean annual evaporation rate by 345 mm, from a present 1,563 mm to 1,908 mm, and a marked decrease in surface water temperature of 3.3°C, to 23.4°C. These estimated rates of evaporation are conceived to be conservative and are comparable to those measured at Lake Mead in Arizona, in the United States, which amount to 2,000 mm per year (Sellers 1965).

This study assumes 1,600 mm of mean annual evaporation for present conditions. The evaporation rate after impounding water from the Mediterranean is assumed to be 1,900 mm per year for the co-generation plan proposed in the following sections.

5.4.3 Co-generation plan: Solar-hydro and hydro-powered reverse-osmosis desalination

The proposed solar-hydro development plan would exploit the elevation difference of 400 m between the Mediterranean Sea and Dead Sea. The water in the Dead Sea would be maintained at a steady-state level, with some seasonal fluctuations of about 2 m, between 402 and 390 m below mean sea level, with the inflow into the Dead Sea balancing evaporation.

The Israel/Jordan Mediterranean–Dead Sea conduit plan is a co-generation alternative that would combine solar-hydro and hydro-powered seawater RO desalination (fig. 5.6). It would have the following major components:

» an upstream reservoir (the Mediterranean) at sea level (0 m), with an essentially unlimited amount of water,

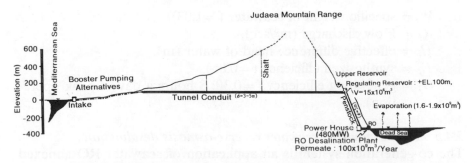

Fig. 5.6 **MDS hydro-solar conduit: development alternatives**

>> a seawater carrier, in tunnel, canal, and pipeline, with a booster pump,
>> an upper reservoir and surge shaft at the outlet of the seawater carrier to allow for regulating the water flow,
>> a storage-type hydroelectric unit capable of reverse operation to allow the system to also work as a pumped-storage unit if required,
>> a downstream reservoir (the Dead Sea), at a present surface elevation of approximately 402 m below sea level,
>> a hydro-powered RO desalination plant, including a pre-treatment unit, a pressure-converter unit, the RO unit, an energy-recovery unit, a post-treatment unit, and regulating reservoirs for distribution.

5.4.4 Estimate of hydro-power

The theoretical hydro-potential to exploit the head difference between the Mediterranean Sea (0 m) and Dead Sea (-400 m) by transferring 56.7 m^3 of seawater per second (1.6×10^9 m^3 per year) is estimated to be 194 MW, or, with an installed capacity for peak-power operation at 495 MW, to provide 1.3×10^9 kWh of electricity per year. Another option for exploiting the gross head at 444–472 m (Tahal 1982) by transferring 43 m^3 of seawater per second would have 198 MW of theoretical hydro-potential, or, with an installed capacity for peak-power operation at 505 MW, to provide 1.33×10^9 kWh of electricity per year. These estimates are based on the following conventional equations for theoretical hydro-potential (P_{th}) and installed capacity (P), both in kW, and potential power generation (W_p) in kWh per year:

$$P_{th} = 9.8 \times W_s \times Q \times H_e,$$
$$P = P_{th} \times E_f,$$
$$W_p = 365 \times 24 \times G_f \times P,$$

where

W_s = specific weight of seawater ($=1.03$),
Q = Flow discharge (m^3/sec),
H_e = effective difference head of water (m),
E_f = synthesized efficiency ($=0.85$),
G_f = generating efficiency ($=0.30$; 8 hours a day of peak operation).

5.4.5 Hydro-powered seawater reverse-osmosis desalination

The co-generation system is an application of seawater RO annexed to a solar-hydro-power system requiring eight hours a day of peak operation. Marginal operation of the RO system is designed to use the hydro-potential energy in the pipeline-tunnel (penstock) system (481.5 m of differential head of water) for 16 hours a day during the off-peak time. The feed-water requirements to produce 100 million m³ of permeate per year with 1,000 mg of TDS per litre are estimated to be 333 million m³ per year, assuming at least a 30% recovery ratio. The installed capacity is estimated to be 322,300 m³ per day, with a load factor of 85%. The energy recovery from the brine reject is estimated to be 24,000 KW, with annual generation of 134.7 million kWh of electricity, with a load factor of 68%. The recovered energy (electricity) will be used to supply electricity for the post-treatment process or other purposes, as shown in fig. 5.7.

COST ESTIMATES. The total investment cost for the proposed hydro-powered seawater RO desalination unit, based on 1990 prices with 8% interest during three years' construction, is preliminarily estimated to be US$389,355,000, with an annual capital cost at US$18,568,000, with the following major elements:
— pre-treatment, US$44,195,000,
— desalting plant, US$70,414,000,
— RO membrane and equipment, US$84,835,000,
— control and operating system, US$5,952,000,
— appurtenant works, US$27,013,000,
— power line and substation, US$11,427,000,
— energy recovery/turbine, US$2,999,000,
— *sub-total* (US$246,835,000);
— design and construction management, US$62,250,000;
— financial expenditure, US$80,270,000.
   The annual cost of operation and maintenance is estimated to be US$44,387,000, with the following major elements:
— labour, US$3,718,000,
— material supply, US$1,860,000,
— chemicals, US$7,440,000,
— power (pumped-storage for RO feed water), US$3,100,000,
— membrane replacement, US$28,269,000.
   These cost estimates are based on 1990 prices and the following assumptions:
— plant life, 20 years;
— membrane life (replacement), 3 years;
— cost benefit from energy recovery not included;
— costs for source water and pipeline/distribution not included.

223

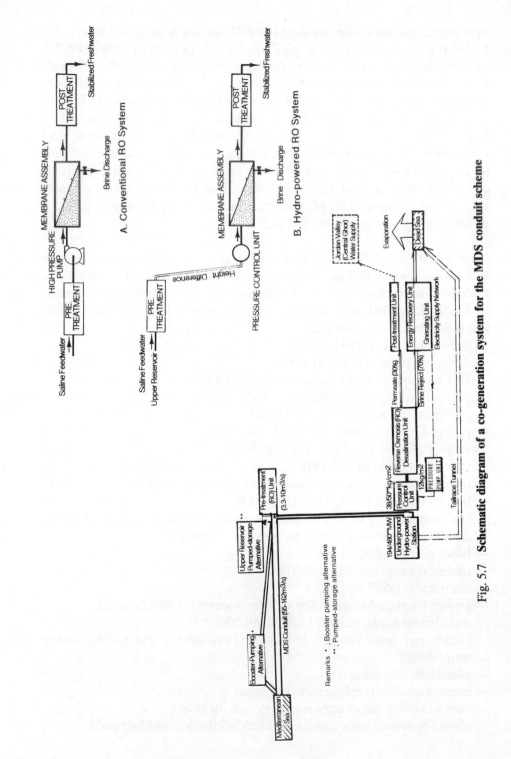

Fig. 5.7 Schematic diagram of a co-generation system for the MDS conduit scheme

A. Conventional RO System

Saline Feedwater → PRE. TREATMENT → HIGH PRESSURE PUMP → MEMBRANE ASSEMBLY → POST TREATMENT → Stabilized Freshwater

Brine Discharge

B. Hydro-powered RO System

Saline Feedwater
Upper Reservoir → PRE. TREATMENT → PRESSURE CONTROL UNIT → Height Difference → MEMBRANE ASSEMBLY → POST TREATMENT → Stabilized Freshwater

Brine Discharge

Jordan Valley (Central Ghor) Water Supply

Evaporation

Dead Sea

Permeate (30%)
Brine Reject (70%)

Post-treatment Unit
Energy Recovery Unit
Generating Unit
Electricity Supply Network

Reverse Osmosis (RO) Desalination Unit

12 kg/m²
PRESSURE PUMP UNIT
Tailrace Tunnel

Pressure Control Unit
38/50 kg/cm²
(3.3-10 m³/s)

194/480 m.MW
Underground Hydro-power Station

Upper Reservoir Pumped-storage Alternative

Pre-treatment (RO) Unit

Booster-Pumping Alternative

MDS Conduit (55-162 m³/s)

Mediterranean Sea

Remarks * : Booster pumping alternative
        ** : Pumped-storage alternative

Table 5.1   **Water and electricity tariffs in six world metropolises**

	Water		Electricity	
	Yen/month[a]	US$/m³	Yen/month[a]	US$/kWh
Tokyo	4,070	1.23	4,962	0.18
New York	746	0.23	12,000	0.44
Los Angeles	4,800	1.45	3,600	0.13
London	2,860	0.87	3,913	0.14
Paris	2,513	0.76	4,700	0.17
Cairo	12,892	3.91	1,055	0.04

Source: LAJ 1989.

a. Japanese yen for 22 m³ of water and 180 kWh of electricity per month.

The unit water cost of the hydro-powered seawater reverse-osmosis desalination for the design annual product water of 100 million m³ is estimated to be US$0.68/m³, which may be reasonable value when compared with international water tariffs, as shown in table 5.1.

The project cost of the Israeli MDS canal for the hydro-power scheme was estimated at US$1.9 × 10⁹, as described in section 5.4.1 above.

5.4.6   Method of sharing and allotment

The Dead Sea surface, which is the source of evaporation for the MDS solar-hydro scheme, is the joint heritage of the riparian states: Israel (300 km², 30%) and Palestine and Jordan (700 km², 70%). The route of the MDS conduit would pass through Palestine (Gaza) (10 km) and Israel (90 km).

The water balance of the Dead Sea for the co-generation scheme to produce 500 MW of electricity and 100 million m³ of fresh water is estimated follows:

— evaporation after impounding seawater, 1,900 million m³,
— seawater intake for MDS hydro-power at steady-state level, 1,220 million m³,
— brine reject water from proposed hydro-powered RO plant, 233 million m³,
— inflow from catchments, 447 million m³.

The riparians, Israel, Palestine, and Jordan, share the resources and must find a way of sharing the benefits. If the cost sharing were to be

225

split fifty-fifty between the riparian states to assure fifty-fifty benefit allotment, project formulation including financing, construction, operation, and maintenance could be done by an international consortium sponsored by an international agency such as the Middle East Development Bank. The possible benefits and their allocation are discussed further in Appendix D.

5.4.7 Remarks

This study of hydro-solar development has been made to test the technical feasibility of exploiting seawater resources by taking into account the distinctive nature of the arid zone hydrology and topography in and around the Dead Sea. Reverse osmosis is the cheapest process for desalination today, but it may not be the optimum solution in the twenty-first century. Further research will be needed to evaluate its technical feasibility, including (1) the actual rate of evaporation from the Dead Sea surface after impounding, (2) the design of materials to avoid corrosion of hydraulic structures from seawater and brine reject water, (3) tunnel-boring-machine methods of construction for the seawater conduit tunnel, (4) application of low-pressure-type (30–50 kg/cm^2) RO-membrane modules for seawater desalination, (5) an improved energy-recovery system in RO, (6) methods of hybrid desalination, and (7) the potential development of technology for power generation by a solar pond.

5.5 Integration of development alternatives in an inter-state water master plan

An integrated water-resource development and management plan for the Jordan River system, including the Mediterranean–Dead Sea conduit scheme for co-generation and the Al-Wuheda dam scheme, which aims to mitigate the historical complexities, commonalties, and conflict between Israel and Jordan, has to be considered to provide for sharing resources and joint development of the Jordan River.

Before discussing a new inter-state basin-development plan for the Jordan system, the following three major existing development alternatives are examined to assess their status and priority in a master plan.

5.5.1 Alternative 1: Inter-state water transportation by pipeline

Two inter-state water-transportation projects have been proposed for either bilateral or multilateral promotion: the Euphrates–North Jordan transmission scheme and the Peace Pipeline. These schemes were set aside, however, because of fears of political constraints, including inter-state riparian-rights questions on the Euphrates River, where the fear of water being used as a political weapon was increasing.

The Peace Pipeline project has now been emphatically rejected by all Arab states, who have said that if necessary they will depend on non-conventional waters in their territory including seawater desalination. However, neither Israel or Jordan, which are not oil-producing countries, have been able to adopt seawater desalination by the thermal method, which requires substantial energy or electricity.

With the opening of the Middle East peace negotiations in Madrid in October 1991, the political emphasis on water's potential as a vehicle for inter-state regional cooperation has taken on new importance. A new proposal for transferring water from water-rich Turkey into the fragile and desiccated core region of the Jordan basin (Wolf 1993) is being discussed to puts forth a multidisciplinary study of techno-political viability in the twenty-first century.

5.5.2 Alternative 2: Water transportation by tanker, barge, or bag

The transport of water by tankers, barges, and towed floating bags has been discussed mainly in the oil-producing Gulf countries and/or small islands.

Israel and the Gaza Strip have a long coastline along the Mediterranean, with major coastal population centres such as Tel Aviv, Haifa, and Gaza. Water transportation by tankers, barges, or bags could provide significant relief to all the coastal towns and cities in the Middle East. Provision of water by Turkey for the Israeli water-bag scheme should go a long way towards developing credibility for its good intentions as regards the Euphrates and Tigris and will reduce one of the most serious problems for Israel in discussion with Palestine (Savage 1990). Turkey also holds the key to future full use of the river systems of the Euphrates, Tigris, Ceyhan, Seyhan, and Manavgat.

Jordan has only a short sea coast at Aqaba, while the water demand is located 400 km north of the highland desert at an elevation of 800–1,000 m, including the population centres of Amman and Zarqa. This alternative may not be attractive since it would require a water pipeline of more than 400 km and a high pumping head, exceeding 1,000 m.

5.5.3 Alternative 3: Non-conventional water-resources development

Priority is likely to be given to marginal, non-conventional waters in the water-resources development of Israel, Palestine, and Jordan, taking into account not only the technical, financial, and economic but also the political feasibility.

Israel provides an example of a country which has long experience with almost all the non-conventional technologies, including the use of saline water for agriculture. From experimental experience in the late 1970s to the mid-1980s, Israel recognized that the reuse of urban waste water in the Dan Waste-Water Recovery project had been less successful than had been hoped owing to difficulties in removing certain contaminants, and seawater desalination was too expensive except for specific projects.

Non-conventional water resources are generally more complex in development and operation than conventional sources, and are almost always more expensive. However, there are no further opportunities for the development of renewable waters in Israel, including its present dependence for about 50% of its renewable water on occupied Palestine and other Arab territories. There is a clear linkage between the Israeli occupation policy on Palestine and the water-resources issue. The Israeli dilemma is based not only on the quantity and quality issues of water resources but also on occupation policies contrary to the United Nations Security Council Resolution 242 of November 1967.

5.5.4 Mediterranean–Dead Sea conduit scheme in the context of inter-state development and Jordan River basin management

The Dead Sea has a huge hydro-solar (evaporation) potential, which is shared by Israel, Palestine, and Jordan. Accordingly, Dead Sea hydro-solar development must be discussed in the context of a master plan for inter-state water and power development and management with sharing of resources, and to provide the basis for peaceful collaboration between Israel and its neighbours.

The four main alternative routes considered for the MDS canal as originally conceived (see fig. 5.5) are described in table 5.2. The shorter of the two southern routes—Southern route 1—would have the advantage of minimizing the constraints of both cost and environment. This study supports the concept of such a multilateral plan, which, it has been suggested, should be managed by an international agency such as the United Nations, as proposed in Appendix D.

The MDS conduit scheme, which includes solar-hydro and hydro-powered RO desalination by joint development by Israel, Palestine, and Jordan, is a key proposal studied in this book. The stream flows into the Dead Sea from the Jordan River and Wadi Mujib will be minimized to maximize the seawater diversion capacity from the Mediterranean and to maximize the hydro-potential. To make a reality of the physical basis, the following alternatives are included to minimize the winter flows in the river and wadi systems:

>> the Al-Wuheda multipurpose storage-dam scheme on the Yarmouk River, which has been postponed since 1989, owing to Israeli opposition on downstream water-allocation questions;

>> storage-dam schemes on the rift-side wadis on the East Bank, including the Wala and Nukheila dams on Wadi Mujib and Tannour dam on Wadi Hasa, which have no political constraints but need financial support from international aid agencies.

>> Flood-retention, groundwater-recharge dam schemes on the side wadis on the West Bank (occupied Palestine), where limestone geology is predominant, as illustrated in the schematic profile of the hydrogeology and groundwater of Palestine in fig. 5.8, with the aims of cutting flash floods, which are being dumped into the Jordan River or the Mediterranean Sea, and recharging the underlying aquifer system to sustain regional groundwater development. This may lead to improvement of the hard situation whereby Israel has to depend for 40%–50% or more of its present water supply on an aquifer underlying the West Bank.

Jordan's last major river development, the Al-Wuheda dam scheme, with an effective storage of 195 million m^3, is urgently needed for the national water supply grid to add 155 million m^3 per year. This will also reduce the amount of winter flow into the Dead Sea. Meanwhile to the west the Jordan valley downstream of the Al-Wuheda dam, including Palestine and a portion of Israel, needs more fresh water to

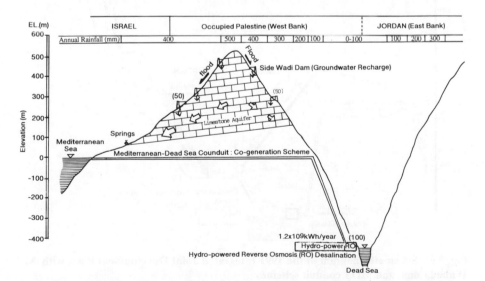

Fig. 5.8   **Schematic profile of the hydrogeology and groundwater of Israel/Palestine**

extend irrigation development, and to the south-east almost all the population centres in Jordan are located on highland desert at an elevation of 800–1,000 m, which suggests the priority use of the Yarmouk River water for M&I water supply by diverting it from Al-Wuheda (elevation 100 m) to Amman (elevation 800 m), as illustrated in the schematic profile of the Jordan valley and Yarmouk River system in fig. 5.9.

Co-generation by coupling solar-hydro with hydro-powered RO desalination in the MDS conduit scheme will generate two products:
— electricity, either 200 MW for base load or 500 MW for peak load,
— fresh water, 100 million m³ per year by desalination.
A schematic of the MDS co-generation system is also shown in fig. 5.9. The capital/investment costs of the hydro-power and the RO desali-

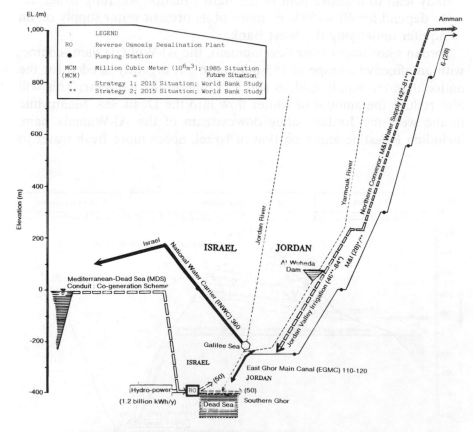

Fig. 5.9 Schematic diagram of the 1991 Integrated Joint Development Plan, with Al-Wuheda dam and MDS conduit schemes

nation elements are preliminarily estimated to be US$1,900 million and US$400 million respectively (see section 5.4). The annual potential outputs such as 1×10^9 kWh of electricity and 100 million m^3 of fresh water for M&I water supply from the co-generation system are estimated to be equivalent to US$80 million per year each (US$160 million in total), assuming an electricity tariff of US$0.08/kWh and a water tariff of US$0.80/m^3. These cost indices simply suggest one feasible approach to joint development by the riparian states.

Power generation in Israel in 1991 was 20.8×10^9 kWh, which was about ten times as much as that of Jordan. The installed capacity of 500 MW would be equivalent to 8.5% of Israel's grid capacity of 5,835 MW in 1991. The electricity from the Dead Sea hydro-power would, however, be a resource to be shared by Israel and Jordan to supply peak demands to optimize their power-supply systems.

By the end of the 1990s, Israel, Jordan, and the West Bank, or Palestine, will overcommit or deplete virtually all of their renewable sources of fresh water if current patterns of consumption are not quickly or radically altered. In the circumstances, the Jordan River system, which includes the Al-Wuheda dam scheme on the Yarmouk River, unquestionably holds the greatest potential for either conflict or compromise. In the southern Ghor of the Dead Sea catchment, the driest area of the Jordan valley, with annual rainfall less than 50–100 mm, there has been substantial water demand to develop the region, but no alternative source of fresh water has been found in the area. M&I water demand in and around the Dead Sea is about 100 million m^3 per year, including increasingly demands for the mining industry (potash works), agro-industry, and resort hotels. The product water of 100 million m^3 per year from hydro-powered RO desalination could be mainly used for M&I water supply with the exclusive aim of supplying water in the southern Ghor (Jordan valley) in the twenty-first century.

All the water-resource development schemes on the Jordan River system, including the proposed Al-Wuheda dam and side-wadi dams, should be linked with the Mediterranean–Dead Sea conduit scheme in the context of an interstate basin-development master plan to promote economic development in Jordan, Palestine, and Israel through sharing of resources and benefits.

The basic framework for allocation of Jordan River water is enshrined in the "Main Plan: 1953" and the "Johnston Plan: 1955," which were negotiated by the United Nations but never formally endorsed by the governments concerned. Flow diagrams and water allocation of the Jordan River system are illustrated in figs. 5.10–5.13,

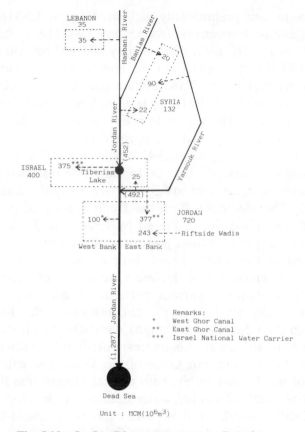

Fig. 5.10 **Jordan River system water allocation—
Johnston Plan: 1955**

including the 1955 Johnston Plan (fig. 5.10), unilateral Jordan River
development as now (fig. 5.11), ongoing or postponed projects that
involve political and/or financial constraints (fig. 5.12), and new
schemes proposed for a 1991 integrated joint development plan that
includes the MDS conduit scheme for co-generation and side-wadi
dam scheme for flood retention and groundwater recharge in the West
Bank (fig. 5.13). The framework for a new inter-state Jordan River
development plan for the twenty-first century as conceived in this
study would build into the 1955 Unified (Johnston) Plan the new
engineering proposal for hydro-powered RO desalination in the MDS
conduit scheme, which would not only provide additional fresh water
and clean energy (electricity) in the driest area but would promote
integrated economic development between Israel, Palestine, and Jordan as a basis for lasting peace.

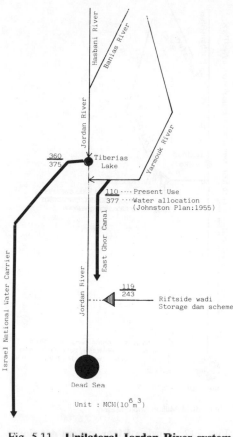

Fig. 5.11 **Unilateral Jordan River system development—current situation**

It should be recognized that issues of the security of water resources and inter-state riparian problems of the Jordan River system, including Israel's heavy dependence on water supply from the underground aquifer that underlies the West Bank, have been some of the reasons why Israel could not withdraw from the areas occupied since 1967. Thus, without resolution of these inter-state water resources problems, no settlement of the Palestine–Israel and Arab–Israel problems can be achieved.

Table 5.2 shows a proposed model of inter-state water allocation including the proposed non-conventional development alternatives.

Implementation of inter-state basin development and management of the Jordan system will not be a complicated matter of water politics, for which some ideas of inter-state regional economic development are further discussed in the following section and Appendices C and D.

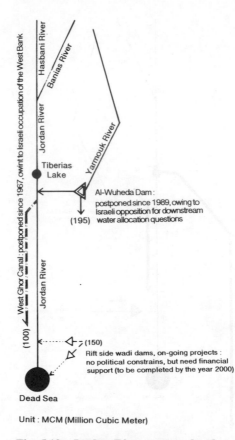

Unit : MCM (Million Cubic Meter)

Fig. 5.12 **Jordan River system development—ongoing and postponed projects**

5.6 Techno-political non-conventional water-energy development alternatives in inter-state regional planning for Aqaba

The historic peace accord between Israel and the Palestine Liberation (PLO) in Oslo on 13 September 1993 produced a Declaration of Principles which included a proposal for an inter-state regional economic development plan (Israel/PLO, 1993). Regional economic development was conceived as a key element to sustain the peace process in the region. The protocol on Israel–PLO relations suggests that priority be given to certain projects including development of the Dead Sea region and the Mediterranean Sea (Gaza)–Dead Sea canal as discussed in sections 5.4 and 5.5 (Murakami 1991; Murakami and Musiake

234

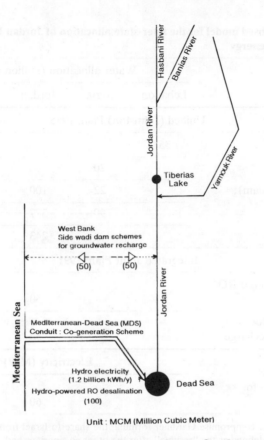

Unit : MCM (Million Cubic Meter)

Fig. 5.13 **Proposed new schemes for the integrated development of the Jordan River system**

1991). The weak point of the bilateral peace agreement was that it did not at that stage include Jordan, which is a major riparian state of the Dead Sea.

It is now necessary to re-examine the techno-political non-conventional water-energy development alternatives in the inter-state Aqaba region, including Jordan, Israel, and Egypt, in the context of sharing resources and benefits. It also has to be recommended that Saudi Arabia is contiguous and could share resources and benefits.

5.6.1 Water-energy issues in a framework of the peace master plan
Energy issues like water are critical matters in the development of non-oil-producing countries like Israel, Palestine, and Jordan. These

Table 5.2 **Proposed model for the inter-state allocation of Jordan River system water and solar-hydro energy**

| | Water allocation (million m³/year) | | | | |
	Lebanon	Syria	Jordan	Israel	Total
Unified (Johnston) Plan: 1955					
Hasbani	35				35
Banias		20		·	20
Jordan (main stream)		22	100	375[a]	497[a]
Yarmouk		90	377	25	492
Side wadis			243		243
Integrated Joint Plan: 1991					
MDS hydro-powered RO desalination			50	50	100
Side-wadi dams for groundwater recharge			50	50	100
Electricity (MW)[b]					
MDS solar-hydro for peak power			60	440	500

a. According to the compromise Gardiner formula, the share to Israel from the main stream of the Jordan was defined as the "residue" after the other co-riparians had received their shares. This would vary from year to year but was expected to average 375 million m³.
b. Installed capacity of hydro-power plant, which may generate 1.26×10^9 kWh of peak-power electricity per year.

countries are the major riparians of the Jordan River system, and all have increasing demand for desalination and the reuse of treated waste water, which consume substantial quantities of energy or electricity.

The region is currently heavily dependent on crude oil (2.5 million tons) and coal (2.3 million tons of oil equivalent) as its energy source for the generation of electricity (table 5.3). Israel produced 20.9×10^9 kWh of electricity at an installed capacity of 5,835 MW in 1991. Israel has a plan to replace its steam-power generating system with nuclear power by steps in the twenty-first century. A significant deficit in peak power supply has been a long-standing problem, while substantial off-peak electricity is being wasted. Although international networking of the electric supply is being discussed with adjoining states, including

Table 5.3 **Energy sources for the production of electricity in Israel**

Sources	Requirement (TOE[a])
Crude oil	8,304,000
Coal	2,549,000
Solar energy	379,000
Natural gas	23,000
Electricity[b]	−33,000
TOTAL	11,255,000

a. Tons oil equivalent.
b. Export to occupied Palestine.

Table 5.4 **Electricity consumption in Israel, 1985–1991 (million kVA)**

	1985	1986	1987	1988	1989	1990	1991
Industry	4,406	4,581	4,939	5,092	5,296	5,496	5,723
Household	3,331	3,614	4,050	4,890	5,190	5,317	5,606
Trade	2,979	3,384	3,781	4,120	4,477	4,762	4,979
Water pumping	2,197	1,717	1,894	2,038	2,113	1,825	1,528
Agriculture	602	658	765	864	906	934	967
TOTAL	13,155	13,954	15,429	16,990	17,982	18,334	18,803

Source: Statistical Abstract of Israel, 1992.

Egypt, no alternatives have been suggested other than building a new pumped-storage unit and/or gas turbine generating units.

The energy supply is closely related to Israel's water supply, which consumes substantial electricity for water pumping. The pumping demand amounted to 1,528 kVA in 1991 (see table 5.4), whose cost accounts for 30% of total expenditure on water supply by Mekorot, Israel's national water company. Taking into account the recent advances in desalination, Israel is planning to introduce large-scale seawater desalination by the year 2000. Although this is likely to be dependent on low-energy types of reverse osmosis, the energy cost will still be 30%–50% of the total, depending on the price of electricity. Consequently the potential use of off-peak electricity will be a key element in minimizing the cost of water management and operation.

5.6.2 Geopolitics of inter-state regions: The Dead Sea and the Gulf of Aqaba

The interregional economic development planning will have to cover two regions: the Dead Sea (Israel/Palestine/Jordan) and Aqaba (Egypt/ Israel/Jordan/Saudi Arabia). These two regions will be gateways for cooperation between the countries of the Middle East.

Because of the geopolitical uniqueness of the Dead Sea, joint regional development planning has a prominent place in the 1993 peace agreement between the PLO and Israel and the October 1994 peace treaty between Jordan and Israel.

The lower Jordan River system, including the Dead Sea, shared by the three riparians Israel, Palestine (the West Bank), and Jordan (the East Bank), will be a focus area for confidence-building measures. A proposal is here offered, as a strategy for the short to medium term, for salvaging brackish water from saline springs and irrigation returns in the area between Lake Tiberias and the Dead Sea, not only to protect the water quality in the lower Jordan main stream but also to produce new potable fresh water. The incentives for using water for peace are taken into account in assessing the techno-political feasibility of the scheme, which would include (1) collecting saline water from Israel; (2) constructing an 80-km-long drainage canal along the lower Jordan on the West Bank with an RO desalination plant at its terminal with an installed capacity of 100,000–200,000 m^3 per day, which would convert harmful saline water to safe potable water at a cost of US$0.40–0.50/ m^3; and (3) sharing the fresh water produced among the three riparian states. This Peace Drainage Canal scheme, protecting the water-quality environment and the eco-system of the lower Jordan, should have the highest priority in a master plan for the environmentally sound, sustainable development of the water of the basin for peace.

Geopolitically, the Aqaba region is shared by four states—Jordan, Israel, Egypt, and Saudi Arabia—and in the short and medium term could be even more important. The region of the Gulf of Aqaba has great potential for the development of international tourism, commerce, and industry if some of the principal infrastructure can be shared. Owing to the hyper-arid climate of the region, however, water supply will be the main constraint to development.

5.6.3 Water-energy co-generating schemes for an inter-state regional economic development plan

Water and energy will be the key elements in any regional development, which will also include tourism/resorts, industry, and commerce.

This study suggests two core projects for co-generation of water and electric power: the Mediterranean–Dead Sea conduit scheme and the Aqaba seawater pumped-storage scheme, as discussed below. These would take into account the following possible scenarios for sharing resources and benefits:

>> an inter-state electricity grid or network including Egypt, Israel, Palestine, Jordan, Saudi Arabia, Syria, and Lebanon, to provide cheap off-peak electricity to pumped-storage schemes, incorporated in the plan to provide peak energy and balance the grid;

>> techno-political project priority given to (1) the MDS conduit co-generating scheme in the Dead Sea regional development plan and (2) the Aqaba co-generation hybrid seawater pumped-storage scheme in the Aqaba regional development plan;

>> an inter-state water pipeline, to connect the three states along the Aqaba coastline, to share fresh potable water from a hydro-powered RO desalination plant in an enlarged Aqaba co-generating pumped-storage scheme;

>> an inter-state sanitation and environmental management programme, including waste-water reclamation for tree-crop irrigation and sustaining the clean water environment of the Gulf of Aqaba.

The Aqaba region was outside the scope of the bilateral peace negotiations between Israel and the PLO in 1993, in which the Dead Sea regional economic development and MDS conduit scheme had strategic priority in terms of geopolitics. In a broader context, Aqaba regional development and hybrid seawater pumped-storage with hydro-powered RO desalination is possibly of even greater importance for the economic development of the whole region. The Aqaba hybrid pumped-storage scheme for co-generation will be even more competitive when compared with a single-purpose hydro-power scheme such as Dead Sea pumped-storage or a Red Sea–Dead Sea canal.

5.6.4 Aqaba hybrid seawater pumped-storage scheme with hydro-powered reverse-osmosis desalination

Construction of any new thermal or nuclear power stations in the region will benefit from a pumped-storage scheme for efficient energy use during off-peak time. A hybrid water-energy co-generation system is an application of RO desalination annexed to a seawater pumped-storage scheme. The Aqaba scheme would use seawater, which would be pumped directly to an upper reservoir on top of an escarpment 600 m above sea level, and from there would flow into a penstock to yield a water pressure of 60 kg/cm^2 to generate 600 MW of electricity as potential base energy and 100 million m^3 of fresh potable water. Off-peak electricity to boost the water to the 600 m elevation would be supplied from either a steam-power plant at Aqaba or from the most economical alternative source, whether steam or nuclear power plants in Egypt or Israel or other electricity grids in the region.

A schematic profile is shown in fig. 5.14. The specification for the hydro-powered seawater RO desalination unit would be similar to that developed for the MDS conduit scheme for co-generation.

The design discharge is preliminary estimated to be 116 m^3/sec ($=600 \times 10^3/(9.8 \times 1.03 \times 600 \times 0.85)$), assuming a specific weight of seawater at 1.03 and synthesized efficiency of 0.85.

The pumped-storage scheme would be designed to generate peak power for 4–8 hours a day. The marginal operation of the RO system could make use of the hydro-potential energy in the penstock pipeline with 600 m of head difference for 16–20 hours a day during off-peak time.

The feed-water requirement to produce 100 million m^3 of permeate per year with 500–1,000 mg of TDS per litre is estimated to be 333 million m^3 per year, assuming a 30% recovery ratio (70% for brine reject). The installed capacity of the RO unit is estimated to be 322,300 m^3 per day with a load factor of 85%.

The energy recovery potential from the brine reject is estimated to be 28,900 KW by the following calculation, which assumes a friction loss of 20% in the RO circuit:

$$9.8 \times 1.03 \times [(233 \times 10^6/365)/86,400] \times (600 \times 0.95 \times 0.8) \times 0.85$$

The annual production of electricity from the RO brine reject is estimated to be 172 million kWh, with a load factor of 68%. The recovered energy would be used to supply electricity for the post-treatment or other pumps to save electricity from the national grid.

The total investment cost of the proposed hydro-powered seawater RO desalination unit, based on 1990 prices, is preliminarily estimated to be US$389,355,000, comprising the following major elements:
— pre-treatment, US$44,195,000,
— desalting plant, US$70,414,000,
— RO membrane/equipment, US$84,835,000,
— control and operating system, US$5,952,000,
— appurtenant works, US$27,013,000,
— powerline and substation, US$11,427,000,
— energy recovery/turbine, US$2,999,000,

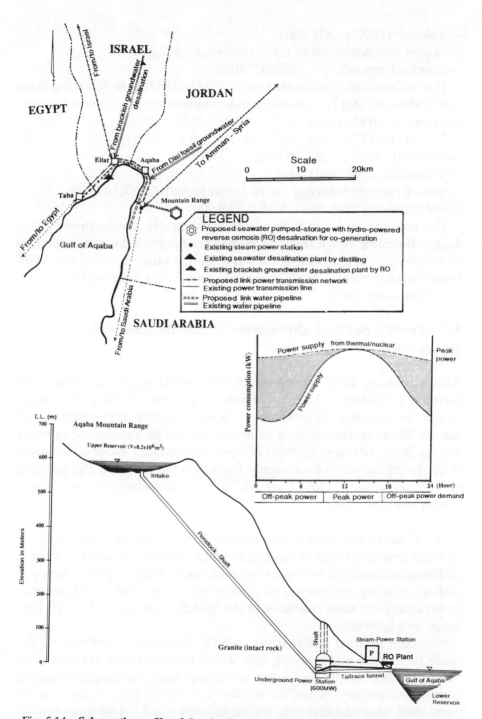

Fig. 5.14 **Schematic profile of the Aqaba co-generation seawater pumped-storage scheme with hydro-powered RO desalination**

241

— *subtotal* (US$246,835,000);
— design and construction management, US$62,250,000;
— financial expenditure, US$80,270,000.

The annual cost is estimated to be US$18,568,000 in financing costs and US$44,387,000 in operation and maintenance costs, including the following main elements:
— labour, US$3,718,000,
— material supply, US$1,860,000,
— chemicals, US$7,440,000,
— power (pumped storage for RO feed water), US$3,100,000,
— membrane replacement, US$28,269,000.

The unit water cost of hydro-powered seawater desalination to produce 100 million m^3 of fresh water per year is preliminarily estimated to be US$0.68/m^3, assuming the same design criteria as for the MDS hydro-powered seawater RO desalination scheme discussed in section 5.4 (Murakami 1993b).

5.7   Techno-political alternatives in Middle East water perspectives

After exploiting all of the renewable fresh water resources within their national boundaries, Israel, Palestine, and Jordan have no choice except to develop transboundary waters and/or non-conventional waters. Water conservation is an important and essential issue in water management, but development of non-conventional water alternatives is becoming imperative to supply fresh potable water to the growing population in the Middle East and within the framework of a water master plan for peace.

5.7.1   *Non-conventional water-resources development alternatives*
Conventional alternatives have the highest priority in water-resources planning where there are still renewable fresh waters to be developed without creating any inter-state riparian questions. This ideal situation does not exist in most countries of the Middle East apart from Turkey, Syria, and Lebanon.

Non-conventional alternatives, which comprise desalination, the reuse of treated waste water, and water transportation by tanker or barge or bags, will be key issues to sustain water development in the twenty-first century, when no further renewable fresh water can be developed without exceeding the sustainable yield, while non-conventional water resources are generally more complex in development and operation than conventional sources and are almost always more expensive. The great advantage of desalination and the reuse of treated waste water is that there are no political constraints on their development. The unlimited supply of seawater is another advantage for desalination, especially since 70% of the Arab and Israeli populations live along the sea coast. This situation favours Israel and the Gaza Strip, but not the West Bank and Jordan except for the Aqaba coastal plain.

Fossil groundwater by contrast is far too valuable an asset for use except as a strategic reserve that can be used for a short time for relief during extreme drought or emergencies.

5.7.2 Project feasibility and techno-political alternatives

Any water project in the Middle East, whether conventional or non-conventional, will have to be reviewed for technical and environmental feasibility, economic and financial feasibility, and social and political feasibility.

Project priority among the techno-political alternatives will be evaluated by taking into account the project time-schedule priorities on a short-term or emergency, mid-term, and long-term basis (see fig. 5.15). The following priorities are proposed on the assumption that equal weight will be given to each feasibility element.

(1) Short-term relief—highest priority and urgent countermeasures in water development and management, no political constraints:
   — water conservation and water management,
   — reuse of treated waste water (for supplemental irrigation),
   — desalination (for potable water supply, mainly by reverse osmosis);

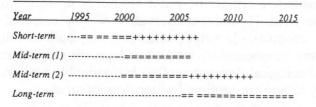

Fig. 5.15 **Schematic time schedule for evaluation of project priorities.** Short dashes (- - -) represent period of study, negotiation, and development; "equals" signs (= = −), project implementation; "plus" signs (+ + +), supplemental implementation if any.

(2) mid-term relief 1—high priority in water-energy development, to be included in a strategic peace agreement between Israel, Palestine, and Jordan that may facilitate peace negotiations, with benefits for multilateral regional economic development opportunities in the Dead Sea and Aqaba regions:
— Mediterranean (Gaza)–Dead Sea conduit scheme with hydro-powered RO desalination for co-generation,
— Aqaba seawater pumped-storage scheme with hydro-powered RO desalination for co-generation,
— Red Sea–Dead Sea or MDS canal hydro-electric scheme,
— Dead Sea pumped-storage scheme;

(3) mid-term relief 2—medium priority in the water-supply alternatives with some bilateral negotiations with water-rich countries such as Turkey, Albania, Iran, and South-East Asian countries:
— interstate water transportation by tankers, barges, and/or bags;

(4) long-term relief—medium to low priority (but not any less important) with complicated multinational riparian negotiations and/or technical-economic-financial complexity. Inter-state water transportation by pipeline, canal, and other means is illustrated in fig. 1.2, including:
— Nile–Gaza/Israel water pipeline,
— Iraq–Jordan water pipeline,
— Litany (Lebanon–Israel) basin water transfer,
— Iraq–Kuwait water pipeline,
— mini-peace pipeline (Seyhan–Ceyhan–Jordan River system),
— peace pipeline or canal,
— peace canal,
— Iran–Qatar submarine water pipeline,
— Turkey–Israel submarine water pipeline,
— megawatershed (Rift Valley groundwater development).

After exploiting renewable water resources up to the limits of the sustainable yield, (1) water conservation will be essential to manage the water resources; (2) water politics and negotiations will be priority issues in any transboundary water-development project; and (3) innovative technological development with reasonable cost reduction will be the key to non-conventional water development.

6

Summary of conclusions, and recommendations for further study

Chapter 6 focuses on the conclusions of the application studies in chapters 3–5. Remarks on the technical feasibility and cost-effectiveness of the proposed new technology of hydro-powered reverse osmosis (RO) desalination and its application to non-conventional water-resources development alternatives are summarized in the context of national and/or inter-state water master planning. This summary also takes into account the concluding remarks of the review studies in section 2.12 of chapter 2.

6.1 Conclusions

From the case study on non-conventional water-resources development in Kuwait, the unit cost of brackish-groundwater RO desalination was estimated to be US$0.40/m^3 with and US$0.60/m^3 without the hydro-potential energy in the water pipeline system (200 m of differential head). The cost of hydro-powered brackish-groundwater RO in these circumstances is estimated to be as low as one-sixth to one-fourth of the cost of conventional seawater desalination either by MSF (US$2.70/m^3) or RO (US$1.70/m^3).

The potential of brackish waters, both groundwater and surface water, which have long been neglected in water-resources studies, has

245

to be evaluated in the context of national water master planning, taking into account the water quality in the aquifers and the promising progress being made in RO desalination technologies.

The case study of national water-resources master planning in Jordan identified two schemes, the Al-Wuheda dam and Disi fossil groundwater development, as key projects to sustain national water-resources development after the 1990s. The fossil groundwater in the Disi aquifer, however, should be conserved for emergency use only. After completion of the Al-Wuheda dam on the Yarmouk River by the end of the 1990s, non-conventional water-resources development, including desalination of brackish water and the reuse of treated sewage effluents, will become the key technologies in future water plans for Jordan.

The proposed co-generation approach to brackish-groundwater development with hydro-powered RO desalination using the existing Disi–Aqaba water-supply system will conserve the fossil groundwater in the Disi aquifer and produce both hydro-electricity and fresh water, including 14.6 million m^3 of fresh water per water with potential hydro-power generation at 15,900 MWh per year. The sustainable management or conservation of the non-renewable fresh groundwater in the Disi aquifer is possible by developing the brackish groundwater in the Kurnub aquifer, which has never been tapped. The unit cost of brackish-groundwater desalination by hydro-powered reverse osmosis is estimated to be US$0.41/m^3.

The proposed integrated co-generation approach, coupling the Mediterranean–Dead Sea (MDS) solar-hydro scheme with hydro-powered RO desalination, will be able to produce 100 million m^3 of fresh water per year and 500 MW of electricity, which is about 10% of Israel's national grid's capacity of 5,835 MW in 1991. The 1×10^9 kWh of electricity generated per year would have to be shared by the two riparians, Israel and Jordan, to supply their peak demands, while the product fresh water is to be exclusively used and shared in the water supply for the central Ghor (Jordan valley). The unit water cost of seawater desalination by hydro-powered reverse osmosis is estimated to be US$0.68/m^3. The much discussed MDS conduit scheme could thus be realizable by introducing new technology and the non-conventional concept of sharing resources in the context of an inter-state water-resources development master plan.

The Al-Wuheda dam project and other side-wadi dam schemes such as flood retention or groundwater recharge dams, together with RO desalination to salvage brackish water from saline springs and irrigation return in the lower Jordan River system, all of which would enhance the solar-hydro potential of the Dead Sea, should be linked with the MDS conduit scheme in a sharing of valuable inter-state resources and benefits in the context of an integrated development plan. This would not create any new political conflicts but rather promote peace and economic development for Jordan, Palestine, and Israel. Any storage or retention dam schemes and the lower Jordan Peace Drainage Canal scheme with RO desalination will have prominent priority in a short- to medium-term strategy.

The proposed joint inter-state basin-development master plan for the Jordan River system would now seem to be a practical possibility, being not only technically and economically feasible but also politically desirable and urgent.

The interregional economic development planning will need to cover the Dead Sea (Israel/Palestine/Jordan) and Aqaba (Egypt/Israel/Jordan). These two geopolitical regions have a prominent place in the peace process and will be a gateway to cooperation among all the countries of the Middle East. The Mediterranean–Dead Sea or Red Sea–Dead Sea conduit scheme and Aqaba hybrid seawater pumped-storage with hydro-powered RO desalination for co-generation are possibly of even greater importance for economic development, including tourism, housing, commerce, and the industry of the whole region.

6.2 Recommendations for further study

Further research will be needed to evaluate the technical and institutional feasibilities of the Mediterranean–Dead Sea or Red Sea–Dead Sea conduit scheme and Aqaba hybrid seawater pumped storage with and without hydro-powered RO desalination.

Technical issues requiring study include:

» reassessment of the actual evaporation that will occur from the surface of the Dead Sea after impounding seawater from the Mediterranean, including in-situ tank trials and laboratory model tests;

» environmental assessment to predict the climatic change and the ecological effect on life in the area;

» prototype trials of low-pressure-type (40–50 kg/cm^2) membrane modules for seawater RO desalination, including the extension of life from the present three years up to five to seven years;

» design of materials to avoid corrosion of hydraulic structures from seawater and brine reject water.

Institutional issues include:

» riparian-rights issues relating to multinational use of the Dead Sea surface, including the allocation of potential energy from evaporation from its surface;

» long-term demilitarization of the Mediterranean–Dead Sea or Red Sea–Dead Sea conduit route and arrangements for project management by an international agency such as the United Nations, including the establishment of the Middle East Development Bank.

Appendices

Appendices

A

Reverse-osmosis desalination

A.1 Background

Desalting techniques are primarily intended for the removal of dissolved salts that generally cannot be removed by conventional treatment processes. Distillation units have been used on some American ships for more than 100 years. Desalting was used on a limited scale for municipal water treatment in the late 1960s. The past four decades can be divided into three phases of desalting: The 1950s were a time of discovery; the 1960s were concerned with research; and the 1970s and 1980s have been the time of commercialization. Beginning in the 1970s, the industry began to concentrate on commercially viable desalination applications and processes (Buros 1989).

The first commercial plant for the production of potable water from a saline source using electrodialysis (ED) and ion-exchange membranes was put into operation in 1954 (Powell and Guild 1961). In 1968, use of membranes for brackish-water treatment started with the construction of an ED plant in Florida, in the United States. This process was not favourably received in view of its inability to adequately reduce dissolved solids. The first reverse-osmosis (RO) water treatment plant was constructed in 1970 for a condominium project on Longboat Key, Florida (Dykes and Colon 1989). Significant advances in membrane technologies in the last 20 years have improved the cost-effectiveness and performance capabilities of the processes. RO membrane processes are increasingly used worldwide to solve a variety of water treatment problems.

A.2 World desalination

The arid region, with its very limited fresh-water potential, has generally used high-salinity waters such as seawater as major water supply sources. More than two-thirds of the world's desalting capacity is located in the arid, oil-rich areas of North Africa and Western Asia, or the Middle East (Buros 1989):

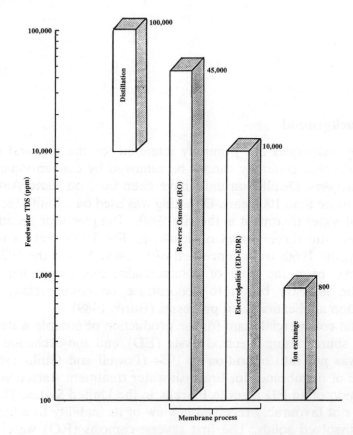

Fig. A.1 **Typical feed-water TDS operating ranges for desalting processes** (Source: AWWA 1989)

— Western Asia (Middle East), 63%,
— North America, 11%,
— North Africa, 7%,
— Europe, 7%,
— Pacific, 4%,
— Caribbean, 2%,
— (former) USSR, 2%,
— others, 4%.

A.2.1 Desalting technology and processes

The major desalting technologies used today are distillation (several types of evaporative process), reverse-osmosis (RO), electrodialysis (ED), electrodialysis reversal (EDR), and ion-exchange demineralization. The typical concentration ranges of total dissolved solids (TDS) in the feed water for distillation, RO, ED, and EDR demineralization are: between 10,000 and 100,000 mg/l for distillation and other thermal (non-membrane) processes, up to about 35,000–45,000 mg/l (seawater concentrations) for RO membrane, up to approximately 10,000 mg/l for ED and EDR membrane (AWWA 1989) (see fig. A.1). Ion exchange, in which anion and cation resins are used to exchange ions for hydrogen and hydroxide, is primarily used in industrial applications for which very pure water is required and the feed-water TDS is relatively low. Distillation and other thermal processes are used primarily for seawater conversion and special industrial applications, such as brine concentration.

A.2.2 Desalination capacity by process

As shown in table A.1, 70% of the world's desalination capacity is dependent on the distilling process. In the Middle East and North

Table A.1 **Distribution of desalination capacity by process**

	Share of capacity (%)	
	World	United States
Distillation	70	21
Reverse osmosis	25	73
Electrodialysis	5	6

Source: Buros 1989.

Africa, distillation of seawater is the main process being used, while the processes favoured in the United States and other countries are quite different, reflecting the numerous applications for the desalination of brackish water (Buros 1989).

In 1985 the total worldwide installed capacity of land-based desalting plants with a capacity exceeding 100 m³ (25,000 gallons) per day was more than 11.4 million m³ (3 × 10⁹ gallons) per day, which is more than three times the capacity in 1975. Seawater and brackish-water sources with salinity in a range between 1,000 and 40,000 ppm of TDS account for nearly all of this installed capacity, comprising approximately 75% of seawater and 23% of brackish-water sources. Membrane processes represent about 30% of this total capacity and nearly all of the brackish-water treatment capacity (AWWA 1989).

A.2.3   Economics and environment

The cost of desalination has generally decreased from more than US$3/m³ to as low as US$0.50/m³ over time as a result of both technological advances and market processes (Buros 1989). The historical cost of desalting brackish water and seawater with available

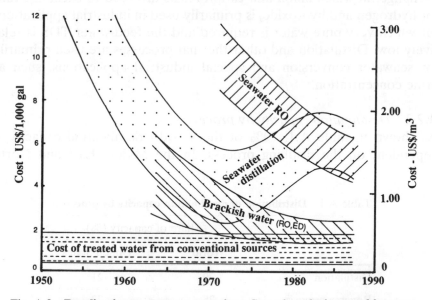

Fig. A.2   **Desalination cost ranges over time.** Cost of producing potable water, by distillation or reverse osmosis, including both capital and operating costs (at 1985 prices), for plants producing 3,700–18,000 m³ per day. The increasing cost of distillation from the early 1970s reflects international crude-oil prices. (Source: Buros 1989)

technologies is shown in fig. A.2, which is based on a recent cost-assessment study by the Office of Technology Assessment for the US Congress.

Improvements in RO membranes have been the main technological change in desalination in recent years. The United States and Japan are the world's leading countries in innovative research to develop the membrane industry. A high level of competition on both a national and international basis has also played a significant role in containing prices for capital equipment. The following percentages illustrate the distribution of overall costs for the operation of a brackish-water desalting plant (Dykes and Colon 1989):

— capital-cost recovery, 41%,
— membranes, 12%,
— energy, 26%,
— labour, 11%,
— chemicals, 7%,
— other expendable items, 3%.

As can be seen, the main item of cost is capital recovery, which represents almost half of the overall cost. The next most significant cost items are energy, membranes, and labour.

The dominant cost element in seawater RO desalination is the energy, or electricity, which accounts for 50% or more. Substantial cost reduction can be achieved by taking into account the following:

» technology improvement and research to increase membrane life—from three years to up to now five to seven years;
» the development of low-pressure-type or low-energy-requirement membranes;
» the development of a pumped-storage-type RO desalination system using off-peak cheap electricity from nuclear power plants or other thermal power plants; hydro-powered RO desalination is another option (Murakami 1991, 1993a).

Generally seen as benign, desalination is not without environmental concerns of its own. From a regulatory standpoint, the big advantage to desalination is that it takes out water that is unusable, leaving fresh water available for other uses. But there is some question about how to dispose of the concentrated brine that is the by-product of desalination. The very highly concentrated brine from distilling plants poses a major problem to be solved, including a sufficient analysis of the potential impact on the marine environment, while less saline brine from RO plants may have a relatively minor adverse impact on the marine ecology.

Table A.2 **Installed capacity of desalination plants in Arabian Gulf countries (million m³ per day)**

	MSF	RO	Other	Total
Saudi Arabia	2,316	77	2	2,395
Kuwait	1,409	—	—	1,409
U.A.E.	709	—	—	709
Qatar	295	—	—	295
Bahrain	115	45	—	160
Oman	105	1	1	107
TOTAL	4,949	123	3	5,075

Source: Akkad 1990.

A.3 Seawater desalination in the Arabian Gulf countries

In extremely arid countries, where good-quality water is not available, seawater desalination is commonly used to supply water for municipal and industrial uses. In spite of the high cost of desalinated water, a vast quantity is produced to meet the demand for domestic water in the Gulf countries.

A.3.1 Installed capacity of desalination plants

The installed capacity of desalination plants in Saudi Arabia, Kuwait, the United Arab Emirates, Qatar, Bahrain, and Oman is estimated at 5.08 million m³ per day in total, including 2.4 million m³ per day in Saudi Arabia, which is approximately half of the total for the Gulf countries. Dual-purpose multi-stage flash (MSF) is the most commonly used technique to desalt seawater, representing 97% of the total installed capacity, as shown in table A.2 (Akkad 1990).

A.3.2 World's largest water pipeline and seawater distillation for municipal and industrial water supply

Saudi Arabia has commissioned several desalination plants to meet the rapidly increasing demand for domestic water since 1970. They are located mainly along the Red Sea and Arabian Gulf coasts and produce 2,183,607 m³ of potable water per day and 4,147 MW of electricity (see fig. A.3). The Al-Jubail–Riyadh pipeline, whose water

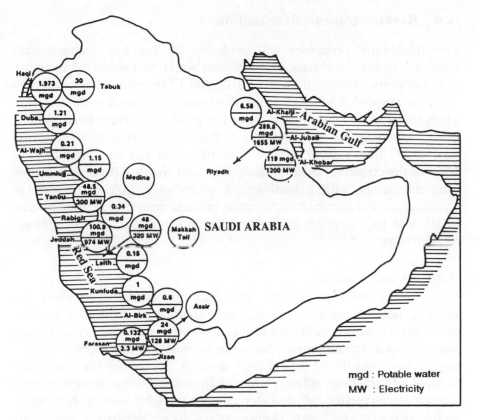

Fig. A.3 **Desalination plants in Saudi Arabia** (Source: SWCC 1988)

source is wholly dependent on seawater distillation, is one of the world's largest high-pressure pipeline systems. It has a diameter of 1.5 m (60 inches), a length of 465 km, a differential head of 690 m, and a design flow rate of 830,000 m³ day. There are six pumping stations with 430 MW capacity in total and a terminal reservoir with 300,000 m³ storage at Riyad (Abanmy and Al-Rashed 1992).

A.3.3 Remarks on seawater distillation
The problem with seawater distillation is the high cost of producing fresh water by the MSF process, which is the most prevalent type of thermal distillation in the Middle East. The process is largely dependent on the rate of energy consumption, which is high and influenced by the unstable world market price of crude oil (fig. A.2).

A.4   Reverse-osmosis desalination

The membrane processes will probably be the key technological approach to the desalination of brackish water and seawater over the next ten years. Although the RO, ED, and EDR membrane processes are used worldwide to solve a variety of water treatment problems, it is likely that RO will continue to have the greatest market share. Where fresh water supplies are limited or must be imported over long distances, RO desalting of nearby brackish water can be cost-effective. Most of the countries in the Middle East and North Africa have rather long sea coasts, with a total length of about 25,000 km. Seawater desalination will continue to increase in these countries, either by distillation or RO, depending on site-specific conditions and technology development.

A.4.1   Brackish water

Good-quality water is neither abundant nor available to meet the growing demand in most of the coastal areas in arid to semi-arid countries. However, sufficient brackish water is normally available on site to support development. Since the early 1970s, advances in desalination have mostly been directed towards improving the abundant sources of brackish water rather than towards the comparatively expensive conversion of seawater. Significant advances in membrane technologies in the last twenty years have improved the cost-effectiveness and performance capabilities of the RO process. Brackish-water desalination usually costs only one-fifth to one-third as much as seawater desalting (Buros 1989).

A.4.2   Seawater

For environmental reasons, thermal distillation plants, which are largely dependent on high specific energy consumption, are likely to be replaced progressively by low-specific-energy-consumption types of RO desalination plants. At the end of 1989, the world's largest seawater RO desalination plant, with an installed capacity of 56,500 m^3 day, was constructed at Jeddah, on the west coast of Saudi Arabia, to replace a 20-year-old MSF distilling plant that was being phased out (fig. A.3). It may be noted that a case study on the Doha desalination plant in Kuwait in 1989 estimated the unit cost of seawater desalination at US\$2.70/m^3 by MSF and US\$1.70/m^3 by the RO membrane process (Darwish et al. 1989).

A.4.3 Reclamation of treated waste water

The application of membrane-separation technology to salvage treated waste water includes three alternative processes: (1) micro filtration, (2) ultra filtration, and (3) loose reverse osmosis. Both the micro-filter and ultra-filter are used to control better water quality in the tertiary treatment process and/or the final water purification process. Another application is being tested to be used directly in the primary or secondary waste-water treatment process. The loose RO process is being developed to reclaim treated waste water for strategic reuse in the agricultural and/or industrial sector.

Although it is clear that membrane desalting is a cost-effective alternative to importing fresh water over long distances, the use of the membrane process to remove turbidity, organic matter, and hardness has typically been more expensive than conventional treatment. However, with the continuing improvements in membrane-separation technology, increasing competition among manufacturers of capital equipment, and the ever-escalating cost of meeting increasingly stringent water quality standards by conventional approaches, the cost gap is decreasing (AWWA 1989).

A.4.4 Key applications in the twenty-first century

Membrane-separation technology, using low-energy and/or energy-saving types of membrane, are expected to continue to be popular in arid coastal regions and other areas wherever saline waters are available but good-quality fresh water is limited or not available. Application of the membrane-separation technology in the arid countries will be mainly for seawater and brackish-water desalination. Reverse-osmosis, ultra-filter, and micro-filter membranes are being used to reclaim either saline water or waste water for reuse, which could indeed be the technology to take the drinking-water and sanitation industries gradually into the twenty-first century.

A.5 Principle, method, and process of reverse osmosis

A.5.1 Principle

Osmosis is a natural process whereby a solvent (water) diffuses through a semi-permeable membrane from a solution of lower concentration to one of higher concentration (part A in fig. A.4). The membrane readily passes the solvent but acts as a barrier to the solutes (dissolved solids). At equilibrium conditions, the pressure differential

259

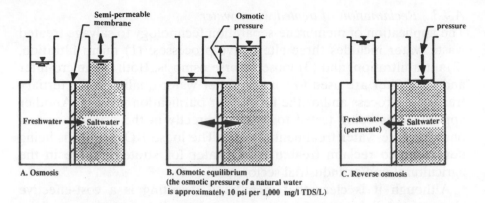

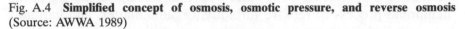

Fig. A.4 **Simplified concept of osmosis, osmotic pressure, and reverse osmosis** (Source: AWWA 1989)

across the membrane is called the osmotic pressure (part B, fig. A.4). For example, the osmotic pressure of brackish water containing about 2,000 ppm TDS at a typical water temperature of 25°C is only about 1.6 kg/cm^2, whereas it is 27.7 kg/cm^2 for standard seawater of 35,000 ppm TDS at 25°C. In reverse osmosis, a pressure greater than the osmotic pressure is applied to the concentrated solution (saline water), and a dilute permeate (product water) is produced (part C, fig. A.4).

Fig. A.5 is a flow schematic of a simplified RO unit. The pressure of the feed water, pre-treated to meet certain established RO membrane feed-water quality guidelines, is boosted before the water enters the RO membranes. Two flows exit the membranes: (1) the combined product (permeate), and (2) the combined concentrate (reject). The fraction of the feed water that results as permeate is called the recovery and is usually expressed as a percentage. The maximum allowable ratio of permeate to reject depends on the water's scaling potential, which is a function of the feed-water quality. This ratio is maintained by the use of a control valve on the reject piping, which controls the flow rate of the reject, thus forcing the permeate flow rate to the desired value.

A.5.2 RO membranes
The first commercially available membranes, developed in the mid-1960s, were made of cellulose acetate (CA) manufactured in flat sheets. Modern CA membranes are modifications of the cellulose acetate structure, including blends and different surface treatments,

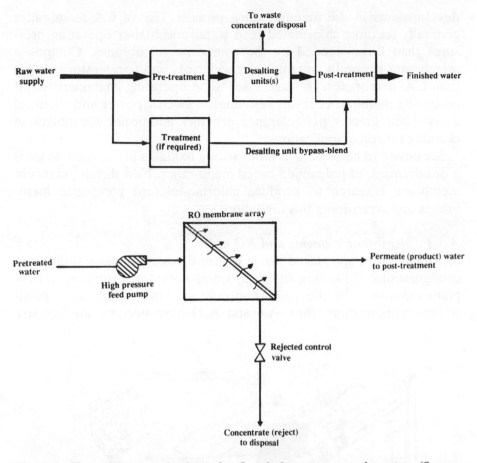

RO membrane array

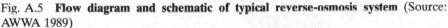

Fig. A.5 **Flow diagram and schematic of typical reverse-osmosis system** (Source: AWWA 1989)

and are called cellulosic or symmetric membrane. Non-cellulosic membranes, called thin-film composite membranes, have been developed since the 1970s. These include polyamide membranes with relatively thick asymmetric polyamide support structures and composite membranes with thin-film polyamide or other membrane materials on a porous support structure.

Each membrane material has advantages and disadvantages. The CA-based membranes are now generally the least expensive per gallon of installed capacity (first cost). The price difference between CA and composites is decreasing, however, as the number of manufacturers supplying the composite-type membranes increases and with new

261

developments in the manufacturing process. Use of CA membranes generally requires chlorinated feed water and higher operating pressures than those needed by the composite membranes. Composite membranes generally operate over wider pH and temperature ranges than CA membranes. In some cases these operating characteristics of composite membranes result in savings in electric power and chemical costs. Their greater pH tolerance provides additional advantages in cleaning for some applications.

Sensitivity to chlorine and other strong oxidants in the feed water is a disadvantage of polyamide-based membranes. New developments in membrane research to produce chlorine-tolerant composite membranes are overcoming this limitation.

A.5.3   Membrane elements and RO units

RO membranes are placed inside pressure vessels in several different configurations: (1) hollow-fibre, (2) spiral-wound, (3) tubular, and (4) plate-and-frame. In the past twenty years, hollow-fibre and spiral-wound configurations (figs. A.6 and A.7) have become the industry

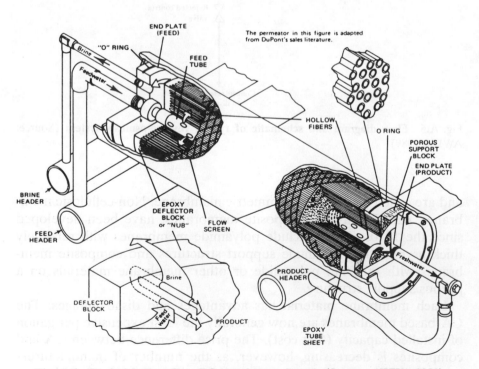

Fig. A.6   **Typical hollow-fibre RO membrane element** (Source: AWWA 1989)

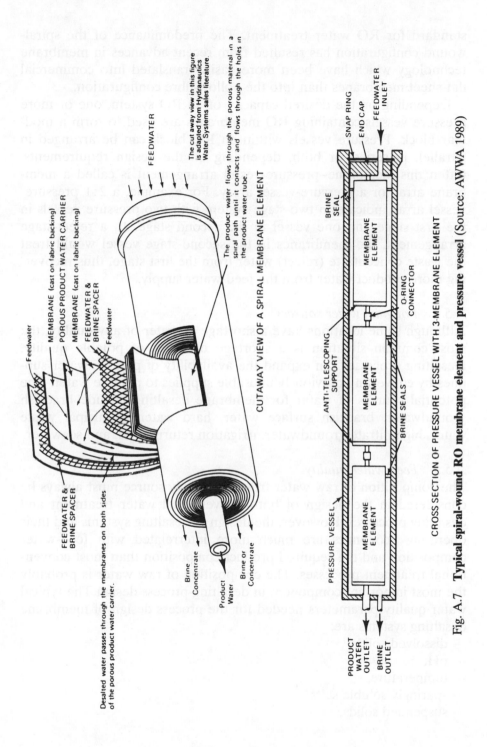

Fig. A.7 Typical spiral-wound RO membrane element and pressure vessel (Source: AWWA 1989)

263

standard for RO water treatment. The predominance of the spiral-wound configuration has resulted from recent advances in membrane technology which have been more easily translated into commercial flat-sheet membranes than into the hollow-fibre configuration.

Depending on the desired capacity of an RO system, one or more pressure vessels containing RO membranes are used to form a modular block. Pressure vessels within an RO block can be arranged in parallel, in series, or both, depending on the design requirements. Often this membrane–pressure-vessel arrangement is called a membrane array or a pressure-vessel array. For example, a 2:1 pressure-vessel array indicates a two-stage system with two pressure vessels in the first stage and one vessel in the second stage. In a reject-stage arrangement, the membranes in the second-stage vessel would treat the waste concentrate (reject) water from the first stage, thus recovering more product water from the feed-water supply.

A.5.4 Potential water sources

Although some locations have a shortage of water of any quality, the most common situation is a shortage of water of potable quality. Desalting processes can expand the availability of potable water supplies by converting previously unusable supplies to potable water. The potential sources of water for membrane desalting include brackish groundwater, brackish surface water, hard water, municipal waste water, high-nitrate groundwater, irrigation return flows, and seawater.

A.5.5 Feed-water quality

The composition of raw water from the supply source must always be considered in the design of both conventional water treatment and desalting processes. However, the design of desalting systems and their operating economics are much more interrelated with feed-water composition and the required product composition than most conventional treatment processes. The composition of raw water is probably the most important component in desalting-process design The typical water-quality parameters needed for the process design of membrane desalting systems are:
— dissolved solids,
— pH,
— temperature,
— sparingly soluble salts,
— suspended solids,

— iron and manganese,
— microbial growth,
— organic.

A.5.6   Pre-treatment

Pre-treatment is usually required to protect the membrane system, to improve performance, or both. The type of pre-treatment required depends on the feed-water characteristics, membrane type, and system design parameters. Pre-treatment requirements can be minimal, such as cartridge filtration of well water, or extensive, such as conventional coagulation, sedimentation, and filtration of surface water supply.

For RO systems, standard pre-treatment usually consists of adding chemicals for scale control, followed by cartridge filtration (usually 1-, 5-, 10-, or 20-μm nominal rating) for membrane protection. The feed water is often acidified to lower its pH; this step is nearly always required for cellulosic membranes. Scale inhibitors such as sodium hexametaphosphate or proprietary chemicals are also added to reduce carbonate and sulphate scale potential.

A.5.7   Pump system

The pump system raises the pressure of the pre-treated feed water to the level required for operation of the desalting system. For RO, the pump system discharge pressure typically is 8.8–28.1 kg/cm^2 (125–400 psi) for low-TDS and brackish-water systems and 56.2–84.3 kg/cm^2 (800–1,200 psi) for seawater systems. The pump system for RO might also include energy-recovery devices, particularly for seawater systems.

A.5.8   Post-treatment

Post-treatment to supply drinking water commonly includes product-water pH adjustment for corrosion control and chemical addition for disinfection. Typically entrained gases such as carbon dioxide and hydrogen sulphide (if present) are removed before final pH adjustment and disinfection.

Removal of these gases is normally accomplished by stripping in a forced-draft packed column. In the most cases, carbon dioxide must be removed to stabilize the RO product water. If hydrogen sulphide is present, degassing of the product water is usually done to control odour and minimize the amount of disinfectant (e.g., chlorine). The final product-water pH is often adjusted by caustic soda, soda ash, or lime. A non-corrosive water can be produced by using these alkaline chemicals and, in some cases, other chemicals and blending with raw or other water supplies that may also feed the distribution system.

Post-treatment disinfection is normally accomplished with chlorine. However, if the desalting process allows the passage of trihalomethane (THM) precursors, chlorine dioxide, or chloramines, some additional post-treatment may be required to comply with THM drinking-water quality standards.

B

Physical geography of Jordan and Israel

B.1 Jordan

For this overview of the physical geography of Jordan, including its geology and hydrogeology, Bender (1975) is used as the core reference.

B.1.1 Topography

In contrast to the more uniform and monotonous morphology of most of the Arabian peninsula, the territory of Jordan is morphologically distinctive and may be divided into seven "physiographic provinces," which coincide with the geological provinces shown in fig. B.1 (RJGC 1986):

— southern mountain desert,
— mountain range and northern highlands east of the Rift,
— central plateau, including the Al-Jafr and Al-Azraq–Wadi as-Sirhan basin,
— northern plateau basalt,
— north-eastern plateau,
— Wadi al-Arabah–Jordan Rift,
— highlands west of the Rift.

The most remarkable physical feature of the country is the Jordan

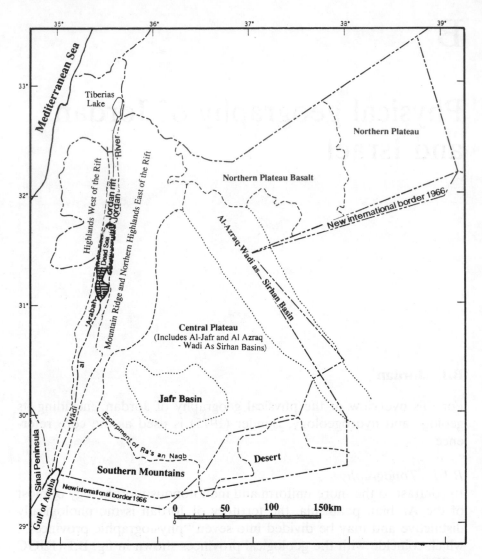

Fig. B.1 **Physiographic-geological provinces of Jordan** (Source: Bender 1975)

Rift valley, which is a narrow depression extending from the Gulf of
Aqaba for approximately 360 km north to the upper Jordan River.
Much of the land in this graben, as it is called, is below sea level, with
the lowest levels in the Dead Sea at −794 m. The Jordan River flows
into the Dead Sea, which has no outlet. The Rift valley, however,
continues to the Gulf of Aqaba, where Jordan has 20 km of coastline.
To the east of the Rift valley, the land rises steeply to a plateau with an

average altitude of about 800 m above mean sea level and with peaks rising to over 1,500 m in the south. Ninety per cent or more of the surface water resources, which include two-third of the country's total potential water resources, are drained into the Dead Sea.

B.1.2 Hydrology

Jordan lies in a transitional zone between the Mediterranean climate in the west and the arid climate to the east and south. The synoptic climatic zone of Jordan is part of the Mediterranean bio-climatic region, an essential feature of which is the concentration of rainfall during the cool winter season and a very marked summer drought. This relatively simple climatic regime is due to the interaction of two major atmospheric circulation patterns. During the winter months Jordan is within the sphere of influence of the temperate-latitudes climatic belt, and moist, cool air moves eastward from the Mediterranean over the area. In the summer months the area lies within the sub-tropical high-pressure belt of dry air; temperatures are relatively high and no rainfall occurs. Regional distribution of rainfall within the area is related to the orographic effect of the western highlands, which are oriented normal to the direction of movement of moist air during the winter months. This produces high rainfall zones coincident with the higher mountain ranges and a marked rain shadow in the lee of the hills. Altitude has also a strong effect on temperature. Frost is common during the winter months, and snowfalls occur in most years in the western highlands from December to March.

The highest rainfall zones correspond to the major mountain blocks of the western highlands, including the highest mean annual rainfall of 664 mm at Ajlun station in the northern part of the western highlands. The mean annual rainfall is relatively abundant, in the range between 200 and 600 mm in the western highlands, but it decreases rapidly from the western highlands into the Jordan valley, Dead Sea, and Wadi Araba. From the northern end of the Dead Sea southwards and from Wadi Araba to Aqaba, the mean annual rainfall decreases to less than 100 mm and 50 mm respectively. North from the Dead Sea to Lake Tiberias rainfall increases to up to 400 mm per year. In most of the central plateau and in the eastern desert the mean annual rainfall decreases to less than 50–100 mm where the land slopes gently to the Arabian desert. Rainfall occurs between October and May and is at its highest between December and March, when more than 80% of the annual rainfall occurs. The annual rainfall varies from year to year; the range is most marked in the central plateau and in the southern part of the western highlands, where there have been extreme records of only 2 mm per year and a maximum of 233 mm per year. The distribution of annual rainfall is shown in fig. B.2.

Owing to the hyper-arid climate with a substantial deficit in soil moisture, actual evaporation from the desert land is estimated to be very small and is less than the amount of annual rainfall plus residual soil moisture, while the potential evaporation, which as measured by class A-pan, is as high as 2,400–7,400 mm per year. The highest rate of 7,400 mm per year occurs in the eastern and southern Bayir, while it is less than 3,000 mm per year in the northern and central mountain ranges and less than 2,800 mm in the mountains of Shoubak and Tafila (RJGC 1986). The highest potential evaporation occurs during the hottest months of the year, from June to August; the months with lowest evaporation are December to February.

The average annual volume of rainfall within Jordan is estimated to be 8,500 million m³. With high evaporation losses, however, the average net annual run-off is only about 1,120 million m³, including 242 million m³ in the form of groundwater and 878 million m³ in surface flow.

The eastern Jordan valley basin, which includes the Syrian share of the Yarmouk River basin—including the Yarmouk River, Wadi Arab, Wadi Ziqlab, Wadi Jurum, Wadi Yabis, Wadi Kufrinja, Wadi Rajib, Wadi Zarqa, Wadi Shueib, and Wadi Kafrein—has an annual average run-off estimated to be 607 million m³ in total, which includes 357 million m³ of base flow.

The Dead Sea basin, which includes Wadi Zerqa Ma'an, Wadi Wala, Wadi Mujib, Wadi al-Karak, and Wadi Hasa, has an annual average run-off estimated to be 191 million m³ in total, including 141 million m³ of base flow.

A small amount of surface flow occurs in the Wadi Araba basin south of the Dead Sea. The Wadi Araba basin includes Wadi Feifa, Wadi Khuneizir, Wadi Fidan, Wadi el-Buweirida, and Wadi Musa. The annual average run-off is estimated to be 31 million m³ in total, including 21.6 million m³ of base flow.

Other desert basins are mostly located in the eastern and southern part of Jordan, of which the wadi systems are not clearly defined.

The Yarmouk River, which runs along the northern border of Jordan with Syria, provides almost half (400 million m³ per year at Adasiya) of Jordan's surface water resources. The total stream-flows of Jordan are estimated to be about 878 million m³ per year, including 540 million m³ of base flow.

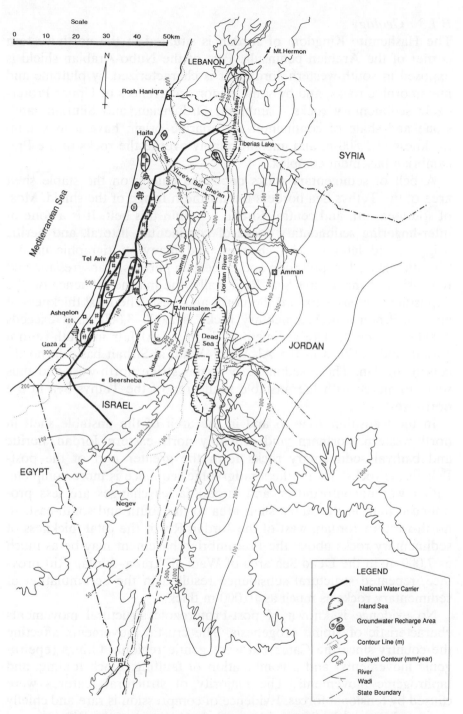

Fig. B.2 **Mean annual rainfall map of Israel and the Jordan Rift valley**

B.1.3   Geology

The Hashemite Kingdom of Jordan is situated in the north-western corner of the Arabian peninsula. Part of the Nubo-Arabian shield is exposed in south-western Jordan. It is characterized by plutonic and metamorphic rocks, and by some minor occurrences of Upper Proterozoic sedimentary rocks. Cambrian, Ordovician, and Silurian sandstone and shale of continental and marine origin have a maximum thickness of 1,800 m and unconformably overlie the rocks of the Precambrian basement complex.

A belt of sedimentary rocks deposited chiefly on the stable shelf area of the Tethys Sea borders the northern fringe of the shield. Most of south-eastern and central Jordan is within this belt. It is a zone of inter-fingering sedimentary rocks of continental, littoral, and neritic origin, rapid lateral facies changes, and many stratigraphic unconformities caused by pulsation and, at certain periods, transgression and regression of the Tethys Sea. Regionally, the marine influence on the deposition increases toward the north and west. The total thickness of all post-Proterozoic sedimentary rocks is 2,000–3,000 m; it exceeds 4,000 m in the baylike sedimentary basin of Al-Jafr in south-central Jordan and 5,000 m in the Al-Azraq–Wadi al-Sirhan basin in north-central Jordan. These sedimentary basins strike north-west and thus seem to merge with the unstable shelf area of the Tethys Sea in the north-west.

In the transition zone to and in the area of the unstable shelf in north-western, northern, and probably north-eastern Jordan, neritic and bathyal sedimentary rocks form the greater part of the post-Palaeozoic rocks. There, the stratigraphic sequence is more complete, with fewer unconformities, and lateral facies changes are less pronounced than in the stable shelf area to the south and south-east. In north-western Jordan, west of the Jordan River, the total thickness of sedimentary rocks above the Precambrian basement may be as much as 7,000 m; in the Dead Sea area of Wadi al-Araba–Jordan Rift province, repeated structural subsidence resulted in the accumulation of sedimentary rocks as much as 10,000 m thick.

No evidence is known of post-Proterozoic structural movements characteristic of alpine orogenesis. The crustal movements affecting the country since the Cambrian were gentle regional tiltings (epeirogenic movements) and a combination of faulting, block folding, and taphrogenic movements. The majority of structural features were caused by tensional forces. Evidence of compression is rare and chiefly restricted to west Jordan and to north Jordan east of the Rift.

Major volcanic activity occurred during (1) the Late Proterozoic and Early Cambrian (quartz porphyries; Wadi al-Araba), (2) the Late Jurassic (?) and Neocomian (mafic and intermediate eruptive rocks; Wadi al-Araba and west of the Jordan River), and (3) the Neogene Tertiary (includes Miocene and Pliocene) and Pleistocene (extensive basalt volcanism) (Bender 1975).

B.1.4 Hydrogeology
The main aquifers have been recognized in the pervious sequences in the formation of (1) the basalt system, (2) Rijam (B4) system, (3) Amman–Wadi Sir (B2/A7) system, (4) Lower Ajlun (A1–6) system, (5) Kurnub system, and (6) Disi system (see fig. B.3).

BASALT SYSTEM. The basalt system of Pleistocene age is a regional shallow aquifer system to the north of Azraq. High rainfall on the Jabel Druze mountains in Syria is a source of groundwater recharge, which discharges southwards to the Azraq depression. The aquifer is formed by permeable scoriaceous zones in the basaltic rock unit.

RIJAM (B4) SYSTEM. The Rijam (B4) system of Eocene-Palaeocene age is a regional shallow aquifer which is formed in the central parts of the Jafr and Azraq basins. The Rijam formation has a thickness of 50–150 m or less, which is underlain by the chalky marls or chalks of the upper Muwaqqar (B3) formation. The aquifer is in an isolated-independent hydrologic system, forming a water-table condition in general. Within the basin the saturated zone of the Rijam formation occurs in an area of very low rainfall, less than 50 mm per year. The aquifer receives limited recharge by infiltration of flash floods through the wadi courses, which flow in an easterly direction. The wadi system and groundwater flow in the Jafr basin have no outlet. The Rijam formation of the Azraq basin comprises part of a composite aquifer system with a basalt system which discharges at the Azraq springs and swamps. The permeability of the Rijam formation is variable, owing to varying degrees of karstification. The water is highly saline in the areas of stagnant environment and in the discharging area, while it is fresh in the areas along the wadi courses where direct infiltration from the flash floods occurs. The Rijam aquifer is a local aquifer with limited potential.

AMMAN–WADI SIR (B2/A7) AQUIFER. The most important aquifer system is the Amman–Wadi Sir (B2/A7), which consists of limestone,

273

Era	Period	Epoch	Group	Formation	Thickness (m)	Aquifer Potential	Lithological Description
CENOZOIC	QUATERNARY	RECENT		Alluvium	0–300	Poor–Excellent	Gravel, sand, clay
		PLEISTOCENE		Lisan	0–300	Poor Good	Calcareous clay, gravels
				Samra		Poor	Calcareous reddish clay and gravels
		PLIO-MIOCENE		Neogene		Poor	Conglomerates
	TERTIARY	OLIGOCENE		Volcanics (basalt)	–100	Moderate–good	Basalt and conglomerates
		EOCENE PALEOCENE		Falej Rijam (B4)	–300	Moderate–excellent	Limestone, chert, marl, chalk, shale
MESOZOIC	CRETACEOUS Upper	DANIAN MAESTRICHTIAN	Berqa	Ramtha	–190	Poor	
				Muwaqqar(B3)	250	Poor	Chalky marl, bituminous marl, limestone, marls
		CAMPANIAN		Amman (B2)	100–150	Moderate–good	Limestone, silicified limestone chert, marl
		SANTONIAN COXIACIAN		Ruseifa(B1)	10–250	Poor	Chalk, marl, chert, limestone
	Middle Lower	TURONIAN	Ajlun	Wadi-Sir(A7)	70–200	Good	Limestone, sandstone, dolomite
		CENOMANIAN Upper		Shueib(A5/6)	70–150	Poor	Marl, limestone
		Middle		Hummar(A4)	30–200	Good–excellent	Dolomite, limestone
				Fuheis (A3)	80–150	Poor	Marl, chalk, limestone
		Lower		Naur (A2)	–120	Good	Limestone, marl, chalk
				(A1)	–300	Excellent	Dolomitic limestone, marl
	JURASSIC			Kurnub Upper	–200	Poor	Fine sandstone,
				Lower	–110	Moderate–good	White coarse sandstone
	TRIASSIC			Zarqa Upper	–300	Good	Limestone, dolomite, sandstone
				Lower	–70	Poor	Shale, gypsum, marl
							Unconformity (Main)
PALEOZOIC		SILURIAN ORDOVICIAN (Upper)		Khreim	–400	Poor	Fine-grained sandstone, mudstone, shale
		ORDOVICIAN (Middle) (Lower)		Disi	–250 130–350	Good	Bedded brownish sandstone Massive whitish sandstone
		CAMBRIAN (Lower)			190–350		Massive brownish sandstone
		CAMBRIAN (Lower)		Um Saleb	50–60	Moderate	Bedded arkosic sandstone
		PRECAMBRIAN		Aquaba	–	Poor	Granite, diabase

Fig. B.3 General hydrogeological section of Jordan (Source: Harshbarger 1966)

silicified limestone, chert, arenaceous limestone, and sandstone of Middle to Upper Cretaceous age. This system extends throughout the entire country, with a thickness of about 100–350 m. The depth of the groundwater table below the ground surface generally ranges from 50 to 250 m on the uplands. Good groundwater recharge occurs in the western highlands, where annual rainfall ranges from 200 to 600 mm. To the east, the aquifer is confined by a thick marl layer such as the Muwwaqar (B3) formation, and water salinity is increased.

LOWER AJLUN (A1–6) AQUIFER. An intermediate aquifer system is the lower Ajlun (A1–6), which consists of alternating limestone, marl, shale, chert, and sandstone of Middle Cretaceous age. This system is underlain by the Amman–Wadi Sir formation, which is mostly confined by its relatively impervious layer of marl and shale in the A5/6 of the upper unit of A1–6. The lower Ajlun formation extends throughout the country with variable thickness and litho-facies. Southwards, the aquifers in the lower Ajlun formation become more sandy with less salinity. The system is mostly untapped, owing to its complicated hydrogeology and deep formations.

DEEP SANDSTONE AQUIFERS: KURNUB/ZARQA AND DISI. Deep sandstone aquifers are the Kurnub/Zarqa of Lower Cretaceous age and the Disi of Palaeozoic age, which are unconformably separated by a less permeable layer of sandstone, siltstone, and shale. The Kurnub formation intercalates frequent argillaceous layers in the south, while the Disi is composed of massive and rather homogeneous arenaceous. Groundwaters in these aquifers are mostly non-renewable because of limited groundwater recharge through small outcrop areas. The quality of the groundwater in the Kurnub/Zarqa system varies from fresh to brackish. Excellent quality with low salinity, however, is found in the Disi aquifer in the southern part of the country, which has been exploited for the water supply of Aqaba and local experimental irrigation. The aquifer complex forms a huge groundwater reservoir extending under the whole of the country, which may offer opportunities for short-term or emergency uses.

B.2 Israel

B.2.1 *Topography*

Israel is one of the smallest states in the Middle East, covering an area of approximately 21,000 km². Its shore-line is on the eastern border of the Mediterranean Sea, and its territory extends northwards through the Golan Heights and southwards through the Negev to Eilat on the Gulf of Aqaba. Israel has four geomorphologic provinces: (1) the coastal plain, (2) mountains and hills, (3) the Negev desert, and (4) the Rift valley (see fig. B.2).

The Mediterranean coastal plain, which is fertile land relatively rich in water resources from wells and springs, stretches from Rosh Hanikra south to Ashkelon, with a length of about 200 km. The source of valuable groundwater recharge for the coastal plains is mainly dependent on rainfall over the mountains and hills with permeable strata dipping westwards. The 'Emek Yizre'el is a graben with a north-west/south-east direction, of which the alluvial plain is floored by a thick layer of rich, heavy soils (fig. B.2).

The mountains and hills include the regions of upper and lower Galilee, Samaria, and Judaea. Upper Galilee is structurally part of the mountains of Lebanon, a picturesque limestone plateau dominated by Mount Hermon (2,814 m). Lower Galilee, to the south, is a mountainous block broken into many smaller hills of lower altitude with gentle slopes. Galilee as a whole is the wettest region of Israel, where both springs and streams are more numerous and richer than in Judaea. Samaria, which roughly corresponds to the heartland of the ancient Kingdom of Israel, between the 'Emek Yizre'el and the plateau of Judaea, is dissected into hills and valleys (fig. B.2). Samaria is lower in elevation than Galilee or Judaea and has rainfall up to 630–750 mm, but surface water is not plentiful. The boundary between Samaria and Judaea is not physically well-defined, but may be thought of as passing some 15 km north of Jerusalem. Judaea is more like a high plateau, between 450 m and 900 m high, with dominating bleaker and barer rocky landscapes. The mountains of Judaea rise to nearly 1,000 m, with precipitation of up to 700 mm; to the east it becomes dry, with under 300 mm of rainfall.

The Negev, which forms a large triangular desert region, constituted about half of the area of pre-1947 Palestine and more than 60% of pre-1976 Israel. A ridge of mountains and hills runs across the central Negev at heights between 500 m and 600 m, rising towards the Egyptian border to above 900 m in places. The north-western part of the Negev receives fair but unreliable rainfall, while the rest of the Negev receives from 200 to less than 50 mm of mean annual rainfall. The Negev has never been thickly populated, but its economic significance is considerable since almost all of Israel's important mineral resources such as copper, phosphates, natural gas, and glass sand are found there.

The Jordan Rift valley is about 360 km long and is the northern part of the world's largest graben system, known as the Rift Valley, which connects East Africa and northern Syria over a total length of about 6,000 km. The Wadi Araba–Jordan rift strikes N15°E from the Gulf of Aqaba to the Dead Sea, and forms the "south graben," which has a length of approximately 200 km. The floor of the rift rises gradually from the Gulf of Aqaba to altitudes of 250 m above sea level at the watershed of Jabal al-Rishah in the center of Wadi al-Araba. From there the floor falls gently northwards to the surface of the Dead Sea at 400 m below sea level. The maximum depth of the Dead Sea is 793 m below sea level. It covers an area of 1,000 km² and has two basins, which are separated by the Lisan Straits, namely the "north sea" and the "south sea," with areas of 720 km² and 230 km² respectively.

The rift turns from N15°E to about N5°E to Lake Tiberias to form the "north graben." From the mouth of the Jordan River, at 400 m below sea level, the 105-km-long Jordan valley rises to 212 m below sea level at Lake Tiberias (the Sea of Galilee). The Jordan River, which runs on the floor of the north graben, separates the West Bank areas of the Palestine block to the west and the Trans-Jordan block, or East Bank, to the east.

The catchment includes parts of Lebanon, Syria, Israel, Palestine, and Jordan. The watershed between the Dead Sea and the Mediterranean extends approximately north-north-west from the Al-Khalil (Hebron) region through Bethlehem, Jerusalem, and Ramallah to the Nablus region and reaches altitudes of about 1,000 m. The shortest distance between the Dead Sea and the Mediterranean is 72 km, which corresponds to the proposed central alternative canal/tunnel route, Tel Aviv–Jerusalem–Qumran, for the Mediterranean–Dead Sea solar-hydro scheme (fig. B.2).

B.2.2 Hydrology

For about eight months of the year Israel enjoys warm and sunny weather. Winter rains fall between December and March, sometimes even in April, usually in storms of two or three days' duration. Precipitation is confined to the winter season and varies from an average of 1,000 mm in Galilee in the north to 500 mm on the coastal plain near Tel Aviv, 200 mm near Beersheba, and less than 50 mm at Eilat in the south (see fig. B.2). Rainfall varies considerably from one winter season to another, from around 25% of the long-term average in dry years to 160% of the long-term average in particularly rainy years. Over half of Israel's area receives less than 180 mm of precipitation annually (Gisser and Pohoryles 1977).

The southern part of Israel is desert, namely the Negev desert, which has a high potential evaporation, in the range between 1,700 and 2,700 mm per year, and whose relative humidity and solar radiation register 40%–60% and 195–201 kcal/cm^2 per year respectively (Buras and Darr 1979). Owing to the low levels of precipitation and high potential evaporation, large water deficiencies have been experienced in the southern part of the Israel. Droughts are not infrequent, particularly in the southern part of the country.

The climate of the Rift valley ranges from "hot-arid" with a mean annual rainfall of less than 100–300 mm in the bottom of Jordan valley to "Mediterranean semi-arid" with more than 300–700 mm in the surrounding highlands. The climate of the Dead Sea and the southern graben is hyper-arid. Sodom, which is situated just beside the southwest shore of the Dead Sea, has an average annual rainfall of 47 mm (1931–1969), with monthly means of daily minimum temperature of 12°C in January and maximum of 39°C in August. The mean relative humidity is rather high, at 56% in January and 38% in August. To the south of Dead Sea, the climate becomes drier. Eilat, on the shore of the Gulf of Aqaba, has an average annual rainfall of 25 mm, with a mean daily minimum temperature of 10°C in January and maximum of 40°C in August. The mean relative humidity is as low as 46% in January and 28% in August. Climatic data for selected locations, including Tel Aviv on the coastal plain, Jerusalem in the mountain range, Deganya in the Rift valley, Sodom on the Dead Sea, Beersheba in the Negev desert, and Eilat on the Gulf of Aqaba, are given in table B.1.

Surface drainage is largely controlled by a few streams flowing east and west, some of which have cut deeply into the highlands with their numerous head streams. The largest river, the Jordan, is entirely landlocked, terminating in the Dead Sea.

The Dead Sea is a closed sea with no outlet except by evaporation from the surface, which amounts to 1,500–1,600 mm per year (Calder and Neal 1984). In the past, the evaporation losses were replenished by an inflow of fresh water from the Jordan River and its tributaries, as well as from other sources such as wadi floods, springs, and rainfall. The mean volume of water flowing into the sea before 1930 was about 1.6×10^9 m^3 per year, of which 1.1×10^9 m^3 was contributed by the Jordan River (Weiner and Ben-Zvi 1982). Under these conditions, the Dead Sea had reached an equilibrium level of around 393 m below sea level, with some seasonal and annual fluctuation due to variations in the amount of rainfall. However, since the early 1950s, Israel, and later Jordan, have taken steps to utilize the fresh water flowing into the Dead Sea for intensified irrigation and other purposes, which has

Table B.1   **Climatic data for selected locations in Israel**

	Altitude (m)	Average annual rainfall (mm)	Mean relative humidity (%)	
			Jan.	Aug.
Tel Aviv	20	564	74	73
Jerusalem	810	486	65	54
Deganya	−200	384	70	54
Sodom	−390	47	56	38
Beersheba	280	204	65	58
Eilat	12	25	46	28

	Mean daily temperature (°C)				
	January		August		
	Min.	Max.	Min.	Max.	Period
Tel Aviv	8	18	22	31	1949–58
Jerusalem	6	13	20	30	1951–60
Deganya	9	18	24	37	1949–58
Sodom	12	21	29	39	1961–70
Beersheba	7	17	19	33	1961–70
Eilat	10	21	26	40	1956–65

reduced the amount of water entering the sea by 1×10^9 m³ per year. As a consequence, the level of the Dead Sea has declined in recent years, reaching as low as 402 m below sea level today, which is almost 15 m lower than its historic equilibrium level. The surface area of the Dead Sea and the volume of evaporation vary by only a few percent between the elevations from −406 to −390 m, while the water levels fluctuate considerably. The Dead Sea and its variations of water level from 1840 to 1980 are shown in fig. B.4.

The sea is a brine water body with vast mineral wealth, including

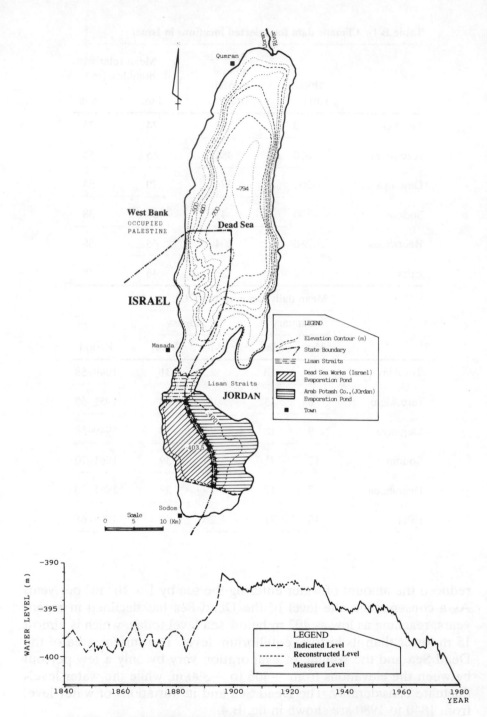

Fig. B.4 **The Dead Sea and water-level changes** (Source: Weiner 1982)

potash, common salt, bromide, magnesium chloride, and calcium chloride. The extremely high salinity amounts to 230,000–300,000 mg of TDS per litre. The specific gravity of the brine water has been estimated to be 1.22–1.23.

B.2.3   Geology
The territory of Israel and the occupied areas of Palestine is part of a physiographic region consisting of marine sedimentary formations lying along the western margins of the ancient Arabian land mass, which were folded in Miocene and Early Pliocene times to form a long anticline running roughly parallel with the Mediterranean coast. According to the "Geological Map of the Arab World" (AOMR 1987), the geology is mostly of sedimentary origin, ranging in age from Triassic to Neogene-Quaternary, except in the vicinity of Lake Tiberias, where volcanics of Miocene-Quaternary age widely cover the area. The sedimentary succession, which has a thickness of more than 1,000 m, is due mainly to a series of regional regressions and transgressions of the Tethys Sea. The stratigraphic sequence of the sedimentary rocks includes Quaternary, Pliocene-Miocene, Eocene-Palaeogene, Upper to Middle Cretaceous of Cenonian and Cenomanian-Turonian, Lower Cretaceous, Jurassic, and Triassic. The lowest formation of the Palaeozoic-Precambrian system, which consists mainly of acid intrusives, outcrops in some small areas in the southern Negev near Eilat. The sedimentary sequences comprise mainly carbonate rocks and sandstones from Triassic to Plio-Pleistocene. Fig. B.5 is a geological map (AOMR 1987). The main aquifer is found in the Cretaceous (Cenomanian-Turonian) formations, which consist largely of dolomite and limestone intercalating some clay and chalk layers and have a maximum thickness of about 600–700 m (Schneider 1967), as indicated in fig. B.6, a schematic geological profile crossing central Israel.

The taphrogenic structural movements which initiated the formation of the present graben apparently occurred along old structural zones of weakness, started during the Late Eocene (?) to Oligocene. The area east of the south graben in the Trans-Jordan block was structurally elevated in the late Oligocene to Miocene. In the graben area itself, marine sediments were deposited during the Oligocene and Neogene. The thick evaporite series of Late Miocene (?) to Pliocene age in the Dead Sea area may demonstrate the gradual decrease and termination of marine deposition in a part of the graben.

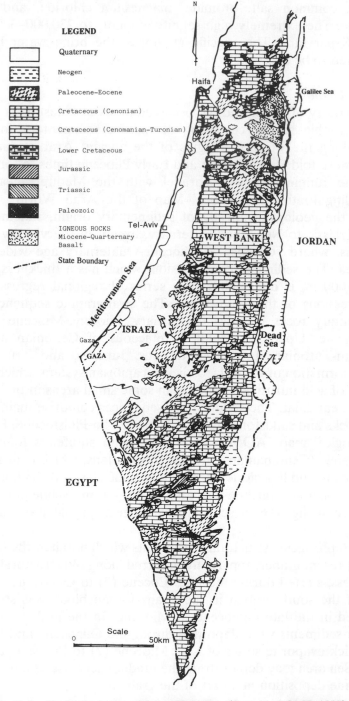

LEGEND

- Quaternary
- Neogen
- Paleocene-Eocene
- Cretaceous (Cenonian)
- Cretaceous (Cenomanian-Turonian)
- Lower Cretaceous
- Jurassic
- Triassic
- Paleozoic
- IGNEOUS ROCKS
  Miocene-Quarternary
  Basalt
- - - - State Boundary

Haifa

Galilee Sea

Mediterranean Sea

Tel-Aviv

WEST BANK

JORDAN

Gaza

ISRAEL

GAZA

Dead Sea

EGYPT

Scale

0   50km

Fig. B.5   **Geological map of Israel/Palestine** (Source: AOMR 1987)

282

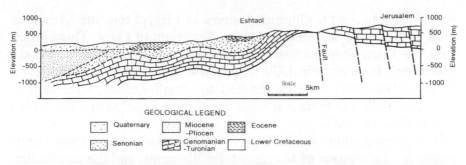

Fig. B.6 **Typical hydrogeological profile of central Israel** (Source: Schneider 1967)

The Lisan formation, which consists mainly of shale and marl inter-calating gravels and some gypsums and native sulphurs, unconformably overlies all older rock sequences in the Rift province. The Lisan formation was deposited in a fluctuating oligohaline and miohaline lacustrine environment in the Late Pleistocene age. The ancient Lisan Lake covered the entire Rift valley from Lake Tiberias to approximately 80 km south of the Dead Sea. Along the margin of the Rift province, the Lisan formation intercalates with coarse clastic and sandy deposits derived from the elevated areas bordering the Rift valley.

The Rift valley is covered with Holocene and Pleistocene fluvial, aeolian, and lacustrine sediments (AOMR 1987).

B.2.4   Israel and the occupied areas: Palestine issues
During the latter half of the nineteenth century more than half of the Jews in the world lived in eastern Europe and in tsarist Russia, where their conditions were as miserable as they had been everywhere in Europe for many centuries. In the 1880s their distress was added to by a series of anti-Jewish riots in southern Russia, which resulted in large-scale emigration. This caused the first wave of Zionists to reach Palestine in modern times. It was their conviction that the only possible solution to the plight of Jewish communities in the East and the threat of assimilation in the West was the formation of a Jewish state. Pre-1948 Jewish colonization in Palestine thus laid the foundations for the emergence of Israel in 1948.

After the First World War and the break-up of the Ottoman Empire a "Mandate" for Palestine was entrusted to Britain by the League of Nations and continued until the eve of the birth of Israel in 1948. The boundaries of Palestine in the east followed the natural divide of the Jordan valley and the Araba depression. In the south-west the 1906 boundary between the Ottoman Empire and Egypt remained, from the Gulf of Aqaba to the Mediterranean Sea south of Gaza. This border, with the Gaza Strip enclave on the coast, was restored with Israel's withdrawal from Sinai in 1979. The northern and north-eastern boundaries of Palestine were established by Anglo-French agreement in 1920 and 1923 and remained unchanged until Israel seized the Golan Heights in June 1967.

The configuration of Israel's pre-1967 boundaries was largely determined by the location of Jewish rural settlements, and the distribution of the Jewish population was the basis of the UN's partition proposals. Jewish colonization of the Arab territories of Sinai (with the Gaza Strip), the Golan, and the West Bank began after the Six Day War of June 1967. Here again, the geopolitical dimension of the settlement strategy is of great interest, but the real significance of the occupied area settlements is that they may hold the key to the future of the state of Israel (see fig. B.7).

Although substantially larger than the area popularly thought of as biblical Palestine, the Mandated territory was one of the smallest geopolitical units in South-West Asia. Its total population was only 752,000 at the 1922 census. Yet throughout history, control of this part of the earth's surface has been the ambition of successive powers, not only because of its unrivalled strategic significance at the crossroads of Asia, Africa, and Europe and between the Mediterranean and the Red Sea, but also because Palestine is revered by millions of Muslims, Christians, and Jews for its religious associations.

In many ways the West Bank is by far the most important of the remaining occupied areas, not only being the largest (5,900 km^2) and most populous but also being the natural focus of Palestinian political aspirations. In 1984 the Arab population, including those temporarily abroad, was more than 900,000, an increase of approximately one-third since the Israeli occupation began in 1967. The West Bank is also the focus of intensive Jewish settlement effort, spurred on by a variety of factors.

Israel's stake on the West Bank was so great that voluntary withdrawal seemed inconceivable. After September 1993, however, there is a goodwill opportunity of withdrawing from the occupied territory, including Gaza and Jericho, in exchange for peace.

Apart from heavy financial and political investment in the new settlements on the West Bank, Israel is dependent on the West Bank for some 430 million m^3 per year of its water supply out of a total 1,655 million m^3, a quarter of the annual water potential. Israel's heavy

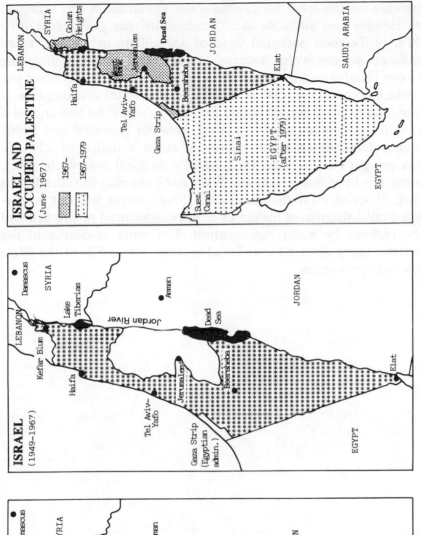

Fig. B.7 Israel and occupied territories

285

dependence on the fresh renewable water resources in the occupied Golan Heights also amounts to 305 million m^3 per year, accounting for 90% of the total potential yield of 330 million m^3. Thus, Israeli dependence on the water sources in occupied Palestine including the Golan Heights and the West Bank amounts to 735 million m^3 per year, which accounts for 45% of its total annual water consumption of 1,655 million m^3 (Zarour and Isaac 1993). This would be less critical if Israel were not already over-exploiting its water potential and facing increasing demands on water supply to cover a deficit of 230–340 million m^3 per year. Since 1982 Israel's national water company, Mekorot, has been integrating the West Bank supplies into the Israeli network. It seems clear that control of these sources will not be surrendered until alternative resources have been secured or the demand can be reduced by water conservation. The water resources of the West Bank being diverted into Israel account for 73.5% of the West Bank's water resources.

C

Historical review of the political riparian issues in the development of the Jordan River and basin management

The political riparian issues in development of the Jordan River and basin management between 1948 and 1967 are described in this appendix. Basic information for understanding the riparian-rights problems in the inter-state basin development of the Jordan River system are provided, with respect to UNRWA's pioneering work on the Main Plan and the Johnston Plan in 1951–1955 (table C.1). The source of this information is the book *Water in the Middle East* from the Middle East Research Institute, University of Pennsylvania (Naff and Matson 1984). The research was unclassified and derived from totally open sources of information. Some recommendations for the future planning of joint development and management are described in Appendix D to conclude the study on the joint development and management of the Jordan River system.

C.1 Unilateral planning and action after the first Israel-Arab war

The 1948 Arab-Israeli war aggravated already-existing difficulties of cooperative water management. The fragile armistice agreements signed by the Arab states and Israel in 1949 did not deal with water, nor was the post-war atmosphere conducive to negotiation. In con-

Table C.1 **Development schemes for the Jordan River system**

	Plan	Agency/Organization/Sponsor
1913	Franhia Plan	Ottoman Empire
1922	Mavromatis Plan	Great Britain
1928	Henriques Report	Great Britain
1935	Palestine Land Development Company	World Zionist Organization
1939	Ionides Survey	Transjordan
1944	Lowdermilk Plan	USA
1946	Survey of Palestine	Anglo-American Committee of Inquiry
1948	Hays-Savage Plan	World Zionist Organization
1950	MacDonald Report	Jordan
1951	All Israel Plan	Israel
1952	Bunger Plan	Jordan/USA
1953	*Main Plan*	UNRWA/United Nations
1953	Israeli Seven-Year Plan	Israel
1954	Cotton Plan	Israel
1954	Arab Plan	Arab League Technical Committee
1955	Baker-Harza Plan	Jordan
1955	*Unified (Johnston) Plan*	USA
1956	Israeli Ten-Year Plan	Israel
1956	Israeli National Water Plan	Israel
1957	Great Yarmouk Project	Jordan
1964	Jordan Headwaters Diversion	Arab League
1991	Integrated Joint Development Plan	Japan (University of Tokyo)
1993	Declaration of Principles: PLO/Israel	Israel and PLO (Annex III, IV)
1994	Treaty of Peace: Jordan/Israel	Jordan and Israel (Article 6, Annex II)

Sources: Naff and Matson 1984, and Murakami 1991.

sequence, each of the riparians moved to utilize the Jordan River system unilaterally.

Israel resumed water planning immediately after 1948. The comprehensive All Israel Plan, completed in 1951, included the draining of the Huleh swamp, the diversion of the Jordan River, and the construction of a carrier system. Subsequently consolidated into the National Water Carrier (hereafter called the "Carrier"), this plan was to became the keystone of Israel's water development, diverting waters of the Jordan to the coastal plains and the Negev desert.

The first part of the project, the draining of the Huleh swamps, began in 1951. Israel delayed construction of the first leg of the Carrier for foreign-policy reasons. Work on the Huleh swamp, which infringed the demilitarized zone with Syria, provoked a number of military incidents, which were the first of many clashes between Israel and Syria and between Israeli and Arab residents in disputed territories and demilitarized zones (table C.2). Some incidents were designed to harass and remove unwanted population elements or protect personal property; others were intended to interfere with the development of water resources in ways that the contesting party viewed as inimical to its interests. In some cases, over a period of some two decades, water-related actions were used as a mask for other conflicts (e.g., shooting on Lake Tiberias in 1954–55 was escalated to incursions that took hostages to exchange for prisoners of war held by the other side). Throughout the period, incidents threatened to shatter the armistice agreements. Some analysts have held that water was a major factor leading to the 1967 war.

Jisr Banat Yaqub (Hebrew: Gesher Bnot Yaacov), the targeted diversion point for the large-scale Israeli project, was located in the demilitarized zone between Israel and Syria. Israel was apprehensive that this fact would provoke Arab opposition and international condemnation. It delayed the decision to proceed with the larger diversion scheme until July 1953.

By the early 1950s, both the Jordanian government and UNRWA (the United Nations Relief and Works Agency for Palestine Refugees in the Near East) were working on irrigation schemes to improve Jordanian agriculture and resettle the Palestinian refugees. In 1950 Jordan received a commissioned study from the British consultant Sir Murdoch MacDonald which proposed diverting the Yarmouk River into Lake Tiberias and constructing irrigation canals down both sides of the Jordan valley. A 1952 plan for UNRWA by American engineer M. E. Bunger envisaged a dam on the Yarmouk River at Maqarin with a storage capacity of 480 million m^3. The impounded water would be diverted by a second dam at Addassiyah into gravity-flow canals along the east Ghor in Jordan. Bunger reckoned the work would irrigate 435,000 dunums (43,500 ha) in Jordan and 60,000 dunums (6,000 ha) in Syria. Hydroelectric plants at the two dams would generate 28,300 kWh per year for Jordan and Syria. Experts estimated that the Bunger Plan would settle 100,000 people.

In March 1953 Jordan and UNRWA signed an agreement to implement the Bunger Plan. In June 1953 Jordan and Syria agreed on sharing the Yarmouk water. Actual work on the project began in July 1953. However, even before it began, Israel protested that its riparian rights to the Yarmouk were not recognized in the Bunger Plan. The Yarmouk Triangle demilitarized zone controlled by Israel had only 10 km of frontage on the Yarmouk.

Table C.2 **Water-related cease-fire violations in the Jordan River system, 1951–1967**

Date	Incident	Immediate issue	Underlying issue	Resolution
Spring 1951	Shooting in DMZ; both sides invade; Israel expels Arab villagers from DMZ; Israeli air force bombs Al-Himah	Arab resistance to Israeli land seizure, expulsion from DMZ	Huleh drainage in DMZ	Security Council orders return of Arab villagers, but villages had been razed
3 Sept. 1953	Shooting in DMZ	Water diversion by Israel in DMZ	Sovereignty over DMZ	UN orders work halted; USA threatens to end aid: Israel moves intake out of DMZ
12 Dec. 1955	Israelis hit Arab villages northeast of Lake Tiberias, killing 50 (followed by two days' fight on lake)	Fishing rights	Israeli saboteurs captured (1954) inside Syria	Security Council condemns Israel; Syria rejects Johnston Plan; prisoners returned two months later
31 Jan. 1962	Israel destroys Lower Tarafiq in DMZ	Israeli drainage ditch in Arab village	Use of land	Syria complains to MAC; Israel boycotts
13 Nov. 1964	Patrols exchange fire; bombing of Tell el-Qadi (source of Dan River)	Road building by Israel in disputed territory	Sovereignty over source of Dan River	Both parties complain to Security Council; Soviets veto

Table C.2—*Continued*

Date	Incident	Immediate issue	Underlying issue	Resolution
1 Jan. 1965	Fatah hits pump station (first in series of attacks on Israel)	Israeli existence	Palestine self-determination	None
Spring 1965	Patrols fire along Israel-Syria border	Road building by Syria in Golan Heights	*Arab water diversion*	None
14 July 1966	Israeli air force bombs Syrian construction vehicles; air battle at Banias	Alleged Syrian provocation	*Arab water diversion*	Security Council
15 Aug. 1966	Exchange of fire on Lake Tiberias	Patrolling, fishing	Land use in DMZ	Syrian note to Security Council
2 Apr. 1967	Fire fight in DMZ	Arab water diversion	*Arab water diversion*	None
7 Apr. 1967	Israeli air force bombs Golan, seen over Damascus	Arab water diversion	*Arab water diversion*	MAC reconvened; no action

Source: Naff and Matson 1984.

In July 1953 Israel began the diversion of the Jordan at Jisr Banat Yaqub. This site was in the demilitarized zone but had two technical advantages over lower alternative sites: (1) it had a lower salinity level than points farther down the Jordan River fork, and (2) the 270 m drop in elevation between the site and Lake Tiberias was sufficient to enable the use of gravity as the means of diversion. The Israeli government underestimated both Syrian and international reaction. In September 1953 the Syrians protested to the United Nations. Unlike the Huleh drainage case, which the UN had allowed to proceed, the UN ruled in favour of Syria. Israel ignored the order to discontinue work. Only an American threat in November 1953 to cut off funds channelled to Israel by the Foreign Operations Administration convinced Israel to terminate construction. Subsequently, a point at Eshed Kinrot on Lake Tiberias was chosen. It was technically inferior to the original site: the water salinity was high and hydroelectric power had to be used to pump the water to the Carrier.

Meanwhile, Jordan had to abandon the Bunger Plan entirely. One factor was Israel's objection on the ground that the original Rutenberg concession gave Israel rights to the Yarmouk. Another factor was a change in American perceptions. King Hussein, in his autobiography, alleges that the United States accepted the Israeli legal position and hence denied funding to the Bunger Plan (Naff and Matson 1984).

C.2 The Johnston negotiations

The US government then moved towards deeper involvement. On 16 October 1953 President Eisenhower appointed Eric Johnston as a special ambassador to mediate a comprehensive plan for the regional development of the Jordan River system. Philosophically based on the Marshall Plan in Europe, it sought to reduce the conflict potential of the region by promoting cooperation and economic stability.

The large number of plans issued between 1953 and 1955 represented bargaining stages in the negotiations over the sharing of the Jordan River system (table C.1). The main bargaining issues pertained to (1) the water quotas for the riparians, (2) the use of Lake Tiberias as a storage facility, (3) the use of Jordan waters for out-of-basin areas, (4) the used of the Litani River as part of the system, and (5) the nature of international supervision and guarantees.

The base plan for Johnston's mission was an UNRWA-sponsored desk study prepared by Charles T. Main, under the supervision of the US Tennessee Valley Authority, with the backing of the American State Department. The plan featured:

— a dam on the Hasbani to provide power and irrigate the Galilee area,
— dams on the Dan and Banias Rivers to irrigate Galilee,
— drainage of the Huleh swamps,
— a dam at Maqarin with 175 million m³ storage capacity to be used for power generation,
— a dam at Addassiyah to divert water to Lake Tiberias and into the east Ghor area,
— a small dam at the outlet of Lake Tiberias to increase the lake's storage capacity,
— gravity-flow canals down the east and west sides of the Jordan valley to irrigate the area between the Yarmouk and the Dead Sea,
— control works and canals to utilize perennial flows from the wadis.

The Main Plan favoured primary in-basin use of the Jordan waters and ruled out integration of the Litani. Provisional quotas gave Israel 394 million m³, Jordan 774 million m³, and Syria 45 million m³.

Israel opened the bargaining by publishing a seven-year plan. Its main features, modelled on the Lowdermilk and Hayes plans (table C.1), included the integration of the Litani, the use of Lake Tiberias as the main storage facility, out-of-basin use of the Jordan waters, and the Mediterranean–Dead Sea canal. Since water flow was based on the combined Jordan-Litani output of 2,500 million m³, Israel sought an initial quota of 810 million m³.

The Israeli proposals were elaborated in the plan prepared for it by Josep Cotton in 1954. The combined annual Litani-Jordan water resources were estimated at 2,345.7 million m³. Israel was to receive 1,290 million m³ per year. The Arab share of 1,055.7 million m³ per year was to be divided by allocating 575 million m³ to Jordan, 450.7 million m³ to Lebanon, and 30 million m³ to Syria.

The Arabs responded to the Main "base plan" with the Arab Plan of 1954, which reaffirmed the Ionides, MacDonald, and Bunger principle of exclusive in-basin use of the water, rejected storage in Lake Tiberias, and rejected integration of the Litani. Because 77% of the water of the Jordan water system originated in the Arab countries, it objected to the quota allocations proposed in the Main Plan. According to the Arab proposal, Israel was to get 200 million m³ per year, Jordan 861 million m³, and Syria 132 million m³. The Arab plan recognized Lebanon as a riparian of the Jordan River system and allocated it 35 million m³ per year.

The Baker-Harza study, published in 1955, was prepared by American engineers commissioned by the Jordanian government to conduct

293

a hydrological survey to determine the amount of water needed to irrigate the Jordan valley. The plan was technically oriented and not directly related to the negotiations. It recommended construction of an elaborate canal system to irrigate 460,000 dunums (46,000 ha) in the Jordan valley. It increased the estimate of cultivable land but decreased the water duty (the amount of water required per unit of land to produce crops).

C.3 Towards the Unified Plan

As negotiations progressed, disagreements were gradually reduced. Israel gave up on integration of the Litani, and the Arabs dropped their objection to out-of-basin use of waters. Lake Tiberias was rejected by the Arabs as a reservoir for Yarmouk water. An alternative Arab proposal to treat Lake Tiberias (without diversion of the Yarmouk) as a regional storage centre to benefit all riparians was rejected by Israel. The Arabs demanded and Israel opposed international supervision over withdrawals of water.

Allocation of water quotas was the most difficult issue. As illustrated in table C.3, the disparity between the opening demands was considerable. After the claim for the Litani was dropped, Israel downgraded its quota demand to 550 million m^3 per year. After extremely hard bargaining the so-called Gardiner Formula was adopted as the final version of the Unified (Johnston) Plan. Compared to the Main Plan figures, the Johnston Plan quotas are significantly different only with regard to Syria and Lebanon. Jordan's share was slightly scaled down, and Israel was to receive the variable residue after other quotas had been met; most estimates place this average residue at 400 million m^3 per year.

The Unified Plan stipulated that supervision would be exercised by a three-member Neutral Engineering Board. The Board's mandate included the supervision of water withdrawal, record keeping, and preserving the spirit and letter of the agreement.

The Unified Plan was accepted by the technical committees from both Israel and the Arab League. The Israeli cabinet discussed the plan in July 1955 without taking a vote. The Arab Experts Committee approved the plan in September 1955 and referred it for final approval to the Arab League Council. The Council decided on 11 October 1955 not to ratify the plan. According to most observers, including Johnston himself, the Arab non-adoption of the plan was not total rejection; while they failed to approve it politically, they were determined to

Table C.3 **Water allocations to riparians of the Jordan River system (million m³ per year)**

Plan/water source	Lebanon	Syria	Jordan	Israel	Total
Main Plan		45	774	394	1,213
Arab Plan	35	132	698	182	1,047
Cotton Plan[a]	450.7	30	575	1,290	2,345.7
Unified (Johnston) Plan					
Hasbani	35				35
Banias		20			20
Jordan (main stream)		22	100	375[b]	497[b]
Yarmouk		90	377	25	492
Side wadis			243		243
TOTAL	35	132	720	400[b]	1,287[b]

Source: Naff and Matson 1984.

a. Includes the Litani.
b. According to the compromise Gardiner formula, the share to Israel from the main stream of the Jordan was defined as the "residue" after the other co-riparians had received their shares. This would vary from year to year but was expected to average 375 million m³.

adhere to the technical details. The issue of impartial monitoring was not resolved, which made for problems in the future.

C.4 Unilateral implementation: 1955–1967

The failure to develop a multilateral approach to water management reinforced unilateral development. Though the Unified Plan failed to be ratified, both Jordan and Israel undertook to operate within their allocations, and two major successful projects were undertaken: the Israeli National Water Carrier and Jordan's East Ghor Main Canal.

The National Water Carrier diverted water from the Jordan River fork at Eshed Kinrot to the coastal plain and the Negev desert. Although sections of it were begun before 1955, it was only completed in 1964. The initial diversion capacity of the National Water Carrier without supplementary booster pumps was 320 million m³, well within the limits of the Johnston Plan.

Design of the East Ghor Canal was begun by Jordan in 1957. It was intended as the first section of a much more ambitious plan known as the Greater Yarmouk project. Additional sections included (1) construction of two dams on the Yarmouk (Mukheiba and Maqarin) for storage and hydroelectricity, (2) construction of a 47-km West Ghor Canal, together with a siphon across the Jordan River near Wadi Faria to connect it with the East Ghor Canal, (3) construction of seven dams to utilize seasonal flow on side wadis flowing into the Jordan, and (4) construction of pumping stations, lateral canals, and flood protection and drainage facilities. In the original Greater Yarmouk project, the East Ghor Canal was scheduled to provide only 25% of the total irrigation scheme. Construction of the canal began in 1959. By 1961 its first section was completed; sections two and three, down to Wadi Zarqa, were in service by June 1966.

Shortly before completion of the Israeli Water Carrier in 1964, an Arab summit conference decided to try to thwart it. Discarding direct military attack, the Arab states chose to divert the Jordan headwaters. Two options were considered: either the diversion of the Hasbani to the Litani and the diversion of the Banias to the Yarmouk, or the diversion of both the Hasbani and the Banias to the Yarmouk. The latter was chosen, with the diverted waters to be stored behind the Mukheiba dam.

According to neutral assessments, the scheme was only marginally feasible; it was technically difficult and expensive. Its estimated cost was between US$190 million and US$200 million, comparable to the cost of the entire Israeli National Water Carrier. Financial issues were to be solved by contributions from Saudi Arabia and Egypt.

Political considerations cited by the Arabs in rejecting the 1955 Johnston Plan were revived to justify the diversion scheme. Particular emphasis was placed on the Carrier's capability to enhance Israel's capacity to absorb immigrants to the detriment of Palestinian refugees. In response, Israel stressed that the National Water Carrier was within the limits of the Johnston Plan. It declared that, as a sovereign state, it had the right to set immigration policies without external interference, and refused to make concessions regarding Arab refugees.

The Arabs started work on the Headwater Diversion project in 1965. Israel declared that it would regard such diversion as an infringement of its sovereign rights. According to estimates, completion of the project would have deprived Israel of 35% of its contemplated withdrawal from the upper Jordan, constituting one-ninth of Israel's annual water budget.

In a series of military strikes, Israel hit the diversion works. The attacks culminated in April 1967 in air strikes deep inside Syria. The increase in water-related Arab-Israeli hostility was a major factor leading to the June 1967 war.

C.5   The militarization of the water conflict

The 1967 war increased the trend towards competitive unilateral utilization of the Jordan River system.

Israel improved its hydrostrategic position through the occupation of the Golan Heights and the West Bank. The occupation of the Golan Heights made it impossible for the Arab states to divert the Jordan headwaters. The 1967 cease-fire lines gave Israel control of half the length of the Yarmouk River, compared to 10 km before the war. This made development of the Yarmouk contingent upon Israeli consent. Even small-scale unilateral impoundment by Jordan can easily be detected by Israel and attacked militarily.

The ability of Arab riparians to proceed with unilateral schemes decreased in proportion to Israeli gains. When the war started, about 20% of the Greater Yarmouk project was completed. In the wake of the war, the two most important projects, the Mukheiba and Maqarin (renamed Al-Wuheda in 1987) dams had to be abandoned. The Mukheiba dam had been planned to store 200 million m³ of water and the Maqarin dam to store up to 350 million m³ and to generate 25,000 kWh of electricity annually.

When the Palestine Liberation Organization (PLO) emerged under new leadership after the 1967 war, it mounted an intensive campaign against Israeli settlements in the Jordan valley. These attacks included raids against water installations, such as that on the Nafaraim pumping station in the summer of 1969. Israeli-PLO skirmishes soon deteriorated into Israeli conflict with Jordanian and Iraqi detachments stationed in the east Jordan valley.

After unsuccessful military efforts to stop PLO activities, Israel raided the East Ghor Canal in 1969 and put most of the system out of commission. Israel appears to have conjectured that extensive damage to the irrigation system would pressure King Hussein to act against the PLO. Conflict over the East Ghor Canal was mediated by the United States. After secret negotiations in 1969–1970, Jordan was allowed to repair the canal; in exchange Jordan reaffirmed its adherence to the Johnston Plan quotas and pledged to terminate PLO activity in Jordan. King Hussein expelled the PLO from Jordan in 1970–1971.

D

Recommendations for future joint development and management: The Mediterranean–Dead Sea canal and Al-Wuheda dam projects

By the end of the 1990s, Israel, Jordan, and the West Bank, or Palestine, will have exhausted development opportunities for virtually all of their renewable sources of fresh water if current patterns of consumption are not quickly and radically altered. In these circumstances, the Jordan River system, which includes the Al-Wuheda dam scheme on the Yarmouk River, unquestionably holds the greatest potential for either conflict or compromise.

The proposed co-generation system coupling solar-hydro with hydro-powered reverse-osmosis (RO) desalination on the Mediterranean–Dead Sea (MDS) conduit scheme would produce both 1.2×10^9 kWh of electricity per year, or 500 MW of peak electricity, and 100 million m^3 of fresh water per year (Murakami 1991; Murakami and Musiake 1991). The power generated would be shared between Israel and Jordan to supply their peak demands, while the fresh water product of 100 million m^3 per year would be used exclusively for the water supply in the central Ghor (the Jordan valley, in and around the Dead Sea) by Israel, Palestine, and Jordan.

The integrated Jordan River development and management scheme proposed here would include as key project elements (1) the MDS canal with hydro-power plant and hydro-powered RO desalination and

(2) the Al-Wuheda dam and flood-rentention/recharge dams, for which the gross project costs are preliminarily estimated to be US$4.5 $\times$ 10^9, as follows (Murakami 1991):
— MDS canal with hydro-power plant, US$2 $\times$ 10^9,
— hydro-powered RO desalination, US$0.5 $\times$ 10^9,
— Al-Wuheda dam and flood retention/recharge dams, US$1 $\times$ 10^9,
— management, administration, and operation and maintenance costs for all of the above, US$1 $\times$ 10^9.

Recommendations

It is suggested that the techno-political alternatives such as the MDS conduit scheme and the Al-Wuheda dam project should be linked in an integrated Jordan River development master plan which would be beneficial for inter-state regional economic development between Israel, Palestine, and Jordan. The water cycle and benefits of coordinating water development, water potential energy, and water politics are well understood by all the parties concerned.

It is suggested that the United Nations Relief and Works Agency for Palestine Refugees in the Near East (UNRWA), which once played an important role in developing the comprehensive Jordan River development plan (Main Plan and Johnston Plan) in the early to mid-1950s, or other potential UN agencies should be strengthened and enabled to initiate negotiations between the riparians Israel, Palestine, and Jordan, and that a new executive agency should be organized with international funding for the specific purpose of developing the Jordan River basin and inter-state economic regions such as the Dead Sea and Aqaba.

It is suggested also that the Japanese government and/or other G7 countries should play an catalytic role in the above, with consolidation of ideas, strategies, policy making, and planning in association with the United Nations University and the World Bank, by providing a strategic fund of say US$2 billion to the United Nations to cover the initial project costs. The new executive agency with United Nations support would be responsible for managing all aspects of the project, including financing arrangement, investigation, planning, design, construction supervision, operation, and management and administration throughout the project life of say fifty years.

299

Conversion tables

Length

m	in	ft
1	39.37	3.281
0.0254	1	0.08333
0.3048	12	1
0.303	11.93	0.9942

Area

m²	in²	ft²
1	1,550	10.764
0.0006452	1	0.006944
0.0929	144	1
3.3058	5,124	35.58

Volume

m³	in³	ft³	US gallons	Imperial gallons
1	61,024	35.31	264.2	220.0
0.00001639	1	0.0005787	0.004329	0.003604
0.02832	1,728	1	7.481	6.228
0.003785	231	0.1337	1	0.8325
0.004547	277.5	0.1606	1.201	1
0.1804	11,008	6.371	47.66	39.68

NOTE: 1 acre-foot = 1,234 m³.

300

Flow rate

m³/min	m³/hour	l/sec	US gallons/min	Imperial gallons/min	ft³/min
1	60	16.67	264.2	222.0	35.31
0.01667	1	0.2778	4.403	3.666	0.5881
0.06	3.6	1	15.85	13.2	2.119
0.1804	10.82	3.007	47.66	39.68	6.371
0.003782	0.2271	0.0631	1	0.8235	0.1337
0.004547	0.2728	0.0578	1.201	1	0.1605
0.0283	1.699	0.472	7.481	6.229	1

Pressure

kg/cm²	lb/in² (psi)	Standard atmospheric pressure	Mercury column (m)	Water column (m)	Water column (ft)
1	14.22	0.9678	0.7355	10	0.1757
0.07031	1	0.0680	0.0517	0.7031	0.1782
1.0332	14.7	1	0.76	10.33	0.2389
1.359	19.34	1.3158	1	13.6	0.002343
0.1	1.422	0.09678	0.07355	1	0.0003239
0.03048	0.4335	0.0295	0.0224	0.3048	1

Power

French horse power (PS)	British horse power (HP)	kilowatt (kW)	kg-m/sec	ft-lb/sec	kcal/sec
1	0.9859	0.7055	75	542.5	0.1757
1.0143	1	0.746	76.07	550.2	0.1782
1.3596	1.3405	1	101.97	737.6	1.2389
0.01333	0.01315	0.009807	1	7.233	0.002343
0.001843	0.001817	0.001356	0.1383	1	0.0003239
5.691	5.611	4.186	426.9	3087	1

301

Conversion tables

SI unit conversions

Symbol	Unit	Equivalents	
N	newton	J/m	$m \cdot kg \cdot s^{-2}$
Pa	pascal	N/m^2	$m^{-1} \cdot kg \cdot s^{-2}$
J	joule	$N \cdot m$	$m^2 \cdot kg \cdot s^{-2}$
W	watt	J/s	$m^2 \cdot kg \cdot s^{-3}$

Quantity	Unit symbol	Other units and related conversions
Area	m^2	hectare, ha = 10,000 m^2
Volume	m^3	litre, l = 10^{-3} m^3
Weight	kg	tonne, t = 1,000 kg
Density	kg/m^3	
Time	s	minute, m = 60 s
		hour, h = 3,600 s
		day, d = 86,400 s
Velocity	m/s	
Pressure	N/m^2	1 kgf/cm^2 = 1 kp/cm^2 = 98,066.5 Pa

302

References

Abanmy, A.B.A., and M.B.O. Al-Rashed. 1922. Saline Water Conversion Corporation (S.W.C.C.) in the Kingdom of Saudi Arabia. *Desalination and Water Reuse* 3 (2): 11–17.

Abusada, S.M. 1988. The Essentials of Groundwater Resources of Kuwait. Technical Report KISR2665. Kuwait Institute for Scientific Research. P. 34.

Abu-Zeid, M., and A.K. Biswas. 1990. Impacts of Agriculture on Water Quality. *Water International*, journal of the International Water Resources Association, 15 (3): 160–67.

Akkad, A.A. 1990. Conservation in the Arabian Gulf Countries. *Management and Operations*, journal of the American Water Works Association, May, pp. 40–50.

Al-Arrayedh, M., B. Ericsson, and M. Ohtani. 1985. Construction and Operation of 46,000 m³/d Reverse Osmosis Desalination Plant, Ra's Abu Jarjur, Bahrain. Proceedings of the Second World Congress on Desalination and Water Reuse, Bermuda. International Desalination Association. 55: 319–42.

Al-Arrayedh, M., B. Ericsson, M.A. Saad, and H. Yoshioka. 1987. Reverse Osmosis Desalination Plant, Ra's Abu Jarjur, State of Bahrain: Two Years Operational Experience for the 46,000 m³/d RO Plant. Proceedings of the Third World Congress on Desalination and Water Reuse, Cannes. International Desalination Association. 65: 197–230.

Alawin, A.K. 1983. Choosing the Best Desalination Arrangement: The Jordan Petroleum Refinery System—A Case Study. Second Arab Water Technology Conference (organized by *Middle East Water and Sewage Journal*), Dubai, United Arab Emirates, pp. 15.1–15.10.

Al-Faroud, K.H. 1988. The Present and Future Development and Utilization of Water Resources in Kuwait. Middle East–Japan Conference on Development and Utilization of Water Resources. Japan Cooperation for the Middle East, Country Report.

Al-Mutaz, I.S., A.M. Soliman, and M.A. Daghthem. 1989. Optimum Design for a Hybrid Desalting Plant. Fourth World Congress on Desalination and Water Reuse, Kuwait. International Desalination Association. *Desalination* 76 (4): 177–88.

Al-Zubaidj, J.A.A. 1989. Parametric Cost Analysis Study of Seawater Reverse Osmosis Systems Design in Kuwait. Fourth World Congress on Desalination and Water Reuse, Kuwait. International Desalination Association. *Desalination* 76 (4): 241–80.

AOMR (Arab Organization for Mineral Resources). 1987. Geological Map of the Arab World. 1/2,250,000. Rabat, Morocco. Sheet 3.

Applegate, R. 1986. World's Largest RO Desalting Facility to Salvage 72.4 mgd. *World Water News*, May/June, pp. 17–19.

Awerbuch, L., S. May, L. Soo-hoo, and V.V.D. Mast. 1989. Hybrid Desalting Systems. Fourth World Congress on Desalination and Water Reuse, Kuwait. International Desalination Association. *Desalination* 76 (4): 189–97.

AWWA (American Water Works Association). 1989a. Theme Introduction: Membrane Processes. *Management and Operations*, Nov., p. 29.

———. 1989b. Committee Report: Membrane Desalting Technologies. Water Desalting and Reuse Committee. *Management and Operations*, Nov., pp. 30–37.

Bassler, F. 1975. New Proposals to Develop the Qattara Depression. *Water Power and Dam Construction*, Aug., pp. 291–97.

Beaumont, P., G.H. Blake, and J.M. Wagstaff. 1988. *The Middle East: A Geographical Study*. 2nd ed. London: David Fulton Publishers.

Bender, F. 1975. *Geology of the Arabian Peninsula: Jordan*. US Geological Survey Professional Paper 560-I. Pp. 11–136.

Benton, G., and A.M. Estoque. 1954. Water Vapor Transfer over the North American Continent. *Journal of Meteorology* 11: 462–77.

Birch, R.P., and M. Al-Arrayedh. 1985. Bahrain's Fresh Groundwater Situation and the Investigations into Using Bahrain's Brackish Water Resources as a Feedwater for the Reverse Osmosis Desalination Program. Proceedings of the Second World Congress on Desalination and Water Reuse, Bermuda. International Desalination Association. 55: 397–492.

Biswas, A.K. 1992. Indus Water Treaty: The Negotiating Process. *Water International*, journal of the International Water Resources Association, 17 (4): 201–9.

Bulloch, J., and A. Darwish. 1993. *Water Wars: Coming Conflicts in the Middle East*. London: St. Edmundsbury Press. Pp. 124–41.

Buras, N. 1967a. Modern Aquifer Management. Symposium of Haifa: Artificial Recharge and Management of Aquifers. IASH Pub. no. 72. International Association of Scientific Hydrology (IASH). Pp. 469–71.

———. 1967b. Systems Engineering and Aquifer Management. Symposium of Haifa: Artificial Recharge and Management of Aquifers. IASH Pub. no. 72. International Association of Scientific Hydrology (IASH). Pp. 466–73.

———, and P. Darr. 1979. An Evaluation of Marginal Waters as a Natural Resource in Israel. American Geophysical Union. *Water Resources Research* 15 (6): 1349–53.

Buros, O.K. 1989. Desalting Practices in the United States. *Management and Operations*, journal of the American Water Works Association, Nov., pp. 38–42.

——, et al. 1993. Issues Associated with Large Scale Desalination Plants. National Water Supply Improvement Association Biennial Conference, Yuma, Arizona, USA, 27 Aug.

Calder, I.R., and C. Neal. 1984. Evaporation from Saline Lakes. *Journal of Hydrological Science* 29 (1): 89–97.

CBSI (Central Bureau of Statistics, Israel). 1992. Statistical Abstract of Israel: 1992. No. 43, pp. 428–52.

COHMAP Members. 1988. Climatic Changes of the Last 18,000 Years: Observations and Model Simulations. *Science* 241: 1043–52.

Collins, O.R. 1988. The Jonglei Canal: Illusion or Reality? *Water International*, journal of the International Water Resources Association, 13: 144–53.

Darwish, M.A., and A.M. Jawad. 1989a. Technical Comparison between Large Capacity MSF and RO Desalting Plants. Proceedings of the Fourth World Congress on Desalination and Water Reuse, Kuwait. International Desalination Association. *Desalination* 76 (4): 281–304.

——. 1989b. Technical Aspect of Reducing Desalting Water Cost by Distillation Methods. Proceedings of the Fourth World Congress on Desalination and Water Reuse, Kuwait. International Desalination Association. *Desalination* 76 (4): 306–22.

——, and G.S. Aly. 1989. Technical and Economical Comparison between Large Capacity MSF and RO Desalting Plants. Proceedings of the Fourth World Congress on Desalination and Water Reuse, Kuwait. International Desalination Association. *Desalination* 76 (4): 215–40.

Deekker, G. 1972. A Note on the Nile. *Water Resources Research* 8 (4): 818–928.

de Martonne, E. 1926. Aréisme et indice d'aridité. *Academie des Sciences* (Paris), *Comptes Rendus* 182 (23): 1395–96.

——. 1942. Nouvelle carte mondiale de l'indice d'aridité. *Annales de Géographie* 51 (288): 242–50.

Doluca, K., and W. Pircher. 1971. Development of the Euphrates River Basin in Turkey. *Water Power and Dam Construction*, Feb., pp. 47–55.

DSJ (Department of Statistics of Jordan). 1988. Statistical Yearbook: 1988. No. 39, pp. 23–25.

DTCD (Department of Technical Development for Cooperation). 1987. *Nonconventional Water Resources Use in Developing Countries*. Proceedings of the International Seminar, Willemstad, Curaçao, Netherlands Antilles, 22–28 April 1985. Natural Resources/Water Series, no. 22. United Nations. Pp. 31–36.

Dykes, G.M., and W.J. Colon. 1989. Use of Membrane Technology in Florida. *Management and Operations*, journal of the American Water Works Association, Nov., pp. 43–46.

ECAFE (Economic Commission for Asia and the Far East). 1966. A Compendium of Major International Rivers in the ECAFE Region. Water Resources Series, no. 29. United Nations. Pp. 48–64.

Economist. 1990. Survey of the Arab World. *The Economist*, 12 May, p. 12.

Emberger, L. 1955. Afrique du nord-ouest. In: *Plant Ecology: Review of Research*. Arid Zone Research, VI. Paris: Unesco. Pp. 219–49.

References

Folland, K.C., and T. Palmer. 1986. Sahel Rainfall and Worldwide Sea Temperature 1901–1985. *Nature* 320 (6063): 602–7.

Gammon, H.R., et al. 1985. History of Carbon Dioxide in the Atmosphere. *Atmospheric Carbon Dioxide and the Global Carbon Cycle*. DOE/ER-0239. Washington, D.C.: US Department of Energy. Pp. 23–62.

Gischler, E.C. 1979. Water Resources in the Arab Middle East and North Africa. Unesco Working Document no. SC-76/CASTARAB/3. Paris: Unesco.

Gisser, M., and S. Pohoryles. 1977. Water Shortage in Israel: Long-Run Policy for the Farm Sector. *Water Resources Research* 13 (6): 865–72.

Glueckstern, P. 1982. Preliminary Consideration of Combining a Large Reverse Osmosis Plant with the Mediterranean–Dead Sea Project. *Desalination* 40: 143–56.

Goodfriend, A.G., M. Mafarits, and I.C. Carmi. 1986. A High Stand of the Dead Sea at the End of the Neolithic Period: Paleoclimatic and Archaeological Implications. *Climatic Change* 9: 349–56.

Goudie, A., and J. Wilkinson. 1977. *The Warm Desert Environment*. Cambridge University Press.

Gould, D. 1988. The Selling of the Peace Pipeline. *Middle East Economic Digest*, 26 Mar., p. 10.

Hare, F.K. 1964. *The Causation of the Arid Zone*. Paris: Unesco. Pp. 25–30.

Heinl, M., and P.J. Brinkmann. 1989. A Groundwater Model of the Nubian Aquifer System. *Hydrological Science* 34 (4): 425–47.

Howe, E.D. 1962. Saline Water Conversion. *Problems of the Arid Zone: Proceedings of the Paris Symposium*. Paris: Unesco. Pp. 271–97.

Huang, J., and A. Banerjee. 1984. Hashemite Kingdom of Jordan: Water Sector Study, Sector Report. World Bank Report no. 4699-JO. Pp. 35–36.

Hurst, H.E. 1952. *The Nile*. England: Constable and Company. Pp. 237–78.

Kally, E. 1974. Extension of Israel's National Water System as a Function of Artificial Rain Prospects. *Water Resources Research* 10 (5): 917–20.

Kolars, J., and A. Wolf. 1993. Preliminary Proposal: Water Transfer Plans from Turkey to the Jordan River Watershed—An Evaluation of Economic, Technical and Political Feasibility. International Water Resources Association Committee on International Water, Santa Fe Meeting, 29 Sep. (draft).

Koppen, W. 1923. *Die Klimate der Erde*. Berlin, Leipzig: de Gruyters.

Korzun, V.I., et al. 1976. World Water Balance and Water Resources of the Earth. Unesco–USSR Committee for the International Hydrological Decade. (ISBN 92-3-101497-8) Pp. 17–56.

LAG (Land Agency of Japan). 1989. *'89 Water Resources Inventory*. Tokyo: Sankando Shuppan Ltd. P. 184. (In Japanese)

Leitner, G.F. 1989. Cost of Seawater Desalination in Real Terms, 1979 through 1989, and Projections for 1999. Fourth World Congress on Desalination and Water Reuse, Kuwait. International Desalination Association. *Desalination* 76 (4): 201–13.

Loruis, C., et al. 1988. Antarctic Ice Core: CO_2 and Climate Change over the Last Climatic Cycle. *Eos*, June, p. 681.

Lowdermilk, W.C. 1944. *Palestine: Land of Promise*. New York: Harper & Row.

Malik, A.L.A., N.G. Younan, B.J.R. Rao, and K.M. Mousa. 1989. Skid Mounted Mobile Brackish Water Reverse Osmosis Plants at Different Sites in Kuwait. International Desalination Association. *Desalination* 75: 341–61.

Manabe, S., and T.R. Wetherald. 1986. Reduction in Summer Soil Wetness Induced by an Increase in Atmospheric Carbon Dioxide. *Science* 232: 626–28.

Martino, G.D. 1973. The Qattara Depression. *Water Power and Dam Construction*, Jan., pp. 27–31.

Matthews, E. 1983. Global Vegetation and Land Use: New High-Resolution Data Base for Climate Studies. *Journal of Climate and Applied Meteorology* 22: 474–87.

MAWSA (Ministry of Agriculture and Water, Kingdom of Saudi Arabia). 1985. Fourth Development Plan (1985–1990).

———. 1990. Fifth Development Plan (1990–1995). Pp. 169–77.

Mermel, T.M. 1989. Major Dams of the World–1989. *Water Power and Dam Construction Hand Book*. Pp. 50–56.

Meybeck, M., V. Chapman, and H.R. Richard. 1989. *Global Freshwater Quality: A First Assessment*. WHO/UNDP. London: Basil Blackwell, Ltd. Pp. 243–52.

MFJ (Ministry of Finance of Japan). 1991. *White Book: Water Resources of Japan*. Pp. 153–56. (In Japanese)

MPJ (Minstry of Planning of Jordan). 1990. Jordan's Water Sector: Seminar Note. Pp. 1–3.

Muhurji, M., V.V.D. Mast, and H. Imai. 1989. Jeddah I RO Plant—Phase I: 15 MGD Reverse Osmosis Plant. Fourth World Congress on Desalination and Water Reuse. International Desalination Association. *Desalination* 76 (4): 75–88.

Murakami, M. 1991. Arid Zone Water Resources Planning Study with Applications of Non-conventional Alternatives. Doctoral thesis, University of Tokyo, Japan.

———. 1993a. Hydro-powered Reverse Osmosis (RO) Desalination for Co-generation: A Middle East Case Study. Proceedings of the IDA and WRPC World Congress on Desalination and Water Treatment, 2: 37–44.

———. 1993b. Water for Peace Master Plan of the Jordan River System. Proceedings of the IDA and WRPC World Congress on Desalination and Water Treatment, 2: 621–29.

———, and K. Musiake. 1991. Hydro-powered Reverse Osmosis (RO) Desalination for Co-generation. Proceedings of the International Seminar on Efficient Water Use, Mexico City, October. International Water Resources Association (in press).

———. 1992. Integrated Water Master Plan for Jordan River Basin Development and Management. Proceedings of Transboundary River Basin Management and Sustainable Development, Delft, 18–22 May. Unesco/IHP/IWRA/EWPCA/IASH/IAWL/RBA Center (in press).

Mussayab, R. 1988. Water Resources and Development in the State of Bahrain. Middle East–Japan Conference on Development and Utilization of Water Resources. Japan Cooperation for the Middle East, Country Report.

Naff, T., and R.C. Matson. 1984. *Water in the Middle East: Conflict or Cooperation?* Boulder, Colo., USA, and London: Westview Press. Pp. 1–62.

Nicholson, E.S., and H. Flohn. 1980. African Environmental and Climatic Changes and the General Atmospheric Circulation in Late Pleistocene and Holocene. *Climatic Change* 2: 313–48.

NPCJ (National Planning Council of Jordan). 1983. Water Supply Project from the River Euphrates. Vol. 1: Technical Assessment. NPCJ and Howard Humphreys & Partners.

References

NRAJ (Natural Resources Authority of Jordan). 1977. Aqaba Water Supply: Hydro-geological Study Report. Howard Humphreys Co., Ltd.

———. 1978. Report on Pumping Simulation of Proposed Qa Disi Phase I Boreholes. Howard Humphreys Co., Ltd.

———. 1982. Modeling of the Disi Sandstone Aquifer—Southern Desert of Jordan. Howard Humphreys Co., Ltd.

———. 1986. Groundwater Resources Study in the Shidaya Area: Main Report. Howard Humphreys Co., Ltd.

OCWD (Orange County Water District). 1989. Annual Report: Water Factory 21. California State Water Council, USA. P. 10.

Penck, A. 1910. *Versuch einer Klimaklassifikation auf physiographischer Grundlage.* K. Preussische Akademie der Wissenshaften, 1: 236–46.

Powell, J.H., and M.E. Guild. 1961. Salinity Problems in the Arid Zones: Field Operation of Electric Membrane Equipment for Water Desalinating. Proceedings of the Teheran Symposium. Unesco. Pp. 363–70.

RJGC (Royal Jordanian Geographic Centre). 1986. *National Atlas of Jordan.* Part II: Hydrology and Agrohydrology. Pp. 5, 56.

Rogers, P. 1986. This Water Costs Almost Nothing. That's Why We're Running Out. *Technological Review*, Nov.–Dec., pp. 30–43.

Rotty, M.R., and D.C. Masters. 1985. Carbon Dioxide from Fossil Fuel Combustion: Trends, Resources, and Technological Implications. *Atmospheric Carbon Dioxide and the Global Carbon Cycle.* DOE/ER-0239. Washington, D.C.: US Department of Energy. Pp. 63–80.

Savage, C. 1990. Middle East Water. Lecture given to the Royal Society for Asian Affairs, London, 20 March. *Journal of the Royal Society for Asian Affairs.*

Schneider, R. 1967. Geologic and Hydrologic Factors Related to Artificial Recharge of the Carbonate-Rock Aquifer System of Central Israel. Symposium of Haifa: Artificial Recharge and Management of Aquifers. IASH Pub. no. 72. International Association of Scientific Hydrology (IASH). Pp. 37–45.

Sellers, W.D. 1965. *Physical Climatology.* Chicago, Ill., USA: University of Chicago Press. Pp. 100–114.

Shahin, M. 1987. Groundwater Resources in Egypt: Potentials and Limitation. *Water for the Future: Hydrology in Perspective.* Proceedings of the Rome Symposium, April. IASH Pub. no. 164. International Association of Scientific Hydrology. Pp. 179–92.

———. 1989. Review and Assessment of Water Resources in the Arab Region. *Water International*, journal of the International Water Resources Association, 14: 206–19.

Starr, J.R., and C.D. Stoll. 1987. Foreign Policy on Water Resources in the Middle East. Panel Report. Washington, D.C.: The Center for Strategic and International Studies. Pp. 5–8.

Stockton, W.C., and G.C. Jacoby, Jr. 1976. *Long-Term Surface-Water Supply and Streamflow Trends in the Upper Colorado River Basin Based on Tree-Ring Analyses.* Lake Powell Research Project Bulletin 18. University of Arizona, Tucson, Ariz., USA.

SWCC (Saline Water Conversion Corporation). 1988. Kingdom of Saudi Arabia: Saline Water Conversion Corporation (SWCC). *Developing World Water.* Grosvenor Press International. P. 198.

Tahal. 1982. MDS Project: Project Summary. Feasibility Study Report. Tahal, Israel.

Thompson, K.O., and D.H. Marks. 1982. Agriculture vs. Hydropower Tradeoffs in the Operation of the Aswan High Dam. *Water Resources Research* 18 (6): 1605–13.

Thornthwaite, W.C. 1948. An Approach toward a Rational Classification of Climate. *Geographical Review* 39 (1): 55–94.

———, and R.J. Mather. 1957. Instructions and Tables for Computing Potential Evapotranspiration and the Water Balance: Centerton, N.J., Laboratory of Climatology. *Climatology* vol. 10, no. 3.

Wagner, W. 1989. The Yuma Desalting Plant: A Status Report. Seventh Annual Membrane Technology Planning Conference, Cambridge, Mass., USA, 17–19 Nov. Pp. 102–11.

Wangnick Consulting and IDA (International Desalination Association). 1988. 1988 IDA Worldwide Desalting Plants Inventory: Worldwide Inventory of Land-Based Desalting Plants Capable of Producing 100 m^3/Unit or More Fresh Water Daily, Delivered or under Construction as of December 31, 1987.

World Bank. 1989. Jordan Water Resources Sector Study. World Bank Report no. 7099-JO.

Weiner, D., and A. Ben-Zvi. 1982. A Stochastic Dynamic Programming Model for the Operation of the Mediterranean–Dead Sea Project. *Water Resources Research* 18 (4): 729–34.

Wesner, G.M., and R.L. Herndon. 1990. Water Reclamation and Seawater Intrusion Barrier Project. Engineering Report. Orange County Water District, State of California, USA. Pp. 4–6.

WMO (World Meteorological Organization). 1987. Water Resources and Climatic Change: Sensitivity of Water Resources System to Climatic Change and Variability. Rep. WCAP-4, WMO/TD 247. P. 50.

Worthington, E.B. 1977. *Arid Land Irrigation in Developing Countries: Environmental Problems and Effects*. London: Pergamon Press. Pp. 149–52.

WPDC (*Water Power and Dam Construction*). 1980. Israel Decides on Canal Route. *Water Power and Dam Construction*, Oct., p. 4.

———. 1983. Jordan Attacks Dead Sea Project. *Water Power and Dam Construction*, Mar., p. 4.

———. 1986. Libya Plans Groundwater Hydro Plant. *Water Power and Dam Construction*, Sept., p. 3.

———. 1987a. Turkey–Syria Water Accord Signed. *Water Power and Dam Construction*, Sept., p. 3.

———. 1987b. Qattara Project Imperative. *Water Power and Dam Construction*, Oct., p. 3.

———. 1988a. Egypt Moves to Avert Nile Crisis. *Water Power and Dam Construction*, Feb., p. 3.

———. 1988b. Tenders: Chile Groundwater-Hydro. *Water Power and Dam Construction*, May, p. 8.

———. 1989a. Egypt Plans Seawater Pumped-Storage Plant. *Water Power and Dam Construction*, Jan., p. 4.

———. 1989b. Dead Sea P-S Scheme Revived. *Water Power and Dam Construction*, May, p. 3.

Zarour, H., and J. Isaac. 1993. Nature's Appointment and the Open Market: A Promising Solution of the Arab-Israeli Water Conflict. *Water International*, journal of the International Water Resources Association, 18 (1): 40–53.

309